The Collected Poems of Patrick Lane

BOOKS BY PATRICK LANE

Poetry

Letters from the Savage Mind (Very Stone House, Vancouver, BC: 1966)

Separations (New Books, Trumansburg, NY: 1969)

Mountain Oysters (Very Stone House in Transit, Vernon, BC: 1970)

On the Street (Very Stone House in Transit, Vernon, BC: 1970)

Hiway 401 Rhapsody (Very Stone House in Transit, Vernon, BC: 1971)

The Sun Has Begun to Eat the Mountain (Ingluvin, Montreal, QC: 1972)

Passing Into Storm (Traumerei Communications, Vernon, BC: 1973)

Beware the Months of Fire (Anansi, Toronto, ON: 1974)

Unborn Things: South American Poems (Harbour, Madeira Park, BC: 1975)

Albino Pheasants (Harbour, Madeira Park, BC: 1977)

Poems: New & Selected (Oxford, Toronto, ON: 1978)

No Longer Two People (with Lorna Uher [Crozier]), (Turnstone, Winnipeg, MB: 1979)

The Measure (Black Moss, Windsor, ON: 1980)

Old Mother (Oxford, Toronto, ON: 1982)

Woman in the Dust (Mosaic, Toronto, ON: 1983)

A Linen Crow, a Caftan Magpie (Thistledown, Saskatoon, SK: 1985)

Selected Poems (Oxford, Toronto, ON: 1987)

Winter (Coteau, Regina, SK: 1990)

Mortal Remains (Exile, Toronto, ON: 1991)

Too Spare, Too Fierce (Harbour, Madeira Park, BC: 1995)

Selected Poems, 1977–1997 (Harbour, Madeira Park, BC: 1997)

The Bare Plum of Winter Rain (Harbour, Madeira Park, BC: 2000)

Go Leaving Strange (Harbour, Madeira Park, BC: 2004)

Syllable of Stone: Selected Poems (Arc, Todmorden, UK: 2005)

Last Water Song (Harbour, Madeira Park, BC: 2007)

Witness: Selected Poems 1962–2010 (Harbour, Madeira Park, BC: 2010)

Children's

Milford & Me, (Coteau Books, Regina, SK: 1989)

Fiction

How Do You Spell Beautiful? (Fifth House, Saskatoon, SK: 1992)

Red Dog Red Dog (McClelland & Stewart, Toronto, ON: 2008)

Non-fiction

There Is a Season: A Memoir in a Garden (McClelland & Stewart, Toronto, ON: 2004)

Anthologies (Editor with Lorna Crozier)

Breathing Fire (Harbour, Madeira Park, BC: 1994)

Addicted: Notes from the Belly of the Beast (Greystone, Vancouver, BC: 2001)

Breathing Fire 2 (Nightwood, Gibsons, BC: 2004)

The Collected Poems

of

PATRICK LANE

Edited with an introduction by
Russell Morton Brown
and
Donna Bennett

Afterword by Nicholas Bradley

HARBOUR PUBLISHING

Harbour Publishing Co. Ltd.
P.O. Box 219, Madeira Park, BC, V0N 2H0
www.harbourpublishing.com

Cover photograph of the author by Gary McKinstry
Edited by Donna Bennett and Russell Morton Brown
Cover design by Anna Comfort
Text design by Mary White
Printed and bound in Canada

Harbour Publishing acknowledges financial support from the Government
of Canada through the Canada Book Fund and the Canada Council for
the Arts, and from the Province of British Columbia through the BC Arts
Council and the Book Publishing Tax Credit.

 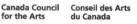 

Library and Archives Canada Cataloguing in Publication

Lane, Patrick, 1939–
    The collected poems of Patrick Lane / edited with an introduction by
Russell Brown and Donna Bennett ; afterword by Nicholas Bradley.

ISBN 978-1-55017-547-9

    I. Bennett, Donna, 1945– II. Brown, Russell, 1942– III. Title.

PS8523.A53A17 2011   C811'.54   C2011-904633-4

Pale moths, soft birds of the night,
move among their grey faces, touch
their small shy feet, cleanse what must be
cleansed in this dark where the dead have come
for blessing. Touch their lips
with your wings so they may sing.
Be to them what the heart is when it sleeps.

CONTENTS

THE SEVENTIES

THE EIGHTIES

THE NINETIES

Winter

THE TWENTY-FIRST CENTURY

Poets, Talking
Patrick Lane

I could wish poems happened more, but wanting them
only leads to the impediment of desire and desire
is never equal to the act. It's much the same as looking back,
expecting a story and finding the characters already dead.
The surprise of that. How the past gets worn down by idle use.
These days the poem comes much as the first bat does
in the false dawn. Its flight the mental stumble that I love.
I have my hungers even as they elude me.
Things are so simple, a bat, and the consequent moth
I create to keep my world whole a little longer.
The poems come to me now as then, occasions, the good ones rarely.
The moth, its wings so white they startle me, escapes.
For the moment.
                I watch the delicate violence of the dance,
the bat, and the moth too, veering.

PREFACE

Russell Morton Brown and Donna Bennett

This *Collected Poems* is a long-overdue book. Bringing together all the poems that Lane wants to preserve (several revised for this publication), it provides an overview of his career and offers an unprecedented perspective on his development. It is the retrospective Lane deserves: not just one of Canada's foremost poets, he is a major figure in anyone's history of Canadian literature.

Lane has been writing for more than fifty years. Along with his twenty-seven books of poetry and several broadsheets, he has published an acclaimed memoir, a children's book, an engaging collection of short stories, and a powerful novel. A member of the generation of poets and fiction writers that emerged in the 1960s to define what we now think of as the Canadian literary tradition, he played a distinctive role. His voice spoke to the nation at large, but more particularly to and about the Canadian west. Independent of schools and movements, his poetry provided an alternative to the directions taken by the Black Mountain-influenced *Tish* poets in British Columbia, the writers in Ontario responding to the ideas of Northrop Frye or the Louis Dudek-influenced Montreal poets. (His allegiances were closest to the realist fiction and the poetry of everyday life that emerged in the prairies and the Atlantic provinces.) He found his way by drawing on his own painful, and even traumatic, experiences to create a kind of poem that, while it wasn't in the confessional mode then being employed in the eastern United States (i.e., that of Robert Lowell, Anne Sexton and others), offered a Canadian analogue to that poetry. Lane's way of writing was important, increasingly so after his early journey to South America, because it spoke for and made visible individuals not then present in Canadian poetry: the disenfranchised and disaffected, the rural poor, the damaged and destroyed souls inhabiting the margins.

This subject matter, combined with the reckless way of life Lane embraced as a young man, earned him a reputation for wildness, but his poems were never careless or governed by the emotions they expressed. Employing an objective eye and exercising careful discipline, Lane worked hard at his craft to create a sense of the visual. But the image was never the end: he was guided by an impeccable ear for sound and rhythm—for the pace, the beat, the pauses and the line-breaks that bring life to the page. Because he never attended university and lived in an age before creative writing was taught in schools and workshops, he had, like Al Purdy, to put himself through his own course of study. Devouring books of all kinds and from all eras, he became, again like Purdy, one of Canada's great autodidacts. Lane's later poetry makes clear how much he steeped himself in his craft: he is a poet whose knowledge of life and nature comes through close study and first-hand contact but who makes sense of his world by sifting through myth and history and drawing frames of reference from Neruda to Zen gardens in Japan, from ancient Chinese literature to Dostoevsky.

His impact on other Canadian writers was felt early. Pat Lowther, whose first book was published by Lane's small press in 1968, shared his concerns for elevating the mundane to the level of poetry. Lane's attention to the working lives of individuals is extended by Erin Mouré in her early collections (Mouré has written: "For me, Patrick's work has always borne a kind of moral force or weight") and in the "work poetry" advocated by Tom Wayman. His close consideration of the

West provided a starting point for poets such as Tim Lilburn. Over the course of his five decades, his travels brought him into contact with most of the Canadian poets of his generation and the next; he engaged them in conversations that went on for years, served with them on juries, wrote poems for and about them and argued with them about poetry and poetics. He also taught and worked with poets still learning their craft, and he edited, with Lorna Crozier, two anthologies of poets early in their careers, giving a boost to the fledgling talents of Michael Redhill, Karen Solie, Karen Connelly, Steven Price, Carmine Starnino, Michael Crummey and others. The largeness of Lane's impact is suggested in Susan Musgrave's observation (in *Because You Loved Being a Stranger*, a book in which fifty-five Canadian poets celebrate Lane's fifty-fifth birthday) that he "must have had more poems dedicated to him than all other poets in the country."

That this volume offers a retrospective on Lane's long career is not to suggest it is over. Rather, it shows his remarkable ability to carry on. He is as creative as he has ever been and, in his later poems, he reassesses earlier ideas and explores new directions while finding new ways to express himself. Remarkably enduring, Lane still has much to tell us.

INTRODUCTION

Russell Morton Brown and Donna Bennett

i

Born March 26, 1939, the third son of the five children of Eileen Mary Titsworth and Albert Stanley ("Red") Lane, Neil Patrick Lane (his first published poems were as "N.P. Lane"), grew up in Nelson, British Columbia. He didn't know his father in the first six years of his childhood. Red Lane, who was suffering from silicosis, quit his job as a hard-rock miner the summer after his son was born and enlisted in the Canadian Army. On his return in 1945, he relocated to Vernon—in the arid lands of the Okanagan Valley in southern British Columbia—to help his lung condition and in an effort to restore a troubled marriage. There the Lanes lived in poverty until the early 1950s, when Red Lane became the sales manager of a heavy-equipment company.

Of his adolescence in Vernon, Lane recalls:

> I lived a socially schizoid life, having two sets of friends, one a small group of "outsiders," an intellectual bunch that listened to classical music and jazz and read the poetry of Pound and Eliot and Williams, and another group that hung around the pool halls and beer parlours, committing petty crimes of

shoplifting and breaking and entering while listening to Ella Fitzgerald, Frank Sinatra, Johnny Ray and Elvis Presley. In the group of young, artistic intellectuals I hung around with was Mary Evelyn Hayden, the daughter of a newspaper editor. When we were in our last year of high school she became pregnant and we got married.*

Lane found himself, at eighteen, taking jobs as a labourer, mill worker and "Cat" driver. He moved with his wife and son Mark to Kamloops in 1959, then to Merritt, BC, where he went to work for a sawmill company as a clerk. After a six-week course in industrial first aid, he was transferred to the tiny village of Avola on the North Thompson River. He lived there with his wife and three young children—Mark, Christopher and Kathryn—until late 1964.

At the beginning of the 1960s Lane began writing poetry. His brother Richard (who, like his father, took the nickname "Red") had met George Bowering while serving in the Royal Canadian Air Force, and was by then playing a Neal Cassady-like role to emerging writers grouped around the poetry newsletter *Tish*, which student poets at the University of British Columbia had founded in 1961. Through Red, Lane met poets in and around Vancouver, including Bowering, Fred Wah, bill bissett, John Newlove, Milton Acorn, Joe Rosenblatt and Dorothy Livesay. Lane had been introduced to poetry in high school by an inspiring teacher, and by this time had already begun reading canonical figures such as Yeats, Pound and Frost, but when his brother gave him a copy of Al Purdy's *Poems for All the Annettes* and, later, *Jawbreakers* by Milton Acorn, he was deeply affected, and began to read widely in Canadian poetry. Of particular impact were Raymond Souster's *A Local Pride* and Irving Layton's *A Red Carpet for the Sun* ("a collection that I loved"), as well as Earle Birney's *Ice Cod Bell or Stone*. His friend Seymour Mayne introduced

---

* Extracts sourced from unpublished email communications with Patrick Lane, November 2010

him to the Latin Americans and Europeans in translation (Neruda and Vallejo, among others). Of all of these, he says, "Acorn and Purdy were closest to my heart, my instinct directing me toward their working-class concerns, their first-person poetry, the anecdotal qualities in Acorn, the echoes of traditional verse in Purdy." Sensitive from the beginning to the question of rhythm in the poetic line, he was also intrigued by Layton's use of metrical conventions in some of his poems.

Around this time a series of events occurred that Lane refers to as "the terrible griefs of the sixties." In 1962, Julie, the four-year-old daughter of his brother John, died of cancer. Two years later, his brother Red died suddenly of a brain haemorrhage. ("My family reeled at the deaths. I think I went mad then," Lane has written, "but so did we all.") In 1968, not long after his wife's mother died, his father was shot and killed by an overwrought customer whose logging equipment had been repossessed. Lane found this last event a devastating blow. His already-troubled marriage dissolved and for the next several years, he drifted between the West Coast and Eastern Canada.

In the mid-Sixties in Vancouver, he and Mayne had joined with bill bissett and the poet Jim Brown to found the small press Very Stone House. The first book they published was *The Collected Poems of Red Lane*, commemorating his brother's tragic death. Following that was their own poetry, including Lane's debut collection, *Letters from the Savage Mind*. (They later published Pat Lowther's debut collection.) The poems Lane wrote during the next few years were gathered in *Separations* (1969), published by New Books—a small press in upstate New York founded by the poet John Gill, the editor of an important little magazine, *New American and Canadian Poetry*. Of the period that followed Lane writes:

> My permanent endless drifting began then, on the move, Vancouver, Toronto, Montreal, New York, San Francisco (with Joe Rosenblatt), the North, Hazelton, Smithers, Prince George, Summerland where I stayed off and on with George Ryga,

everywhere and nowhere. The years mostly a blur, a couple of grants keeping me going. Crashed several cars, lived back in the bush up Babine Lake way in northern BC. I lived in New York City for a while, slept in Central Park and then sought shelter with a woman whose name I don't remember. I passed some time on John and Elaine Gill's commune near Ithaca, where I printed Alden Nowlan's American Selected (*Playing the Jesus Game*) on John's offset machine. Spent a couple of summers in northern BC with Ken and Alice Belford, Ken and I loading boxcars at a local sawmill. Susan Newlove threw me out of her rented basement suite in Prince George in 1969, John and I, disastrously drunk and fighting; wrecked my car; slept in an alley inside a cardboard box, winter, damn near froze to death. Hopped a PGE freight south to Vancouver, ending up in hospital for three weeks with frozen feet. Also spent a month in hospital in Quesnel for a drastic allergic response to god-knows-what. Damn near died. Wrecked my car on Highway 401 with Ray Fraser as a passenger, rolling it eight times according to the cop who hauled the car away and left us on the side of the road in nowhere Ontario, Ray returning to Montreal, and me with a broken collarbone going to Toronto. The third car wreck in three months. Published various chapbooks under the name of Very Stone House in Transit, three of my own, *Hiway 401 Rhapsody* (which tells the story of that car wreck with Fraser), *Mountain Oysters* and *On the Street*. Drifting.

In 1972 Lane collected, in *The Sun Has Begun to Eat the Mountain*, most of the poems he had so far published: Mayne, now in Montreal, brought the collection out under the imprint of Ingluvin, the small press he had founded with K.V. Hertz. Lane then travelled to South America with Carol Beale, whom he had met while in Toronto. They visited Colombia, Ecuador and Peru. The poems that eventually came out of that trip show the effect of his travels: a broadening of horizons, a moving beyond the personal, a passion for history and a sensitivity to the lives of the poor and mistreated.

In 1973 Beale and Lane moved west, living at first in a cheap Vancouver rooming house and then in Vernon, where he published *Passing into Storm* with a small local press, Traumerei Communications.

> Carol went to work in a Vancouver bank on Broadway and I wrote the South American poems, shooting pool nights in the bars down on Granville Street. I'd met Peter Trower and his young friend Howard White, who founded Harbour Publishing around then. Howie hired me on a Local Initiatives Program grant to write for him, though I wrote only one article—on the old fur seal hunts up Alaska way—then lived for six months on the Sunshine Coast on LIP money.

Margaret Atwood asked Lane for a selection of poems for the House of Anansi Press, published in 1974 as *Beware the Months of Fire*. The following year Lane collected the poems that had come out of his South American journeys as *Unborn Things*. That volume marked the beginning of his long association with Harbour Publishing.

In 1974, he and Carol bought ten acres of land on the coast near Madeira Park and moved into a shack there with their young son Michael and the soon-to-be-born Richard. Lane struggled with a novel he never completed and wrote the poems gathered in *Albino Pheasants*. In 1976 he met the poet Lorna Crozier while giving a reading and workshop in Regina.

The year 1978 was significant for Lane. Oxford University Press published his *Poems, New & Selected*, for which he received the Governor General's Award. He accepted the writer-in-residence position at the University of Manitoba. And in the spring, while attending the annual meeting of the Saskatchewan Writers' Guild as keynote speaker, he met Crozier again and fell in love with her. They decided to end their respective marriages and live together. They have, despite everyone's predictions, been together since. (They married in 2001.) Lane says that at first they communicated by poetry and that *No Longer Two People*, the sequence of interwoven poems they collaborated on in 1979, was written "after an argument." Until they moved to Saskatoon in 1986 to teach creative writing and Canadian literature at the University of Saskatchewan, they travelled across the country, living on grants and writer-in-residencies. (In July 1981 Lane journeyed to China with six other Canadian writers.)

The poems Lane published in the first part of the 1980s, collected in *The Measure, Old Mother* (which is divided into "Prairie Poems" and "China Poems") and *Woman in the Dust*, exhibit the strengths of his earlier work, but they also show him experimenting with form and content in ways that break with his earlier poetic practise. In *Patrick Lane and His Works*, George Woodcock praises the "gnomic" qualities newly evident in *The Measure* (1980) and calls attention to the innovative form of Lane's long poem "The Weight" (1982), which, in its structure and dream-like drifting through history, is different from anything seen previously. The poetic form employed in *A Linen Crow, a Caftan Magpie* (1984) suggests the impact of his trip to China—its poems are written in what Lane called a "composite of haiku and ghazal." Marking a full break from Lane's earlier anecdotal lyrics, they provide a further indication of his broadening scope. (Lane identifies his reading of Isaiah, Schiller, Buson and Basho as shaping influences here.) Lane's next book of new poetry, the sequence *Winter* (1990), uses the book as poetic unit in a way that makes it one of the most important volumes of twentieth-century Canadian poetry.

After moving, in 1991, with Crozier to Victoria on Vancouver Island, where they both began teaching at the University of Victoria, Lane extended his range still further in voice, tonalities and concerns by, among other things, writing meditative poems, composing an elegiac sequence and working with prose poetry. He also gathered the affecting short stories he'd been writing over the past decade into the book *How*

Do You Spell Beautiful? (1992). However, though he was now living a more orderly life, the drinking begun in his teenage years was taking its toll. In 1989 he had badly shattered an ankle in a drunken leap from a thirty-foot cliff into shallow water. In 2000, Lane, then sixty-two, entered a rehab facility. After he had completed rehabilitation he co-edited, with Crozier, *Addicted: Notes from the Belly of the Beast* (2001), a collection of essays written by Lane, Crozier, Peter Gzowski, John Newlove, David Adams Richards and others about addiction and its effects. In the months that followed, Lane devoted himself to the half-acre garden he had maintained since moving to Vancouver Island, making it his sanctuary, a space that allowed him to retreat and reconsider his past: the tending of it became a consoling activity that helped him remain sober. His memoir, *There Is a Season: A Memoir in a Garden*, published in 2004, recounts this period—during which he says he sought "to find myself among the things of this world." The book of poems that appeared that same year, *Go Leaving Strange*, is divided into two parts: "After" and "The Addiction Poems." *Go Leaving Strange* is one of four new books of poetry Lane has published since leaving rehab. The most recent, *Last Water Song*, which appeared in 2007, contains a sequence of elegies for the poets who have passed before him. The following year he published his novel, *Red Dog Red Dog*, which owes much in its control of language and images to the skills he honed as a poet. John Kelman observed, in *The Guardian*, that in its portrait of the Stark family, "The tension between the outsider's inner life and the unyielding certainty of his reality has rarely been so incisively documented."

ii

The paradox of Lane's early success as a poet is that the reputation he established obscured his later accomplishments. His poems have been widely praised and anthologized and his books have won a number of awards, but critical discussion of his work has too frequently returned to the idea that this poetry is chiefly "tough, and masculine," or that it is particularly to be valued for its "unflinching honesty about the dark side of human nature," or that it can be summed up as "violent and tragic."

Lane *has* created strong poems to which such descriptions apply, from the early "At the Edge of the Jungle," with its maimed rooster that "beats its blunt head / again and again into the earth," to—more recently—"The War," with its memories of innocents slaughtered. However, as important as these poems are, Lane's work has offered another perspective that is no less significant and that tempers brutality with beauty, including the beauty of the poem itself. And having confronted so much darkness and emptiness in his early years, Lane increasingly turned his gaze elsewhere to focus on overlooked loveliness—as in the simple and untroubled lyric "Her Laughter." In "The Spiders Are Back," consuming nature may be waiting for us in the poem's conclusion but, rather than seeming disheartening, its last lines intensify our appreciation of the poem's lovely opening images. As the poem called "Forms" suggests, decay can reveal a mountain.

Discovering balance in the world's essential duality has been a consolation, but Lane's recent poems go further. They are open to the possibility that to live in this world we must also discover love and learn to praise. In later work such as "What Little Is Left," "Weeds" and "Choices," contemplative passages and meditative utterances come to the fore as the poet realizes that there is more to life than simple endurance. "The Sooke Potholes," for example, opens with an image of nature that seems familiar in its general contours:

> A frog's creak and croak are all that beauty is
> when we're alone. Sometimes a song is all we have.

But what began as a nature poem carries us into much larger realms:

> The waters go on to the ocean, busy,
> happy to find the place where it all began. I think water
> knows more than I of love. Old Hugh Latimer back in 1549

told his king, *The drop of rain maketh a hole in the stone not by violence, but by oft falling.*

Nature offers beauty, but something more is needed:

> Sometimes a gentle soul is what we want.
> What can be saved, I ask, but the moon and the stars,
> the owl and the frog tell me nothing of salvation.
> If my woman were here she'd say all will be well,
> knowing I need love at times a little.
> Her song saves me tonight, no matter love.
> She tells me there are living things.

The reporting and the solitariness of the individual witnessing are no longer enough. The observer must join others to live fully:

> I listen to the waters far below, the scour of stone on stone.
> Like the tree frog's song, I think the earth is singing.
> The owl knows he will starve if he waits for the mouse
> to crawl under his talon, and the tree frog knows
> no lovely frog will come without a song.
> Nor pray for tree nor frog nor man,
> but praise that *we* are a living place,
> the whisper of these waters ours to hold,
> however brief our stay.

In the present collection, such poems are an important element in the larger corpus—which reveals itself as a body of work chronicling its author's quest "to find myself among the things of this world." In recording this quest in his poetry, Lane shows his readers that this necessary journey is not without peril and pain, but he also reveals that it can be accompanied by a deep sense of wonder and lead to a spiritual awakening.

THE SIXTIES

Legacies

I'm smoking one of his cigars tonight
after this one
there's only one left
    a pack of cigars
    Remington shaver
    swagger-stick from the First War
    and nothing else
legacies from the old man.

Once in all his eighty years
I saw him—father of my father,
    forebear
    passing my father to me
    in one sudden moment
    of a prairie night
    begat
    begat

and I sit here and smoke his cigar tonight
while I clean his earthly hairs
from the razor
sit and smoke
sit and consume legacies

Newspaper Walls

And the newspaper walls to keep the heat in.
A diary of packed-in dreams
overland from Kamloops
to a land-locked lake.

    Who split the cedar,
            took beaver poplar
            for table-legs and shelves,
            carved the sash
            at home
            on the North Thompson —
            broken windows and mouse seed?

Thirty-one days of August
1914
stare out at a room—
no sheet crumbled, burned
to find September's turn.

            Where was home then—
            after the deluge?

Cariboo Winter

Snow has burned the rocks

            the ground is cold

---

and a wind
has curled the empty
fields with sheets of ice

       in my gloves
       my fingers
       grasp at nothing

Silent trees are airborne
and hills a shifting
mist in the pallid sky

       my flesh recoils

soon it will snow again

The Bee Cave

Sitting in the bee cave
beneath Okanagan hills
I look out to yellow

of mountain sunflowers
and wrap my closed breath
around the droning

of bees that in
the darkness nest

I bare my belly
to their smooth stings
and measure swelling

by years they are
away on desolate trips
Sing bees of the lonely caves

why do you travel
back into this darkness?

Prospector

Old man you prospected summer
country of caves and gold.
With the rattlesnake and spider
you shared with the sun
a babble of flowers and full
brown flawless centres where
you walked in a wilderness
of golden sleep.

Once I was a child
and saw you touch a mountain
wasp with your finger
tip to wing it didn't move
but shivered gently its petal shells
in the wide corner of August.
You watched solitary wasps
float down sunflower fields.

Old man I dreamed you
wandered the mountains
in spring and planted
the hills with golden flowers.

When they found you
they said you were dead
but I knew that the wasps
had planted their eggs in you
and flowers were growing
out of your sleeping eyes.

Calgary City Jail

Today they took him away
and lonely in my cell I read the walls—
the names the thousand jagged scrawls
in slivers of words
in languages I don't know.

And I think, he's gone
and what the hell?

Yesterday he spent the hours
capturing roaches
in his cramped rachitic hand
and after supper
took a dented can
and smashed them all.

He laughed when I carved my name above my bed.
What does it matter? he said
they'll only paint you over.

Elephants

The cracked cedar
bunkhouse hangs behind me like a grey pueblo
in the sundown where I sit
to carve an elephant
from a hunk of brown soap
for the Indian boy
who lives in the village a mile back
in the bush.

The alcoholic truck driver
and the cat-skinner sit beside
me with their eyes closed—
all of us waiting out the last hour
until we go back on the grade—

and I try to forget the forever
clank clank clank
across the grade
pounding stones and earth to powder
for hours in mosquito-darkness
of the endless cold mountain night.

The elephant takes form—
my knife caresses smooth soap
scaling off curls of brown
which the boy saves to take home
to his mother in the village.

Finished, I hand the carving to him
and he looks at the image of the great
beast for a long time

---

then sets it on dry cedar
and looks up at me:

> *What's an elephant?*

he asks me
so I tell him of the elephants
and their jungles—the story
of the elephant graveyard
which no one has ever found
and how the silent
animals of the rainforest
go away to die somewhere
in the distances
and he smiles at me

tells me of his father's
graveyard where his people have been
buried for years. So far back
no one remembers when it started
and I ask him where the graveyard is
and he tells me it is gone
now where no one will ever find it
buried under the grade of the new
highway.

Wild Horses

Just to come once alone
to these wild horses
driving out of the high Rockies
raw legs heaving the hip-high snow.

Just once alone. Never to see
the men and their trucks.
Just once alone. Nothing moves
as the stallion with five free mares
rush into the guns. All dead.
Their eyes glaze with frost.
Ice bleeds in their nostrils
as the cable hauls them in.

Later, after the swearing
and the stamping of feet
we ride down into Golden:

Quit bitchin.
It's a hard bloody life
and a long week
for three hundred bucks of meat.

That and the dull dead eyes
and the empty meadows.

Cattle Are Stupid

Cattle are stupid.
They'll die standing, waiting for men
to bring in feed. In the stiff morning
I watch the cowboys ride out.
Each pack horse carries
two hundred pounds of hay
for the herd locked in snow
beyond Williams Lake. Clouds of white

mist roll from the horses' mouths
like lead chain borrowed from a wind.
Riders hunch in their saddles.
Before they left, they wrapped
the horses' hooves in burlap bags.
Even so, Joel said, their blood'll mark
the trail through the ice.

Cattle are stupid.
They'll die standing.
Only men and horses curse the day.
I think of the times I wanted to be
a cowboy. Now when it could be,
they won't trust me or my skin
to make the trip. In this weather
all the cowboys are Indians, hard
in the cutting cold on the crusted lake.

Similkameen Deer

Driving through the Similkameen valley
I watch for deer on the road.
Miles roll out beneath me. A telegraph key.
A perpetual line of dots.
                    Men here
have put up signs telling me to watch
for rolling rock under the escarpment
of mountains where they've cut stones
for their convenience.

Soon it will be spring and mountains
will lose their somnolence. Snow will melt
and out of a fading
whiteness of mountain cold
there will be deer somewhere
who will have no time to spend
watching for me.

Ten Miles in from Horsefly

Ten miles in from Horsefly
shoulders sore from my pack
feet blistered, I asked for
and got a job cleaning a barn
for the price of a meal
and the promise I could sleep
out of the unseasonal rain
—and worked like a damn
as horseflies took chunks
of meat from my arms
and mosquitoes sucked my blood.

Shovelling ten months of shit
from a barn clears your head
and allows you to look forward
to sleep without fear or favour from old
sad dreams of enemies and friends.
Just to have one moment
with shoulders free of weight
and feet braced finally still
as you come breathless
to the clear hard boards below.

On the Bum

I told him I was broke.
The mottled bronze of leather glove
sloughed slowly
as if his hand were a snake
gone past the sun, and late,
the hours done,
could only move with pain
to peel it off.

The crushed blue bones
pushed awkwardly
in the swollen bag of flesh
like broken wood.

And all for what?
To bum two bits,
to buy my pride
or pity, or something less
or something more than that?
I know I couldn't watch him
as he braced his wrist against his knee
and pushed his pulped hand
back in the glove like a snake
whose offering was refused.

I think if I'd been a woman
I'd have loved him. As it was
I was a man and lied, not being able
to decide whose sin it was
and left him broke in the dust
on the bum in Edmonton.

Because I Never Learned

For my brother John

Because I never learned how
to be gentle and the country
I lived in was hard with dead
animals and men, I didn't question
my father when he told me
to step on the kitten's head
after the bus had run over
its hindquarters.

Now, twenty years later,
I remember only:
the silence of the dying
when the fragile skull collapsed
under my hard bare heel,
the curved tongue in the dust
that would never cry again
and the small of my father's back
as he walked tall away.

The Water Truck

You're fired, Lane
he yelled and me lying
there and the truck
belching out great gouts
of water and me
half-drowned fifty feet

down from the edge
of the clay bank

and him running down
the ruts of my descent
grabbing me shaking
to my feet and throwing
me down in the mud again
blind without my glasses
where the truck spun out
its bald tires on the
slippery grade
        nothing
like clay when it's wet
you know
            and the boss
madder'n hell at me
for wrecking the truck
gasoline floating on
water and me lying
on wet stones and clay
looking for my glasses
blind as a bat
and the cat-skinner
beside the boss laughing
like hell and the boss
telling him to shut up
and the truck
I can still feel
rolling over and over
me inside holding on
to the spinning wheel
crashing down the bank

with five tons of water
behind bursting out
and the boss daring me
to get up and get out
his hands shaking and
         I find my glasses
finally locate him
standing there and
                    Fuck you
I said
      I quit

In This Field

Squatting in this field
I watch the bare earth —
wonder if there are enough
seeds left over from other years
to start it all again.

Wonder if new grass will grow
and if it will, will it be
the same and will I be
here, squatting on bare earth,
some landlord waiting
to collect my rent.

Fireweed Seeds
For Ken Belford

Red-winged blackbirds
lower in ripe grain.
Fireweed seeds mass
in the wind. It is late
August and already snow
has found the midline
of the mountains. We sit on
the seasoning uncut wood.

Ken has cut the handle off
the axe and is using it
for a wedge. They were talking
about us in the beer parlour
he says. They call us dirty
uneven people. But it doesn't
matter, he says. Wood splits
under his pounding sledge.

Look at the fireweed seeds
in the wind, he says. The air is full
of their growing. In the grain
blackbirds lift and circle
at the sound of his pounding.

Bottle Pickers

I'm empty as a rusted can, crushed
on the side of this long highway,
kicked ten thousand times
by bottle pickers who passed this way.

In the heavy heat of the sun
they moved with their burlap bags
walking the ditches and once
or twice in the miles they bent
to gather a bit of unbroken glass
to sell in some unknown town
I've never passed through.

For one hour at dusk they sat with me
and talked of the long hot days:

. . . tougher all the time
Cans are like losers
and there's no one to buy.

Now it's late.
The bottle pickers have gone.
I lie in a cold ditch and try to sleep
and think of these men and their passing
and me.

Last Night in Darkness

Last night in darkness someone killed our cat.
Dipped her in gas. Set her aflame.
Her scattered kittens adorned the yard
in opaque sacks where she aborted them,
none of them burned in her pain.

As I gathered them in a paper bag
I had to pull off slugs
who'd gathered for the feast.
Their scavenger trails hovered
on her body like a mist.

Just to forget her
I leaned heavy in the morning
thrusting with my shovel
deep into earth behind the daisies
reminded only of the other
graves I'd dug

while my son prepared them
for peace. Took each one
out of their paper coffin.
Drove apple blossoms into their eyes—
even the mother who was so scarred.

Raking Leaves

Raking leaves
and earth clean
taking a hammer
putting in
a new picket
on the fence
clipping off
one old branch
on the apple tree
painting steel
on the oil barrel
stand carefully
putting away
his tools and
walking slowly
into the house

Yesterday
an ambulance
drove up and
took him away
and this after
noon his wife
grey lady cried
alone on the front
porch below yellow
leaves rustling
with wind and
leaves falling
not understanding
or caring

having to fall
and no one there
to clean and make
ready his woman's
tears and the rake
hanging silent
in the garage

There Was a Woman Bending

There was a woman bending
her body on a bed
curved like a statue carved from life.
In her hand was a twisted thing
black as the hair
that hung like a broken wing.
She lived down the hall from me.

Everything about her smelled of death.
I want to tell you of the foetus
speared on a knitting needle
and blood thick as grease
between her thighs.

There was this woman I saw once on a bed
her body curved like a statue, dead.
I've forgotten her name.
It was the walls her eyelids made
that I remember. The silences they bred.

And her eyes
eyes I will never know the colours of.

Who Is My Lover

High in the valley of the Coquihalla
I watch the brown woman who is my lover

cross to the other side. On her head
she balances her bundle of clothes.

She clasps her breasts,
holding her breath at the cold.

They are like two balls of snow
melting in the hands of a child.

In the water a leaf swirls and catches at her.
She trembles and it drifts away.

The Absinthe Drinker (1969)

For years I tried to leave them,
leave them all.
Now they've left me.
Three childish smiles are scars
inside my mind.
                    She took all three.

My head breaks. The hours
slash my skull to splintered bone.

I wish there was a picture
I could hang to break the sight

of the wall across this room
with its hook of stone.

Where is my Degas lady?
I carried her for years inside my poems
and hung her on the wall to comfort me.
Somewhere in a box of broken books
she sits, sipping her absinthe.
Now for the first time
I would drink with her.

Cold

With your finger you trace
your pain trembling along the blue
patterns of your dress. Across the room
your mother's picture hangs
crooked. Later you'll straighten
it and your fingers will jerk so quietly
no one will see. You stand there
and your shoulders bend like wings.

What is it that makes me cold?
Outside it's raining and our cats
have crept into a corner of the fence
for shelter. Their eyes are closed
and their claws clutch at the clay
as if they will crawl inside.

I know I should do something
but she's dead. Soon enough

you'll wear your tears
in a necklace made of stones.
There's nothing I can say.

I should call the cats in.
From this window they look
like they've drowned
in the falling rain.

For Ten Years

Tonight the moon slants cold into the snow.
Ice shudders on the glass and suddenly alone
I'm aware of windows. Was it you who told me
you were gone? Beyond the snow
light rides thin as a broken bow
without a hand to guide it. From this hour
darkness comes shrill as a dying bird.

One night in the North you lay in my arms
and wept for a crying bird. In the morning
you found him dead on the windowsill.
His beak was a crust of ice
that melted as you breathed.
When I threw him away, he didn't fly.
That country of snow we lived in
was a cushion for owls to walk on.
Birds don't understand windows.
They never did.

For Rita in Asylum

In candle-spiked darkness of the coffee house
I watched tonight your last
your temporary lover
who remembered you for me
over a cup of espresso
and the laughter of his friends.
He was happy.
Two weeks had gone by
and he still wasn't diseased.

Now you sleep in asylum.
Tonight I walk between two tenements
where grass grows yellow
and in the wind
bends like strange weeping
hair on your thin white face.
Rita you said
only a fool walks in a singing rain
but tonight I'm sick
and the rain no longer sings.
Cars pass me in the night.
Their tires crease hard wet streets.
Water folds back on their passing.

Saskatchewan

Covering my shaking
I roll this cigarette
hard in the wind.

I left so much in you:
your belly will always hold
the curves I made. You danced
for me, swollen with the second child.
That was eight years ago and now
I can't find you anywhere —
only this flat prairie
and an unhealed bruise
of cloud that won't go down.
As the land retreats
there's nothing to touch,
nothing to hold onto.

Only this shaking
and this last match
I'm afraid to light
in the wind
in the empty land.

Natasha

One second before I crashed
I smashed the soft body of a crow
who was picking dry blood
off the highway.

His smell of dying penetrates
my mind like a clumsy hand.

        I think of your soft body
        at the coast. Wonder
        if I'll make it down alive.

Outside in dark spruces
crows watch me. I can hear
their shuffle of wings.
Only the dark keeps them
from digging out my eyes.

        My belly heaves again
        and again I dry-puke
        across the steering-wheel.

I think of you and my hands
shake as I lock the doors.
Outside, the flesh and stench
of my most recent dead
hangs shredded in the cold.

Surcease

Here in this car is surcease from a thousand dead,
a woman and a bottle and the rain.

Used car chrome crumbles into dust
and broken windows stain with smears of rust,
each rock-scarred shivered pane

creased with a crust of red. Your eyes
in darkness will never see why you're afraid
and why I'm drunk.

Only hours can drain away the sudden
years, pits I've placed my dead in.
I don't want words from you.

Tonight I want to turn with you to neon
blue as the stiff veins under your tongue
and don't say: Give it time
say nothing
to hell with time.
Take off your clothes. Hang
your breasts in my eyes. I want
to ride with your body and celebrate
the darkness and my pain.
Forget the past.

Play with me gently, woman,
I'm made of glass.

My Father's House

I look back at my father's house on the hill
and all my tears are still
held behind my eyes like burning string.
Somewhere I was a child who liked to sing.
Now everything is said and the burying
is a song for the very old

who, covered in a peculiar kind of mould,
have a wish to die.

I fear the way the mourners speak.
Their tongues move clumsy over words
like feet on a broken sidewalk.
The word is *was*—alien to me
as butcher string in a drawer.
They collect each other awkwardly.
Their hands have the feel of grass
struggling in a tract of broken stone.

Must I always be three feet high
running around corners? The crumbling
cracks in concrete stutter songs.
Remember?
        Step on a crack,
you break your father's back.

I run to the edge of town,
clothe myself in a web of couch-grass roots,
cornflowers and clumps of earth.
Somewhere the song began,
the sidewalk ends.

THE SEVENTIES

On the Street

Adjusting my body to the limits
of the backseat of the '57 Chev
in
        Ed's Used Cars—An Honest Trade
I feel again the old
fear as the high whipping scream
of a siren careens through the night

and I remember
a city

        the way my knife cut through his arm
        so soft like steak
        and how he tried to lift it then
        to hit me again
        and when it wouldn't obey
        looked at it
        puzzled
        his blood splashing on the floor
        and his woman who'd been so silent
        when he punched me in the mouth
        screamed
        You never said knives
        and held him then
        stupidly
        My arm
        you damn near
        cut my arm off
        not being able to believe
        he could come apart so easily

and running away
to another city

       the way her mouth worked over words
       as if she had to chew them into shape
       before she spoke
       how I would tell her
       to *Shutup*
       softly so she would understand
       it wasn't necessary
       reading *Sweet Thursday* to her
       at night in bed and how she'd curl
       her fingers in her hair
       and hunch her knees to her chin
       as she listened to the paintings
       in her mind
       cold
       hungry
       and poems to write
       and how she told me she'd been
       on the street
       but how it didn't matter to her
       did it matter to me?
       did it?
       nothing mattering but the poems
       and her money sliding away
       like snow off a warm roof
       the way she said *Thank you*
       when I left
       her words so slow and clumsy
       swelling in my mind
       then nothing

nothing at all just
goodbye

and running away
to another city

the way sounds became so clear
terror as Wade took a bar
jerked at the cash register
mad because it wouldn't open
Pete loading cigarettes in the truck
box by box
piling them like an awkward child
humming urgently his voice high
Let's go
Let's go
saying it over and over
as he hoisted boxes
and me poised on the counter
scared at the time wasted
talking softly to Wade
Leave it, man.
There's nothing there.
and him
Then why'd he lock it? Huh?
finally mad
beating the cash register
with his bar screaming
The bastards — the bastards
and we ran out the back
Wade stumbling over Pete
the truck not starting

that one wild moment looking
at each other as the engine moaned

and running
and running away

to another city
in another used car
      broke, cold, hungry,
      taking my poems and stuffing them
      into my wet shoes to cut the cold
      hiding my head
      as the siren wailed past
into the night and gone.

The Lost Guitarman

Sing whatever song you wish to sing.
It is only fear. The last steel ring
dwindles in the night among fallen trees,
there where the lost guitarman
takes his solitude
and strains his music to a slender string,
brings his lost voice down
as a tree when it cannot take the strain
falls into moss and forgetfulness.

Sing whatever song you wish to sing.
Your frightened hands to bring
those last sounds down to silence.

You are no wanderer.
You have only forgotten where you were
and do not know the way.
It is no simple thing to be lost,
your voice fading into night, alone
and a forest around you
filled with a sighing wind
blue on a dead tree's bone.

The Sun Has Begun to Eat the Mountains

Pines eat mist out of the sky
in the village the old
man with yellow eyes
lies stretched out on the mat
he is dying

Stones change shape as they breathe
in the bush the shaman
scrapes the green bark
from the devil's club
she will purge death
again this spring

You who are near enough to death
please tell me
where the beginning is
look
the sky weeps
the woman comes

Tell me where the sun goes
when the mountains are all eaten
and the world is only a flatness
where eagles fly
cutting the sky to ribbons
with their great wings

Poem for a Gone Woman

I breathe in the mouth
of a blue snake
who lies broken in the mountains.
In his mouth a frog struggles
who cannot escape.

His legs are being digested.
The snake cannot swallow.
The frog cannot escape.
There is only this lesson
I must learn.

You squat beside me
in the mouth of the gorge
and ask me to kill the snake.

I cannot.
It is as if my hands
were wrapped around the sun
and the burning a single note
sung madly in the shelter
of stones and water.

I cannot leave you here
and I cannot go away.

The Bird

The bird you captured is dead.
I told you it would die
but you would not learn
from my telling. You wanted
to cage a bird in your hands
and learn to fly.

Listen again.
You must not handle birds.
They cannot fly through your fingers.
You are not a nest
and a feather is
not made of blood and bone.

Only words
can fly for you like birds
on the wall of the sun.
A bird is a poem
that talks of the end of cages.

The Black Filly

All day light stuttered
as the slow uncertain hills
were captured by dark clouds
rolling out of the Monashee.
It was when the sky split
that the filly screamed
eyes rolling
tail stretched stiff in the wind.

He smelled it coming.
The charred air and her sweat.
Early in the day he tethered her,
drove a peg in deep, leaving her
earth-bound in the pasture.
When the storm struck she braced
and screamed
heaved at the leather rope.

Between them now is a madness.

Today with mountains firm
under a silent sky he approached her
with soft singing and sweet oats
but she ran to her tether's end
driving to break the binding.

Soon enough she'll come
choking with hunger, weak,
the madness gone with the god
who came to her in her last wildness.

Mountain Oysters

Kneeling in the sheep shit
he picked up the biggest of the new rams,
brushed the tail aside,
slit the bag,
tucked the knackers in his mouth
and clipped the cords off clean —

the ram   stiff
with a single wild scream

as the tar went on
and he spit the balls in a bowl.

That's how we used to do it
when I was a boy.
It's no more gawdam painful
than any other way
and you can't have rams fightin,
slammin it up every nanny . . .

and enjoyed them with him,
cutting delicately
into the deep-fried testicles.

Mountain oysters make you strong

he said
while out in the field
the rams stood holding their pain,
legs fluttering like blue hands
of old tired men.

The Dump

In the orange light of burning oil
a woman moves through the wreckage,
the urge of rats and wasps
feasting in the light of the sun.
She cups her flowered dress
for the gathering of apples.

With a loop of twisted wire
her child flays the decayed head of a coyote.
Flies stitch the air between his feet
with a black crooning to the scattered maggots.
She bends, her belly full of fruit,
and ties the child to her waist
with a twist of binder twine.

She asks me what time it is
as the last truck turns on the brink
of the rotting wall
and bleeds into the fire.
I tell her I don't know.

Wild Dogs

I
In the coldest week
of winter hunger
gathers wild dogs
drives the pack

down the Coquihalla
to the edge of town

for months they hunted
in the hills
now their howls
on the boundary road
once so lonely
in the night grated
on our bones like
skinning knives

II
On a hill above
the Nicola I watched
them pull down
a steer

one heavy bitch
swung from his nose
while others ripped
at his legs

tendons torn
he stumbled
in the snow

they didn't wait
but ate him alive
still bellowing
in the drifts

III

Why do you have
to hunt them
my wife asked
I'd have told her
if I thought
she'd understand

How do you explain
what men do

there's a special
hatred for wild dogs
we go to hunt
because we were
their masters

it's not for food
we kill them
or even pleasure
but the fear
we thought we'd lost
so long ago

IV

Trapped on the icy road
the dogs swung round
to run and then
swung round again
to face us
we all took aim
I thought of Spartacus
and his slaves

free in the hills
of Rome

They didn't
try to kill us
but baffled
twisted round
and round
as I wept
and they blew them
to pieces

The God Who Is Goshawk

Listen
I survive another day

       Out on the flat meadow
       where light cannot disease the land with shadow
       your spot on the sun creases the field with fear

       as you slide empty home.

Listen
I survive another day

       Our bodies on the ground
       will rise again to your beak. Lift feathers on your tongue
       and settle them with pride. The hunger cannot hold.

       Joint rips from joint.

Listen
I survive another day

Wrap feathers each to each
around the wind and measure the desolate day.
All the soft animals are hiding. We hunger to remind ourselves

of pain. This cold disdain.

Listen
I survive another day

There is no rest.
I gather the old bones from your nest. My hands
tear on your isolate tree as your talons drag the sky

in search of me.

Listen
I survive another day

A feather from your wing
gives death a child-birth in my mind. Return again.
Here there is only pain where I, a frightened man,

prepare to die.

Beware the Months of Fire
They Are Twelve and Contain a Year

Hung from a stone branch of city wall
a red cloth bleeds ragged in the rain.
A pallid fire in the winter seacoast night.
I see the skirt of a woman walking proud,
hesitant in the crumpled shade of light,
moving to some destination I'll never know.
The casual cruelty of a street lamp
breaks down the rain.

A red cloth drifts triumphant
over ramparts of garbage
where boys wield swords and symbols
in the wet storms of war.
But there was a woman walking proud,
revealing a touch of leg where her dress was,
and there are children sleeping
behind these walls of rain.

Beware the months of fire.
They are twelve and contain a year
of children sleeping and a walking woman
and a torn dress like a lost tongue.
Now just leave it there in the night,
threaded with mould. A thing for birds to plunder
and mice to find wrapped around their bones.

Passing into Storm

Know him for a white man.
He walks sideways into wind
allowing the left of him

to forget what the right
knows as cold. His ears
turn into death what

his eyes can't see. All day
he walks away from the sun
passing into storm. Do not

mistake him for the howl you hear
or the track you think you
follow. Finding a white man

in snow is to look for the dead.
He has been burned by the wind.
He has left too much

flesh on winter's white metal
to leave his colour as a sign.
Cold white. Cold flesh. He leans

into wind sideways; kills without
mercy anything to the left of him
coming like madness in the snow.

Thirty Below

Men on the pond
push logs through constant ice.
Faces stubble with frost.
No one moves beyond the ritual
of work. Torment of metal
and the scream of saws.

Everything is hard. The sky
scrapes the earth at thirty below
and living things pull into pain
like grotesque children
thrown in the wrong season.

Someone curses.
Pulls his hand from the chain.
His skin has been left on steel,
blood frozen into balls.
He is replaced and the work goes on.

Everything is hard.
Cold lances the slow dance
on the pond. The new man trembles
out of control.
He can't hold his pole.
Someone laughs,
says it will be breakup
before they shut this damn mill down.

After (1973)

For Pat Lowther

After the machine on the gypo show
caught his arm in its mouth
and chewed the nerves dead
from elbow to finger-tips
he sat in the bar
telling stories for drinks

His best the one about
how he'd lost the use of his arm
changing it every other day
until he ran out of variations
and no one would listen to him
the arm getting in his way
bumping into things
and hanging useless

until the only way
he had of getting a drink
was to lay the dead piece of meat
across the table
and stick pins in it
saying:

It doesn't hurt at all

men laughing
and buying him a drink
for every pin he could hammer in

with his empty glass

For Riel in That Gawdam Prison

When Dumont rode with his army
there were only muttered words
of praise at the end; the possible
Messiah praying in his prison

      and how he danced in the circus
      waiting for the clowns to dismount
      while hucksters sold his legend
      to the nickel and dime seats.

There on the prairie there were people
waiting to stop moving. Somewhere
west was too far
and the day eased away into language.

      Indians stumbling over buffalo
      in the ring of Madison Square Gardens,
      Gabriel Dumont riding to the dead
      God somewhere over Regina.

Sleep Is the Silence Darkness Takes
    For my father

For breaking forty acres to the plow
pouring my blood into the sun
pulling stone knuckles from the earth
and walking bowed behind a spavined horse
out of the frost of a dead season
following a stone-boat through my thirteenth year

---

for a share in a crop that was denied
by a father who wouldn't pay a son
for a man's work done

Sleep is the silence darkness takes

Turner Valley was where I starved for youth
until a lady crusted in her trade
lifted me out of a pit of boards and sod
to work in a house of bedrooms where she made
life contain the laughter of the riggers
in a world on the wrong side of the sun
who taught me what it was to be a man
earning the bonus of a year's hard work
in the arms of wild Elsie

Sleep is the silence darkness takes

I broke my body in the hard-rock mines
of depression mountains sucking silica dust
into my swollen lungs until they felt
like bags of blood and glass
but the mountains gave me love
and three small sons until the war
when in the fever of the going
I left them all behind to walk alone
through the graceless falling of my friends
for a dream I did not understand

Sleep is the silence darkness takes

Then the hard days of the returning mind —
the body of my friend still frozen

hanging above the turret of his tank
framed in the flame of the guns
where he remained through the nights
of sweat and jerking dreams —
to a woman who was a stranger with three boys
until I learned that love was bred in pain
and through creation began it all again
struggling through the bitter postwar years
of two more children and three to rediscover
knowing that what was lost
could not be found again

Sleep is the silence darkness takes

And then to be a man and pour my soul
into the pockets of those smiling bastard sons
who, because of privilege, birth, or prior right,
stayed behind and built the glass-walled galleys
where I slaved — no, not for nothing,
but why in the last years I should lie
with a bullet in my heart
when I had come so far, so hard,
to rest here bleeding on a floor and die
and not to know my killer — why?

Sleep is the silence darkness takes

We Talk of Women

Sitting in the cookhouse
in the long last hours before sleep
I trade drinks of scotch for tea
with the Chinese cook.
His skin is the texture of rice paper
and his eyes, narrow and black
as a crow's wings against the sun,
move below fine wisps of grey
that float on his forehead
like moss on a yellow pine.

We talk of women
in the cold distance of a winter
that has locked us for weeks
inside barriers of snow.

I tell him of a girl at the coast:

> All I can remember
> is her hands. When they touched me
> they struggled like captive birds.
> Three months and her face
> is the suggestion of light
> in the window beyond us, eyes
> cold as the barbs of stars
> strung on the wire of night.

He nods and sits on the low
mattress by the wall.
Over warm wine heated on a candle
we quietly talk:

If I could tell you
what she is, I would say
she is made of leaves
and her touch is the sound
of the breath I take
when I climb a mountain.

Yes, I said,
but her memory is winter.

Moving like a piece of alabaster
born in stone he motions me.
I follow him into his room.
Lighting a candle he leads me
through a dance of startled moths
to the wall beside his bed
where drawings of a woman
delicate as dry wings
hang against the splintered red
of cedar:

This is my woman.
She is as young as wind
that rises to melt snow
in the wrong season.

Thinking on That Contest

Thinking on that contest women do
with clothespins in the country
having to hold all the pins in one hand
and they could do it
with hands trained by diapers
and blue work shirts in winter
hand-soaping in a steel tub

as if it was a measure of survival
like an axe falling in a far valley
where sound comes late to you
or not at all
they having learned it in harder times
cursing the cold
clothes hanging frozen to the line
for days going on days
bringing them in piecemeal
to hang over the fire
and let them melt there
reassuming the shape of a man
in time for him to shrug into
before going down to the graveyard
shift at the mines

thinking on that time of trouble
turned into a game
how struggle roots itself in ritual
hands full of clothespins
leaning into wind
never dropping a pin into the snow below

That Quick and Instant Flight

Looking through frost on the window
I count the stars and catch a meteor
that falls in the western sky.
Car wheels cut snow as I follow
this twisted track of road
south to Kamloops on the Yellowhead.
Eight hours fighting a wheel.
I run through every song I ever knew
making up the lines that I forget
and search for the passing glint
among the trees. They are
the only company I keep, these eyes
that twitch and blink as I pass by
and think they must think me
a stranger kind of animal, huge
metal thing roaring in the night.

Sing another song I never knew
and search in the sky
for the cutting line of light
a meteor leaves as it dies
that quick and instant flight
among stars. Gravel sprays
into the river on a black ice corner
as I wonder at the new child
born to me in the city.
Two days to know her
then back to the bush
that keeps us all alive
in this winter
spring a year away.

Still Hunting

A single banner of sky between two mountains:
neither the beginning nor the end of clouds.
Somewhere all the animals have happened
and I wait and pray I will know
the difference between the animal and man;
pray for the gift of a death
to break this glacial waste of time —
that when I shoulder the empty body
I will have something to walk with
be it ice, air, stone, or man; pray
I will find the road where I left it
in the treeline far below.

Thirty Miles in from the Coast

In the high valleys when the sun dies
a man waits out the death
of his season in silence
carving dreams into masks of fire
in the light from an oil-drum stove.
Winter is measured by the mind —
words that fell from a woman
in another time.

. . . and when she died in the days of snow
choked roads and fallen lines
I rolled her in a canvas
and stored her in the shed until spring.
Thirty miles in from the coast is up

and frost goes down six feet.
It's too hard to dig.

Winter is silence
when ice gathers on crows' wings
and nothing can be salvaged from dreams.
In times like these I unwrap her again
to stand in the corner of my mind
like a piece of snow-pounded pine.
Her words are trees that in my mind explode
and cast their fragments
frozen onto the belly of the snow.

You Learn

You learn when you wake up
not to open your mouth for fear
of what you might fill it with.
Dying is a serious business.
Almost as serious as snooker
or learning how to balance
the dead weight of your mind
as you choose by not choosing
the road that could lead you anywhere
but where you think you're going.

You keep your mouth closed
as if something inside you
might escape and lift your body
like some broken thing you've seen
and never knew you'd be: a bird

---

breast-shot and rearing
into the sudden cold
of a sky that has turned
forever from blue to black;
that flying, broken, with eyes
staring centre-shot and looking
at a place you've never been.

White Mountain

Trees in glass robes
cold under the moon's cowl.
Arms hold ice.

Wind carries only the howl
of a dog. Ashes of snow
in grey fire.

There is only a faint glow.
Roads of men advance
and retreat.

Tracks fill with snow.

October

All day I worked in the field
bagging potatoes and turnips,
gathering the last gourds

from among the curled black vines.
All the wandering and women,
the strange roads and stranger times
have led to this: a handful of earth,
a boot on the brittle corn.

I look up at the apples
in the branches I couldn't reach.
Already they have withered.
Soon the storms will come.
Hard from the North
they will strip the trees of leaves.
Like dry brown fists on pillows
the apples will fall into the snow.

O Reader You

know
the poet is made of paper
can you hear him inside your eye
the scream of the tree
as you read him

know
the poem is a paper hero
who used to sing
when you prayed him

now
can you find him inside
your book of safety

matches can you feel
his burning can you heal
him when you strike

now
can you feel the dead tree
as you turn his pages away

Unborn Things

After the dog drowns in the arroyo
and the old people stumble into the jungle
muttering imprecations at the birds
and the child draws circles in the dust
for bits of glass to occupy
the eyes staring out of earth
and the woman lies in her hammock
dreaming of the lover who will save her
from the need to make bread again
I will go into the field
and be buried with the corn.

Folding my hands on my chest
I will see the shadow of myself; the same
who watched a father when he moved
with hands on the dark side of a candle
create the birds and beasts of dreams.

One with unborn things
I will open my body to the earth
and watch worms reach like pink roots

as I turn slowly tongue to stone
and speak of the beginning of seeds
as they struggle in the earth,
pale things moving toward the sun
that feel the feet of men above,
the tread of their marching
thudding into my earth.

—ECUADOR

Machu Picchu
For Earle Birney

I

The Hitching Post of the Sun

Father Condor, take me,
Brother Falcon, take me,
tell my little mother I am coming,
for five days I have not eaten or drunk a drop,
Father Messenger, bearer of signs, swift messenger,
carry me off, I beg you: little mouth, little heart,
tell my little father and little mother, I beg you, that
I am coming.
                    —Death song of condemned lovers, from the Quechua

Standing on the highest rung of the city
we place our hands on polished stone
that was a hitching post for the sun.
Now there is nothing but silence.
We watch the sun fall into the Andes.

The first cold shafts of night
reach into the river far below.
In a gathering mist I feel
we are growing out of
the body of something dead.

. . .

Today we lay in the Temple of Virgins
as centuries filled our mouths with moss.
They have stripped away the jungle.
They have torn the winding cloths.
They have scattered bones to the wind.

Strangers walk through the ruins.
They talk of where they come from,
where they are going.
As we lay in this roofless room
they stoned a snake.

It crawled out of the earth
to lie in the brilliant sun.
Coils of its body like plaited hair,
eyes of cracked stone. They left it
broken, draped on a fallen wall.

. . .

We have been cursed with dreams.
This city was meant to be lost.
Those who died here did not want it found.
I pick up our blanket and find a place
to sleep in the Temple of the Sun.

But even he has hidden his face.
Yellow bruise of light, lost to us,
who could heal everything.
We began when the sun fell.
Now there is nothing but shadow.

I imagine women moving with their men.
They surround us with eyes
here in the high Andes
in a city lost and found again
by men who came to unhitch the sun.

II

The Virgins of the Sun

In the jungle tombs they found only women.
One held a child in her womb, hands
brown roots wrapped around his face.
There were no men.
The city belonged to the Virgins of the Sun.
One by one the tombs were broken,
the jungle torn away:

    Manco Cápac
    And his Incas dead.
    The empire fallen.

    Here they tied the sun at the end of seasons.
    Here they tilled the soil beneath the eyes
    of warriors who stood between the portals

of the sun waiting for the Spanish horse.
Here the Virgins were buried.
The Spanish never came.

Betrayed, the last Inca left for Cuzco
to bargain with the Viceroy of Spain.
He died in an ambuscade.

The bridges were cut behind him.
The road forgotten, the jungle grew a mantle
for the dead. The sun rose and fell on the temple

and in the dark tombs the Virgins slept
waiting for the Incas to return
and restore them to the sun.

Let the grave robbers go.
Let the city grow back to jungle.
Back to the speechless things.
The Virgins have left their tombs
with hands like brown roots,
with their unborn child.
Let the city grow back to jungle,
Let the graves like wounds be closed again.

III

Manco Cápac—Last Inca

Today I leave for the great capital.
Much has been said of the wisdom
of this move. In Machu Picchu
I have ruled. It is as if the empire was

still water curled in a jug's curve
spilled like this river into jungle.
Lately numerous stars have crossed
the heaven. As it was for Huaina Cápac

so for me. Huáscar and Atahualpa dead.
They have raised the bloodstone cross
in Cuzco. The people are afraid.
But the Viceroy of Spain has asked me

to return. He wishes me in the Temple.
What is that to me? My people burn
in the great square. My houses are
plundered. The empire come and gone.

The golden rod that was planted in
the beginning is removed, melted
for the Three-in-One in Spain.
My warriors will stand at the bridges

and along the great road. If I do not
return, all will be destroyed.
My people starve in the high passes.
My people die in the streets.

My priests have read the omens.
Still I must go. Perhaps this Spaniard
speaks truth. I no longer know what
their truth is. I have spoken to the dead

by the hitching post of the sun.
I have returned them to their tombs.

I am Manco Cápac, Lord of the Inca.
The words of Pachacutec are my words:

> *Born like a lily in the garden*
> *I grew like a lily*
> *And when the time came*
> *I withered and died.*

—Peru

The Hustler

In a rainbow bus we begin to descend
a gorge that gapes open like a wound.
The women, who chattered like black beans
in a dry gourd, cover their faces and moan
while the men, not wanting to admit the fear
that turns their knuckles white,
light cigarettes and squint their eyes.

The air fills with hands making crosses.
I make the sign of the cross
with a small grey woman
but she doesn't see me. She has no time
for a gringo when the manifold sins
of a lifetime must be confessed.
Her eyes are buried in the hole
three thousand feet below.

The driver stops the bus, adjusts
the plastic Jesus that obscures
half of his windshield and his eyes—

gets out and stands beside each tire
shaking his head. His face is a scowl
of despair. He kicks each tire in turn,
opens the hood and pounds the carburetor
then gets back on the bus
and crosses himself slowly as the women
begin to weep and children scream.

He mutters two *Pater Nosters*
and a dozen *Ave Marias* as he walks
through the bus with hat extended
to the people who fill it with coins.
He smiles then, bravely, as if the world
had been lifted from his shoulders
and like the thief that Christ forgave
walks out the broken doors to a roadside shrine
and empties his hat into the hands of a Mary
whose expression of humility
hasn't changed in a hundred years.

The people sigh and consign their souls to God
and I relax because I saw him as he knelt there
cross his hands on his crotch as if
he were imploring the Mother of God's help
in preserving his manhood on the road to Hell
and pour the collected sucres in his pocket
the price of safety embodied in the vulture
who lifted off her beatific head,
the men shushing their children grandly
and me, peeling a banana and eating,
gazing into the endless abyss.

—ECUADOR

Election Day

Sitting in the Language Institute
I listen to a German tell us of the time
he spent four months in the prison
high above the city. Yucca soup and rats
wet walls and the empty eyes of men
who spend lost lives outside the sun.
Two thousand marks from home had given him
his freedom. In the distance the spastic rattle
of machine guns splatter the night.

For three days we have been locked inside
these rooms looking out over Medellin.
The election has been called
and thousands of students have marched
into the city demanding their rights.
Two nuns, a nurse, and a boy without legs
ask me to teach them English. The German
laughs. What good is language going to be?
It takes money to go to America.

Kennedy grins beside the passion
of Christ and his hopeless Mother.
*Yucca soup and rats, that's all you'll
live for,* he says. The boy with no legs
tells me of his uncle who lives in Miami.
Everything is beautiful there, he says.
The radio squawks out the platitudes
of El Presidente. I begin to teach him
my language: the word *knife*, the word *kill*.

— COLOMBIA

The Man

Drinking bad whiskey in a bar
on the baked coast of a desert
where the wind never stops moving
and the sand never stops moving
and the sweat never stops moving
down his arms, he wonders
what he is doing beside this woman
whose language he can't speak
and whose body he doesn't know
any better than he knows himself.

He doesn't remember where
he met her or why he is still
with her. He has been watching
two vultures fight over the body
of a rat and he has made a bet
with the fat man who owns the bar
that the bird with one leg will win.

It is the last of his money.
He knows she will leave him
if he loses and he is wondering
what he will do with her if he wins.

—Peru

The Woman (1975)

On a small red stool in a bar
on the baked coast of a desert
where the surf and the sand
and the men have always moved
like years inside her mind
she watches the stranger watching
two vultures fight over the body
of a rat. His skin is so white
and all the hardness that was in him
has drained away like wax off a candle.
It isn't him she wants.

He laughs when the bird
with one leg falls over.
She knows he will leave her.
And it isn't the money.

Hijo de puta.

He smiles. God, she says, God.
He cannot even speak my language,
doesn't know what it is I am
saying, trying not to say, and not.

—PERU

Her

He sits beside her
and his face is missing
as if someone had taken a knife
and scraped it bare
leaving only the holes
through which he had known her.
It is not love that's left him
bereft of sense. It is not even
that he remembers what she was
before she was gone but that
he must sit there with his hands
buried in the black hair of her
and know that what he has
will never go again.

—Ecuador

The Children of Bogotá

The first thing to understand, Manuel says,
is that they're not children. Don't start feeling
sorry for them. There are five thousand
roaming the streets of this city

and just because they look innocent
doesn't make them human. Any one
would kill you for the price of a meal.
Children? See those two in the gutter

behind the stall? I saw them put out
the eyes of a dog with thorns because
it barked at them. Tomorrow it could be you.
No one knows where they come from

but you can be sure they're not going.
In five years they'll be men and tired of killing
dogs. And when that happens you'll be the first
to cheer when the carabineros shoot them down.

—COLOMBIA

Pizarro's Tomb

On broad hills, the broken backs of mountains
and the cracks where earth has split from earth
high walls and viaducts, canals and temples
stand rooted in grey stone. But do not speak.
Only the living eye breeds language
where no language is. The words conjured
are only images. The memory of something
in the race that is unknown.

Pizarro stood by these walls
who now lies dried and shrunken
in his tomb beside the sea.
The great cathedral shelters him
where priests walk hooded
beside God. And Pizarro died
who broke an empire into dust.
So it is told in our histories.
And so it was. But the dead do not speak.

Only the living eye breeds language
out of dust. It is what holds this empire
still. This lust for history.

On broken hills the monolithic stones
that once were mountains stand
Men move upon the land. Pizarro
lies in the capital he built.
The men who were his enemies are gone,
their history unknown, their language lost
as ancient times are lost
though they come and go in me
and will until what now I speak
men know as silence.

— PERU

The Caicusca

The legend says three thousand men
died for this stone in the mountains.
Fifteen leagues were traversed to this field
in front of the heaving walls of Sacsayhuamán
where it lies. It is called *the weary stone*.

Two holes for eyes are drilled into the corner.
From these the legend says it wept men's blood.
The people say the blood came from the stone.
But twenty thousand men who hauled it here
are dead and the fortress says nothing,
ruined, sprawled in the sun.
The stone was for the wall,

the wall was for the men,
the men were for nothing:
what are walls but boundaries for death
that man creates to hide himself behind.
Three thousand men were crushed beneath
a stone that now sits quiet in a field.
The will of man is equal to his walls.

It is the myth of his suffering.
The weight that he carries.
It is called *the weary stone*
but names are made by man for men
as walls are made from mountains in his mind.

—PERU

Farmers

Rain falls, the rain has fallen
and will fall again tomorrow.
The slow perceptible sorrow
of the hours and the clamorous
insistence of the rain.
Below black lines of stone
where bits of earth have clung
like flesh to bone the peasants
break this land to seed.

What took a thousand years to be
turns broken into inch-deep graves.
Here only condors live.
The seed goes down and grows

in the ripped skin a harvest
of potatoes like small marbles.
Each plot of land a handful
and no more. It will take
another thousand years to grow
a crop so pitiful again

Ancient fields are crusted
on the mountains and the men
move on to plant again. No one
attempts to own this land.
The rich control the valleys
and the poor are left with this:
the slow perceptible sorrow
of the rain, the earth and the bodies
of earth's children on the Andes
scraping their lives from stone.

—PERU

The Cuzco Leper

In the morning madness of lost languages
the blind leper sits and sings of night.
The grey bones of his eyes roll
as rosaries of flies like stuttering nuns
circle the remnants of his fingers.
He thrusts his empty bowl
at the sound of the market knives.

He has sat through the morning
and received nothing. The alms he exacts

from the people no longer come.
The fear of his falling apart has been
explained by the doctors from America
and he is no longer considered holy.

A woman, dressed in crusted skirts,
crawls from beneath a cutting table
and fills his bowl with blood.
He drinks
as the flayed and bloody animal
heads stare at him
great mouths empty of tongues.

—Peru

At the Edge of the Jungle

At the edge of the jungle
I watch a dog bury his head
in the mud of the Amazon
to drive away the hovering
mass of flies around his eyes.
The swarm expands like a lung
and settles again on the wound.

I turn to where sunflowers gape
like the vulvas of hanged women.
Everything here is a madness:
a broken melon bleeds a pestilence
of bees; a woman squats and pees
balancing perfectly her basket

of meat; a gelding falls to its knees
under the goad of its driver.

Images catch at my skull like thorns.
I no longer believe
the sight I have been given
and live inside the eyes of a rooster
who walks around a pile of broken bones.
Children have cut away his beak
and with a string have staked him
where he sees but cannot eat.

Diseased clouds bloom in the sky.
They throw down roots of fire.
The bird drags sound from its skin.
I am grown older than I imagined:
the garden I dreamed does not exist
and compassion is only the beginning
of suffering. Everything deceives.

 A man could walk into this jungle
and lying down be lost
among the green sucking of trees.
What reality there is resides
in the child who holds the string
and does not see
the bird as it beats its blunt head
again and again into the earth.

—COLOMBIA

As It Is with Birds and Bulls
For Margaret Atwood

Having left their women in the dust
outside the sanctuary of the pit
the men, gambling on the bloodline
of birds, hunch with their cocks.
Legs plucked carefully and spiked with spurs
the roosters, born to killing,
beat the still air with wings
and tear at the gloves that bind them.

The sand is cleaned of blood.
Pit masters rub pepper
under the arched green of tails.
The birds are thrown.

I gamble on the smaller bird
because it is afraid.
Survival lies in the death you make
believe. As it is with birds and bulls
so with men. They do not hate what they are
they hate what they cannot be.

The survivor crows and falls
blood splurting from its bill.
I collect my money
as the sun stumbles over the line of adobe.
The men sit inside and talk of birds.
The women sit outside and talk of men:
mouths full of coca leaf, they squat
beside gaping bags that receive the dead,

quick fingers tearing
the last feathers from the birds.

—COLOMBIA

Mill Cry

Mill cry, metal on metal,
and the winding clank of the chains.
The lumber market's shot to hell
and every mill's shut down
from Prince George to the border.

Cleanup men and millwrights
crawl under quiet blades,
fix a twisted shaft and lift
out shattered bits of wood,
sawdust scattered in every corner.

They've been burning junk all week:
enough to keep a few men busy,
enough to stop the rust
that grows like moss on the machines.
Al opens the small door on the burner,

pulls his barrow into dust.
The pots have got to be cleaned
and he bends into his shovel
as quietly as he can. He doesn't want
to wake the men sleeping on the ash

the only warm place left to rest
in a valley crowded by cold
the bush shut down
the mill just barely busy
on the last shift working in town.

Friday Night

Friday night riding down from Sugar Lake
where a week's been spent pushing logs
and cutting bush road high in the Monashee
we share the best part of a bottle
and push our truck through potholes
into town. The cook sits between us
singing the Sugar Lake Blues.
I answer with a Buddy Reynolds tune.
Everyone's crazy coming out
and we pass and are passed by the crew.
The job should hold all summer.
Saturday night in town.
I spend my paycheque on a girl
I'm going to marry. Ten years from now
I'll be divorced and wander back
and forth across this country
wondering where I went wrong
but for now it's just a bush road
pointing out: I drink and sing
you ain't going to miss me when I'm gone.
Two days, ten years,
pounding the long road out.

A Beautiful Woman

Mountains, like drifters, never arrive.
Women, like wounds, are what you must survive.
And stones, though they resemble bones,
cannot hold flesh. A beautiful woman
is what you know before you speak it.
The shade your skull casts on your brain.
The space in a stone before you break it.

The Carpenter

The gentle fears he tells me of being
afraid to climb back down each day
from the top of the unfinished building.
He says: I'm getting old
and wish each morning when I arrive
I could beat into shape
a scaffold to take me higher
but the wood I'd need
is still growing on the hills
the nails raw red with rust
still changing shape in bluffs
somewhere north of my mind.

I've hung over this city like a bird
and seen it change from shacks to towers.
It's not that I'm afraid
but sometimes when I'm alone up here
and know I can't get higher

I think I'll just walk off the edge
and either fall or fly

and then he laughs
so that his plumb bob goes awry
and single-strokes the spikes into the joists
pushing the floor another level higher
like a hawk who every year adds levels to his nest
until he's risen above the tree he builds on
and alone lifts off into the wind
beating his wings like nails into the sky.

Slash-Burning on Silver Star

For John Waterer

The brutal anger that cannot be relieved
except on things. The stump torn from earth
rolls with hanging clots of dirt
into the fire. My hands rage at the roots.
Fear lies in my own defeat
because I do not dare to leave this place;
the elaborate care I take
in pouring diesel on the limbs,
the pride that takes its pleasure
in the flame, the anger
when the packed wet earth won't burn
and the shaking,
the terrible shaking
when it's time to quit.

The Collected Poems of Patrick Lane

What Little Is Left

What little is left is the darkness
under the leaves: the earth
and the geese on the skyline
riding cold wind.
Wingbeat and cry.

We lie and listen to the falling
of leaves. The yellow plunge of
softness breaking silence.

What little is left
pulls into itself and sleeps
with its burden: a leaf
and above its fall
the call of wild geese
as they drift through our darkness
riding the season south.

Obedience

I learn obedience,
the perpetual serenity of snow.

There is a benign epitaph in things,
the purgatory of stones in ice.

What have I done that I must praise
this ecstasy? Solitude sits within

me like a mountain, profound,
alien as a wish. Truly, I have grieved

for your back in the storm,
grieved at the silence in words. Always

we shall see each other later,
you with your death in that city

broken by a machine and me,
consumed by a terrible patience

as I watch the way ice grows in flowers
on the black and empty windows of the night.

Of Letters

I sit in the solitude of letters.
Words do not slow the sun.
The sky is clear in the west.

Clouds have passed over me.
Their spun silk hangs
on the bones of the Monashee.

A magpie drifts across the sun.
His long tail writes too swiftly
for me to interpret. On my desk

a wasp I killed last week
after it stung me. Who
will write its poem?

I move toward my fortieth year.
Letters remain unanswered.
The sun slides into the west

and in the east clouds collapse
draping with crystal
the waiting arms of the trees.

Stigmata

For Irving Layton

What if there wasn't a metaphor
and the bodies were only bodies
bones pushed out in awkward fingers?
Waves come to the seawall, fall away,
children bounce mouths against the stones
man has carved to keep the sea at bay
and women walk with empty wombs
proclaiming freedom to the night.
Through barroom windows rotten with light
eyes of men open and close like fists.

I bend beside a tidal pool and take a crab from the sea.
His small green life twists helpless in my hand
the living bars of bone and flesh
a cage made by the animal I am.
This thing, the beat, the beat of life
now captured in the darkness of my flesh
struggling with claws as if it could tear its way
through my body back to the sea.
What do I know of the inexorable beauty,

the unrelenting turning of the wheel I am inside me?
Stigmata. I hold a web of blood.

I dream of the scrimshawed teeth of endless whales,
the oceans it took to carve them. Drifting ships
echo in fog the wounds of Leviathan
great grey voices giving cadence to their loss.
The men are gone
who scratched upon white bones their destiny.
Who will speak of the albatross in the shroud of the man,
the sailor who sinks forever in the Mindanao Deep?
I open my hand. The life leaps out.

Albino Pheasants

At the bottom of the field
where thistles throw their seeds
and poplars grow from cotton into trees
in a single season I stand among the weeds.
Fenceposts hold each other up with sagging wire.
Here no man walks except in wasted time.
Men circle me with cattle, cars, and wheat.
Machines rot on my margins.
They say the land is wasted when it's wild
and offer plows and apple trees to tame,
but in the fall when I have driven them away
with their guns and dogs and dreams
I walk alone. While those who'd kill
lie sleeping in soft beds
huddled against the bodies of their wives
I go with spear-grass and hooked burrs
and wait upon the ice alone.

Delicate across the mesh of snow
I watch the pale birds come
with beaks the colour of discarded flesh.
White, their feathers are white,
as if they had been born in caves
and only now have risen to the earth
to watch with pink and darting eyes
the slowly moving shadows of the moon.
There is no way to tell men what we do.
The dance they make in sleep
withholds its meaning from their dreams.
That which has been nursed in bone
rests easy upon frozen stone
and what is wild is lost behind closed eyes:
albino birds, pale sisters, succubi.

And Say of What You See in the Dark

Now with these words the book of the sky
closes. Darkness cries the news to bats
who fly in alphabets no man can read.
The killdeer quiets on her nest
and rests the wing she lied with
when she drew the man away.
Night is the image of running
water and what runs beneath:
stones who know no wind,
trees who lean above
the broken banks their lives.

Darkness crouches. The sky
closes on the animal: the spider

with one leg poised on hunger,
the black fly concealed in leaves.
My fire creates the night
I am surrounded by. The image
and what runs beneath.
The silence following sound.
That which is bound and that
which is undone. This the bond,
the light and the night beyond.

Day after Day the Sun

Day after day the sun hurts these hills into summer
as green returns to stone in filaments as hard as yellow.
Everywhere the old mortality sings.

Sagebrush breaks the bodies of the small.
Desiccated bits of fur huddle in arroyos
as the land drifts away, melted by the heat.

Down by the drying lake a people curl on sand
having nothing more to do with beauty and desire
than to turn their bodies brown. Images of image

they have forgotten the animal who lived in a hole.
Carrion-eater, digger of roots, worshipper of fear.
They burn as an eagle returns from the long week's hunt

and tears from the bone the breast of a marmot
killed in the hills above Kalamalka.
Satiate she hunches on a dead tree's crest

while below her as she sleeps, magpies,
thin in the thorn trees, more ancient than hunger,
dance their dance of the sun.

At the Edge of the

At the edge of the
field the fence gathers
leaves of the year.
Two magpies in the acacia.
They fatten on the last dead,
old field mice
and the heads of moles
left by the hunting cats.
The farmer picks by hand
spare stalks of winter wheat.
He has gone over the ground
again and again
nothing is wasted.

The Witnesses

To know as the word is known, to know little
or less than little, nothing, to contemplate
the setting sun and sit for hours, the world
turning you into the sun as day begins again

To remember words, to remember nothing
but words and make out of nothing the past,

to remember my father, the Macleod Kid
carrying the beat, riding against time

On the rodeo circuit of fifty years ago
the prairie, stretched wet hide
scraped by a knife, disappearing everywhere
to know the Macleod Kid was defeated

To know these things
to climb into the confusions
which are only words, to climb into desire
to ride in the sun, to ride against time

The Macleod Kid raking his spurs on the mare
the cheers from the wagon backs
where the people sit to watch the local
boy ride against the riders from Calgary

To spit melon seeds into the dust
to roll cigarettes, to leave them hanging
from the lip, to tip your hat back and grin
to laugh or not laugh, to climb into darkness

Below the stands and touch Erla's breast
to eat corn or melons, to roll cigarettes
to drink beer, bottles hidden in paper bags
to grin at the RCMP, horseless, dust on their boots

To watch or not watch, to surround the spectacle
horses asleep in their harness, tails switching
bees swarming on melon rinds, flies buzzing
and what if my words are their voices

What if I try to capture an ecstasy that is not
mine, what if these are only words saying
this was or this was not, a story told to me
until I now no longer believe it was told to me

The witnesses dead? What if I create a past
that never was, make out of nothing
a history of my people whether in pain
or ecstasy, my father riding in the Fort Macleod Rodeo

The hours before dawn when in the last of darkness
I make out of nothing a man riding against time
and thus my agony, the mare twisted sideways
muscles bunched in knots beneath her hide

Her mane, black hair feathered in the wind,
that I believe I see, caked mud in her eyes,
the breath broken from her body and the Macleod Kid
in the air, falling, the clock stopped?

Wild Birds

Because the light has paled and the moon
has wandered west and left the night
to the receding sea, we turn into ourselves
and count our solitudes. The change
we might have wished for had we time

to wish is gone. The sacrifice of hours
has endured and we remember nothing of our days.
Neither the hand with the knife nor human gift

is enough to bring fulfillment. Form that was never
ours, the questioning of paradise, the beauty of

our minds. Once beyond the sight of land
I saw a flock of crows battle the wind.
Baffled, returning, knowing the landfall,
they beat their wings against a strength
greater than their own. We are all of us

as those birds I saw at sea blown outward
against our will. I read the books
and dreamed the dream that words could change
the vision, make of man a perfect animal
and so transformed become immortal.

What else was there to dream? Not this,
not this beating against the wind. Chaos
is our creation and the god we wished was man:
to turn again into the thing we are, yet be
black cinders lost at sea, the wild birds failing.

Ice Storm

As if the snow was more than just a prison.
Ice like an eyelid closing on the birds
beneath the snow. As I am more than just

the owner of this field, knowing every bird
I free, I'll find another dozen dead.
My foot jerks back from the cold,

---

angry now, shaking my fists at the rare
explosions below me, feet breaking through
the icy cloud cover of their tombs.

The Trace of Being

Drunk, the poison breathing in my body,
pain, I am no more than the camels
who died here in search of the deserts
they remembered. Think of them wandering
the upland plateau, avoiding the natural
world they were strangers to.

Moose, elk and deer, the cougar's cough
polite before killing, the bear's paw
printed deep in sand beside the sprawling
wrecks of rotting salmon, the trees
stark, bones in snow, and the camels
chimera, ghosts, the last one dead.

Walking the city I read the desires,
obituaries, bitter poems in praise,
memories of the days and nights spent
waiting for desire, for praise.
The beautiful machines. The poems
of desire, of praise, the terrible vanities.

The beautiful women, the uncompromising
men who are their companions, those
who no longer doubt, who are already
ancestors, the pride that worships things,

great monoliths, erected stone, gestures
to the endless vision called property.

I have begun to believe myself.
A tragedy for a poet who wanted to be
a poet. In spite of everything.
In spite. In anger, confusion, pain,
the transfigured, enigmatic, the tears
of ruin, the body wronged from the start.

Why are the McLean Boys in my mind?
Why are they always vicious punks
who murdered out of fear? Why not
heroic like Billy the Kid? Why
was I always them? The dying gods?
Peter's journey to Rome? Fish on stone?

The trace of being, the impossible wreckage
of the human, without respite, without cease,
turning and turning in spite of prophecy,
corrupt, history without holiness, the gone
peoples, the endless rituals, the dead
and those who accompany them, singing.

As I Care

As I care for the opening in the clouds
and the clouds opening before me
like the eyes of a man in a room
who sees for one moment walls
from a bed he cannot rise from

so I care for the open window
and the cries of the man below.

His body has grown older than he imagines
and in the night he begs it
to lift him from where he lies.
His love will not allow him windows.
The wind parts the clouds
so I care though I know nothing
and nothing can be known.

See where the clouds open, see
where the clouds for one moment open
and the moon, gone down to darkness
so far back in the memory
it is as if it has always been gone
returns, tentative, slow
with that first glow of evening

when light is not light
when eyes are for one moment afraid
and the why of what we are reaches out
to touch whatever it is lying next to us
so long as it be alive
so long as it be something
more than nothing but ourselves.

A Murder of Crows

It is night and somewhere
a tree has fallen across the lines.
There was a time when I would have slept
at the end of the sun and risen with light.
My body knows what I betray.
Even the candle fails, its guttering stub
spitting out the flame. I have struggled
tonight with the poem as never before
wanting to tell you what I know —
what can be said? Words are dark rainbows
without roots, a murder of crows,
a memory of music reduced to guile.
Innocence, old nightmare, drags behind
me like a shadow and today I killed again.

The body hanging down from its tripod.
My knife slid up and steaming ribbons of gut
fell to the ground. I broke the legs
and cut the anus out, stripped off the skin
and chopped the head away; maggots of fat
clinging to the pale red flesh. The death?

If I could tell you the silence
when the body refused to fall
until it seemed the ground reached up
and pulled it down, then I could tell you
everything: what the grass said
to the crows as they passed over,
the eyes of moss, the histories of stone.

It is night and somewhere
a tree has fallen across the lines.
Everything I love has gone to sleep.
What can be said?
The flesh consumes while in the trees
black birds perch waiting first light.
It is night and mountains
and I cannot tell you what the grass said
to the crows as they passed over
can only say how when I looked
I lost their bodies in the sun.

How the Heart Stinks with Its Devotions

How the heart stinks with its devotions—
rot my wisdom, I am drowned
in the poisonous storms of the mind.
To remember dying
buried in the surge of the dance.
Empty your eyes of all save form.
It is the green perfection of the space
a leaf includes in its growing,
the delicate birth baffled by the wind.
Ah, heart, I cannot scorn the armies of your pain.
It is night, air, and I am drunk again on words.
One stone would be enough,
one leaf a feast.

From *No Longer Two People*

The space
between my ribs contains
only a loss. As a child
I dreamed the story of the
mother made from me
and lying alone in bed
counted my cage of bone
the stolen life.

In that turning wheel
called darkness
where dreams, impossible
as fish, swim below
the hunched carapace
that is the sky,
I swim, endlessly
imagining my escape.

The image of the heron
holds my mind. Always
in the distance I see
the great brown stumps
of her legs. Her patience
as she waits for my arrival
is the reptile's dance
the eyes that still me
into death where every
escape is a return
an endless entering

where I swim milk-white
among the clustered eggs.

                •   •   •

You have always driven into silence
planted trees to shelter you
on that prairie that made you
naked. Everything is

measured in space. The outland
that made you care. I seed
as the land is bred, see you
chapped and bleeding, walking

into wind as if that silence was
enough. The man I am tears leaves,
strips wood through winter
into spring, leaving only enough

to breed the dead. Caragana, lilac,
belts of shelter you create
to call a home. Naked you come
to silence but when the wind dies

you turn to dreams of rain. Old
wife, old house, old darkness:
as that woman who walks into
the west, dark as memory is, black

with clothing and wrinkles, without
fear, without anything a man could call
love. You go this way, woman, waiting
like a bird wandered onto the prairie

without wings, demanding nothing
but the roots you call claws
curled into earth, your beak
an opening that kills.

· · ·

We have only begun our seasons.
The time of naming. A thing
crawls inside me, sluggish,
cold as snakes are among stones.
I have opened myself
for the last time. A door
is two visions. My hands
tear at the flesh of my belly
and I fold into the wound,
search for the lost
among organs that demand
a life.
                You will find me
like this when you return:
head sewn into belly,
back broken, and the flesh
zippered with needles,
black stitches
tracks of missing birds.

· · ·

Behind your face a fish swims
covered with pale feathers.
At night when you lie
sleeping among the green

dreams your body calls love
I lift your eyelids, watch
his wandering among the white
rivers of your mind.

                .   .   .

We have begun to bury ourselves.
Each day we emerge more slowly,
look at the trees as they strip
themselves for winter. The sky is
filled with falling and everything
that wants to live escapes:
geese, wild wedges burning south,
the swarms of teal,
black scars cut into clouds.

In dark rooms we find our corners,
collect the books and papers
that are someone else's dream.
Prepare for sleep. This season
is as hard as white, the pure bodies
we have thought ourselves into being.
Closing we give each other
the little deaths, afraid of sound,
afraid of the silence that devours.

It is almost never morning. The sun
escapes and night surrounds
us like an ancient wound. It is the time
for rituals, the time of corn and gourds,
locks of hair, the bones of birds.
Trees like broken fingers reach

awkwardly into a sky they hate
and cold, that broken lidless eye
stares down from the perfect north.

We wish for scabs. We want to be
inside where trees of blood
hide among the scars, the flesh
that calls us human. We break,
tear at our skin and watch the red
burn as it searches among
the forests of hair, black trails
reaching for our fingers, the maps
of our living left behind.

      • • •

Beneath your skirts every man
you have ever known
hangs flayed from the hooks
you call your love. Shrunk
to the size of hummingbirds
their plucked bodies smile
loosely like skin bags
whose mouths are openings
without sound. I break you,
tear apart the webbed sex
and rise within, huge
in your empty. Beneath me
you move in a sea of sweat
shaking with violence. The words,
the songs, the rituals, the
death repeated endlessly. Woman
dead three thousand years,

your life can no longer be
called love. You are
the mask, hunter.

. . .

I.
You have never learned
the meaning of the word
gentleness: tell me
you will kill me
for poems. My death
will be by your hand,
the instrument you speak
with. Every age of you
is death. I have seen
your future, black,
birdlike, riding buses
into the heart of the city
where you weave your
tapestry with names
of the past, each one
a perfect word, sewn
like icons, every mouth
closed by the claw
that holds your needles.

II.
I was never afraid of love,
the images you curl in
when you lie. Woman,
the secrets of your hell
are only beginning to move

to the surface; broken teeth
cut through your skin,
flay me as I sink into
the burned feathers
you call a body. This is
the name of fear.
It turns me to mountains
where I create word, the
wall you rage against.

Face called despair, face
of masks, of vacant staring,
your images are eyes, mouths
black and open in the night.
I know the children
who burned in your brass mouth
the men with genitals slit
who bled to death
on the steps of your temple
calling out your name.

       • • •

Out of mountains, out of cold stone
I have fashioned a word
that will destroy you, hunter woman.
You who wear the skins of birds,
who decorate your dark breasts
with the skulls of snakes,
the fragile clicking bones
whose song is crow.

Out of mountains, out of cold passes
I have fashioned a word
that will claim your shadow,
that will climb through your skin
and enter your heart.
I will cast this word in stone.
I will cast this word in sand.
I will cast this word in earth
where your power hides trembling.

Your body will fall, hunter woman.
Your voice will be silence, hunter woman.
Your song will be dust.

Out of cold, out of the distant mountains
I have come with a word
that will destroy you, hunter woman,
and when you are silence
I will reach into your death
and with my spittle
I will fashion from your dust
a word that is not a word
and I will take it back to my mountains
and speak you into life.

· · ·

Now is the time
for patience. All the animals are fallen,
the birds escaped. Furrows, black ruts,
wrinkle the face of the earth.
Only the bound remain, rotting potatoes,
the curled black vines where tomatoes hang

shrivelled by frost.
               There is no forgiveness,
only a blind woman calling out her dead,
the snow, the broken earth.
                   Alone at night
I look down upon your sleeping,
hear the unborn crying for release.
Castrate, stripped of seed, I break
a trail through the snow.
There is no looking behind.
Everywhere the wind covers my passing.

L

THE EIGHTIES

The Measure
For P.K. Page

What is the measure then, the magpie in the field
watching over death, the dog's eyes hard as marbles
breath still frozen to his lips? This quiet repose,

the land having given up the battle against sleep,
the voices crying out beneath the snow.
It is the cold spear of the wind piercing me

that makes me sing of this, the hunger in your eyes.
It is the room of your retreat,
the strain in the hand when it reaches out to touch

the dried and frozen flowers brittle in their vase,
the strain when the mind desires praise,
the music as of soldiers wandering among their dead

or the poor dreaming of wandering as they break
their mouths open to sing as prisoners sing.
Or soldiers marching toward their devotions

or the poor marching or the rich in their dark
rooms of commerce saying this is finally the answer,
this will allow us the right to be and be. To be

anything. In the field the rare
stalks of grass stick stiffly into air.
The poor, the broken people, the endless suffering

we are heir to, given to desire and gaining little.
To fold the arms across the breast and fly
into ourselves. That painless darkness. Or stand

---

in the field with nothing everywhere and watch
the first flakes falling and pray for the deliverance
of the grass, a dog's death in the snow? Look

there. Stark as charred bone
a magpie stuns his tongue against the wind
and the wind steals the rattle of his cry.

Temenos

> *Bide your time for the battle, bird of black pinions;*
> *There you shall find the flesh of mankind to devour in abundance.*
> —Ancient Sibylline Oracle

> *"The blossoms of the apricot*
> *blow from the east to the west,*
> *And I have tried to keep them from falling."*
> —Ezra Pound, "Canto XIII"

1.

What was it I knew, out of my desire
out of the endless pain? Were those deaths
more than any other death? Am I less

than those who lived the field and wept
for what they saw? Am I less
that I could not return them with gifts

to their people, sing their bravery, praise
the order that their fate ordained?
Mean spirit, man who is little in all things.

There is no honour without humility.
Though the ravens cannot count the dead
their beaks are sharp. There is no honour.

2.

Is the eye met with anything it has not seen
before? The tree at its moment is the one tree.
It cannot be seen again as the river cannot be
the same river. To hold the still world,

the strain to have it thus and thus.
What shall I do with the leaf
locked in stone, the earth holding its bones,
a future king who cries his vanity,

the endless torment when the forest moves?
Sybil, is the prophecy less because
it does not meet the eye? Can the name be
changed? Is the circle without centre?

3.

The circle is drawn. I have come down to this.
Break free. It was all I asked in the temple.
That there be a memory. That nothing be forgotten.

Though we break free we scribe another,
each spell bound to hold us in our track.
Must I begin or end or must I turn

---

upon myself and give to apathy its virtues,
the bed, the ease of wine, books, women dancing
with eyes deep as lethargy, deep as love?

Must I be broken to be free? The corpses lie
where the men have fallen. And I said, let them lie
so their bones be testament to our victory.

They are a wall greater than a wall. Red dust.
Does their circle include me?
What is the sacred name of the sacred name?

4.

How many rituals must be lived that they will teach us
our worth? I have come back to the temple
but have not entered there. I have known the light

yet I have seen only shadows playing by the fire,
have cried out this and this, yet the dead plague me.
Not women, wine or words will ease me.

I have asked the priestess to speak.
She has refused me. I will have the temple down.
To what avail? I take her silence as a sign.

Am I profane? The man must do
whether or not the spilled entrails speak.
To what end and is there an end to things?

Honour, virtue, words to give a death a life.
Who was it said there is a truth?
She will not speak though I stand as stone

in the sun. She gives no answer. In the dark
cave there are only shadows on the wall.
Brooding bitch. I lie here with my desire.

5.

Whose words are my words? Is what was said
what is said? Do I repeat myself in what I think
I know? In whose spell am I bound?

In the still centre of the still world
there is no stillness. I would hold the wind.
I would throw my voice and say, I am the wind.

6.

We stripped the dead of their insignia.
We took their shields and sent them back
as a sign for the people. The orators spoke
endlessly our praises. Fat men. Wordsmiths.

We flanked them here and here until the centre broke.
We slaughtered them everywhere.
There is laughter around the fires.
There is not a wall that has not fallen to us.

Why do I lie here? There is an end to the world.
There is an end to battles. What use is it to win
over barbarians? Shall I go east or west?
Why do I lie here waiting for a sign?

7.

I remember the lessons well.
Let me repeat:

Go beyond who you are to who you are not.
What you do to yourself you do to me.
What you say of me you say of yourself.
Will you name the stone, stone?
Between the name that is and the name that is not
is the thing that is. Call it stone.
Call it not-stone. What have you named?

I remember the lessons. I remember them well.
In the shade of the trees.
The philosophers and the poets.
The endless tangle of words.

8.

What would you conquer
if you do not conquer yourself?

I am a river between walls which has but one course
to follow. What use to rage against the walls?

Shall I protect myself against the sword?
Do I not create the sword that kills me?

Why else would it be held against me?
Better to lose your sword than your shield.

A man's protection is the protection of the state.
Am I of use to anyone dead? Alive?

A man can drink from the river
yet the river flows.

9.

This has little meaning yet I mean well.
That I tried to be for my people for better
or for worse. That I tried to be.

It is no mean ambition to choose a death
that will leave you alive in the mouths of men.
I sang the bird inside of all the deaths

I was surrounded by and they were not
made meaningless by what I did.
What I did was a good.

10.

The gift is the honour done to the dead.
What greater honour than to lie where you have fallen.
A raven's eye contains its own humility.

To know they lived the field and died there
or were captured there and came before me
covered with the blood of their defeat

asking for a death with honour. What else
could they do but die by our swords?
Each narrow pass holds a death with honour.

At that moment they were and the circle
around them was the spell that bound them
to me. Temenos. I was not asked to judge

for what judgement can there be if their desire
was to remain on the field? No shame. I sing here
of what I knew though they were only shadows.

11.

With whom do I speak?
Do you want the real?

What is the real that you demand it so?
If you learn nothing

then there is nothing
to learn.

Just Living

It isn't just violence I told them
in the warm white room below the prairie snow.
It's just another story I no longer know
the truth of, tell it now to hide the holes
when conversation dies. The stories
are like fossils locked in Tyndall stone,
just there and no one knows the meaning.

We were five hours over mountain roads,
the tourniquet wet, red, and him in the seat

lifting the stump of his arm each mile
looking by the glow of the dashboard lights.
Jesus, he kept saying between cigarettes.
In the pink ice cream bucket between us
the severed hand sloshed in the melting ice.
He never looked at that.
And then the usual madness, the nurse
wanting his name and birthdate, demanding
his wallet's proof until I lifted his sleeve
and showed her. He grinned at that.
The sight of those veins and tendons
made her turn away. The doctors got him then.
I asked one if he could use the hand
but he said it was probably dead. Too many hours
and, anyway, they couldn't put it back.

On the night-road north
I thought of the saw and the flesh still
hanging from the teeth. They didn't wash it off,
just let it cook in the cants coming down
off the headrig. But that hand in the bucket.
The ice had melted. I emptied the water out,
looked at it curled like an empty cup,
a dark blue spider sleeping. Strange
how the sight of it didn't matter much.
I thought of drying it out and giving it
to him when he got back. I laughed at that,
could see it hanging in the sun
outside his window at the shack.
The light dancing on the nails,
maybe using it for a bird feeder,
whiskey jacks perched on the fingers
eating suet from the palm.

I thought those things.
When you're pushing your life
down a tunnel of light
it goes like that. Night and mountains.

I stopped at Mad River bridge.
I'd been driving then eight hours.
But here's the strange part.
I took it out of the bucket and held it
there in the night. It was just meat
you understand. It could have been
a club or a tool for scraping earth,
like when your arm has gone to sleep
and feeling it you know
there's nothing there. What do you do
with the pieces of yourself you lose?
I knew I couldn't keep it and I couldn't
give it to his wife. Bury it?
What for? The life was gone
and he was still alive.
It was cold and it was night and I
had shift work in the morning.
I threw it high off the bridge
and for one moment it held the moon
still in its fingers before it dropped
into that darkness down below.

It's just a story now.
Sometimes I wish it wasn't me was there.
Violence? Hell, I knew men
who lost more than their hands.
You know, sitting here drinking wine
it all seems so far away. That whole life

was violent but it didn't seem so at the time.
We were just living you see.
Him? Oh, he came back. They'd healed him up.
His wife and kids had left by then,
gone off with the trim-saw man to Edmonton.
He hung around for a few days
but there was no work for a man
with a stump. And Claude, the boss,
didn't want him there. You can see why.

CPR Station — Winnipeg

You sit and your hands are folded in
upon you. The coffee is bleak, black. This
catacomb is lighted with the pale death
our fathers called marble in their pride.
This is an old song. This country.

This country was still a hope.
It is the CPR Station in Winnipeg,
11:30 and no one is leaving again.
The trains are late. The passengers wait
for the passing freight of the nation.

The people have turned to stone, cannot be
moved. The coffee is black. The night is far
above us. Steel passes over in the rumbling
called destinations. The gates are dark.
There is no passing here.

There is no desire to pass. Someone with
a lantern hesitates and moves on.
The river of white marble swirls cold
beneath us. It is worn, worn by the feet
of a nation. Your heavy hands. Your

fingers are huge, swollen with the
freight of years. This country has
travelled through you. The man with the
lantern sits in the far corner, waiting.
If you could lift your head I could go

out into the night with grace. O hell,
you are old. Winter is above us. Steel
wheels. If you could lift your head.
Bleak black. White marble.
And the trains, the trains pass over.

There Are Still the Mountains

It is winter and the sun just barely risen
crawls above the trees. I stand obscure
and swing my arm into the light
scattering wheat across the ice
as the birds descend to feed.
Caged among icicles
the wild cat coughs, measuring hunger
by the freedom he endures. The small
exist just beyond his claws.

In any other season I would gladly see him
dead. Half-torn to pieces by this snow
he scrapes a beauty from my mind,
a thin white solitude. Fragile explosions
the birds ascend into the air,
circle in fury the wild one's head,
driving him empty, dark across the snow.

The Long Coyote Line
For Andy Suknaski

The long coyote line crosses the pure
white and the prairie is divided
again by hunger. The snowshoe hare
thin as January creates a running
circle encompassing a moon of snow
as the lean lope of the coyote
cuts in a curving radius
bringing escape down to a single terror.
It is the long line, coyote, and the man
who stands in your small disturbance
counting the crystals of blood and bone:
three by three, coyote, hare and the howl
where the true prairie begins.

Blue Valley Night

1

It is blue valley night
and the light of the moon
long gone over the eastern ridge.
The last mosquitoes, slowed by cold,
settle into the grass and wait
for the sun. Only the owl is awake
in the arms of the widow-maker.
She cowls her wings and cries,
warning the small of her falling.
The insatiable mice hesitate and then,
driven by hunger, move toward the open.

2

Walking over the hill to Charlie's
the grass in heavy bending
bumps against my thighs.
The day is never long enough
and I pray for the nights
when the moon brings back
to this narrow valley light. The end
of the month is the worst time.
He has moved from wine to extract.
Outside the door I stop
at the gibbous cry of an owl
and then, teeth tight, move
the hanging blanket and go in.
Odours cover me
like mouldy skin. Charlie
lies naked on his bed. The room
smells of acrid lemons.

3

Old Charlie wakes to the smell.
The empty bottles are decorated
with the drowned bodies of flies.
The first-aid man from the mill
has come and gone after washing away
the stench his body made
when everything collapsed.
The stained yellow rags lie
strewn in the grass beside the door.
He does not remember the moon.
The smoke-smeared ceiling,
thick with oil and soot,
shifts and moves above him.
He looks at the loose skin bags
that are his arms and wonders
where his flesh has gone.

4

The graveyard crew, cleaning
for the morning shift, empty
their barrows into the conveyors.
The burner belches fire.
Yellow machines squat on their pads.
The diesels in the power plant
beat out the time of night
as a doe, browsing beyond the tracks,
lifts her head into the hunger
of the hunting owl.

5

I place the first-aid kit
on the floor and begin to wash

away the sticky yellow mess
from his legs and belly. He moans
and thrashes. Mad at all the reasons
that I care, I yell, *Shutup!*
He is beyond hearing tonight.
The flesh comes slowly grey.
I roll him over, clean his back
and thighs, then lift him to the
blanket. He weighs no more
than eighty pounds. I've known him
for two years now and heard him
deliver the whole of "Dan McGrew"
from memory. Cursing the night,
the filth, the job and all my love
I tear the smeared sheets off
and put him back, rolled like a child
in the red Bay blanket. He drools
on my arm. Everywhere is wreckage.
Flies circle the empty bottles.
All I can do is swear.

6
Charlie stands naked on his bed.
Thin yellow gruel slides down his thigh.
He turns awkwardly in a grotesque dance
and stumbles to the floor.
He checks each bottle, scraping off
the flies with his pale white fingers.
It is, as always, the last night.
He licks his arm and tastes the lemon sweat.
The past tumbles through his mind
like pieces of distorted chain.
Laid out on the scarred trunk

his suit with ivory buttons
gleams beside his brushed black bowler.
He sticks his finger down his throat.
Nothing comes up but air
and a long silver loop of spittle.
A bush rat watches, wary in the corner.

7

The scattered dust of stars
gleams bleakly between the mountains.
A last bat flutters
down the windless night, his belly
full of moths. The bull snake's eyes
rest lidless on a stone. The cold
has stiffened him. His body, thick
as a man's arm, winds among boulders,
drawing what little is left
from yesterday's sun. Five frogs,
a garter snake and deer flies
have fed him to silence.

8

I swear again I will go
to the Dutchman and break his face.
He rips off every pension cheque.
His store owns all the workers
in the village, their debt
longer than their lives. Trees
eat into the moon as I walk
back to my cabin. It will take
an hour to get rid of the stink.
Sound trembles in the deadfalls.
Something is dying.

9

Down the long row of bunkhouses
Charlie walks, dressed in the dark
perfection of the ancient suit
he brought with him from Africa
when he was mustered out.
The knob of his swagger stick
blinks silver among his fingers.
Distantly, above the sounds of metal
from the mill, the whistle of the CN
Mainline Passenger calls out
the siding at Wolfenden. A cat
hunches in the grass and spits
at a night filled with the sweet
smell of lemon. Ears torn and bleeding
from a fight beneath the cookhouse
he is heading, sullen, home.
Charlie tries to whistle
but his cracked lips begin to bleed.
He hums instead. His bare feet
find their own way in the gravel.

10

The station agent's dog
lifts his massive head from sleep.
He watches the man weave
toward the circle of light
in front of Mad River Station.
The chain around his neck
clinks softly. He drops back
into his slow dream of running.
A muscle in his shoulder twitches
but the swollen wood tick,

intent on blood, ignores it.
It is almost ready to drop
the purple grape of its body
into the scattered straw of the pen.

11

I sit naked in my chair and watch
the flames consume pitch pockets.
The coffee is bitter, boiled
too long on the stove. In the distance
the hum of the Mainliner
opens into the valley
all that is other.
It is cool and I am tired.
Tomorrow I will try again to talk
to Charlie. He will tell me
of the Boer War and the family
that hated him in Ontario. I will
try to convince him to go on the wagon.
He will look at me, his head cocked
sideways and grin and I, hating
myself, will offer him his single
drink of rye from my bottle.
I sleep and dream I am no longer
the first-aid man to this village
of slaves and broken lives.

12

Charlie sits straight on the bench
in front of the station.
Small white stitches curve
across his shoulders. They are
the tracks of a wood mouse

---

on black snow. Turning his head
he looks at the great eye
of the train as it appears
out of the curve at Poplar Flats.
He straightens his school tie
beneath strands of greasy beard.
A drum of sound drowns the night.
The twin blades of the track
sag into their gravel bed
shifting below the approaching
weight of the east-bound freight.
Charlie grins and whistles,
licks his lips and steps out
in the diesel stillness of the ties.
The wind the train pushes
flattens his suit against his bones.
His body explodes.

13
In the cedars, crows
lift in their feathers,
lift and settle
in their sleep.

Something Other Than Our Own

Sitting on the mainline tracks
we look down into silence as snow,
soft as an owl's flight, drifts and falls
among hunched lumber shoulders of the yard.
The sound of a rifle firing three times

has pulled us from our beds and brought us down
to squat in a row of bodies
strung like spikes along the rail.
Below us in the yard two men hunt:
one naked but for boots and hat
the other wrapped in the formless grey
of the railroad. One with a rifle
and one with a guitar.

The story with a bottle of cheap rye
stutters down the line of men
changing shape with every mouth that forms
the words but holding true to the one thing
each man knows: the one returned
sick from his northern run and found his wife
dancing naked to the other's music. Each of us
had wished as much. His wife was something other
than our own.

The story stutters down.
A young kid throws his hair back:
Bitch, he says,
They should be hunting her!

We say nothing,
watch the millyard down below
and try to catch the bodies where they move.
The moon begins to clear.

They oughta kill that sonufabitch!
the millwright says and each man nods
though none of them will say
which one should die and who are *they*.

It is our theatre of war,
this camp with too few women.
The bottles and the card games aren't enough.
Every dance is broken by a fight. Each man's
wish to hold a woman free as that.

In the yard the two men move.
Neither wants to kill.
It is too cold for that.
The naked one, clutching his guitar,
slips from between two hulks of two-by-six
and stumbles down the line.
The other waits until he disappears
then slopes across the trampled snow
past us into town. *I knew he wouldn't kill him,*
someone says and then we laugh:
He looked so fucking helpless in the snow!
He'll freeze his balls off
long before he makes it to Mad River!

We laugh again and stumble toward our beds
now cold. I dream a woman turning into me.
I sleep and wake with eyes
caught in the smoke of cigarettes
their small hot stars
twisting above the bunkhouse beds around me.

Annie She

tamps the snoose behind her lip
and cocks her heel hard on the edge
of the beer-parlour table. The game is
tight with fifty dollars riding
on the eight-ball caught on the rag
in the corner. It's a bad lie
with a wall intruding on the stroke
so Annie takes her time
while the young logger she battles
laughs from his table
his buddies giving him the elbow.

Yet you can see the lines of white
around his eyes: to lose to a woman
like Annie, a great gut-hung lady
with breasts like bags of suet
and a laugh that lays a curse on any man
who doubts what she can do.
And he is doubtful
has been from the first
when she challenged his table.

He tips his beer across his jeans
and Annie roars: *What's the matter, sonny?*
If your cue was a cock
and the hole a lady waiting
I bet you'd spill your load
two jumps from bed!
And while he suffers
the laughter of his friends
she rises like a whale in spring

and spits her snoose
and with one hand
jig-pokes the ball into the side.

If you wasn't a woman,
the loser mutters as he pays
and Annie takes his money
turning so her breast
catches him on the shoulder
and spins him to his knees,
Woman, Annie says, *woman!*
Why I eat young boys like you
for breakfast!

       And laughs
and tamps some snoose behind her lip
and buys the boys a round
all of them afraid of her
and none of them seeing her eyes
flick their way through the bar
like pale grey bitches on a garbage dump
who, finding nothing to feed upon,
break with their hunger for the hills.

In the Wet Haze

For John Daly and Laura Benwell

The house is locked, the roof is done.
I stop my pounding, gather up my tools
and stare. In the wet haze
a great blue heron slides west
a single line of smoke in the evening air.

The Silence Game
For Michael and Richard

We name the hidden things,
invent shape and colour,
teeth, claws and feathers,
monsters small as needles and birds
huge as the driven clouds
when they are herded by wind
to break against the broken teeth
of the lands we call mountain.
It is called the silence game.

Today they take me into the bush
to show me where the bear sleeps.
It is not the real bear,
the one that eats each day
at the pit behind our house.
All of us know that.
Among trees dark as memory
we stop, squat on our haunches.
We have been together so long now
none of us can remember when
we began to be each other.

The bear that is not a bear
rises from his bed of moss
and shakes his shaggy head.
A fly spins a circle above him.
His tongue lolls softly
across our faces
as he passes between us.
We turn and watch him go.

On the way back we say very little,
stop only once to watch a mushroom grow.
I leave them playing by the alders
and sit with my coffee on the porch.
In a few more years they will enter
the government school where
a young woman from the city
will teach them knowledge.

I think of this now we are
separated by range after range
and a thousand miles of prairie
and again that cool wet tongue
leaves its word upon my cheek.

Fragments

Memory begins with the small,
a piece of paper lodged among roots
in a garden I no longer remember,
a child's body still upon a table
in a room surrounded by singing.
The years are a patience
as if in my mind I am always
there with a language
I can never understand.

What is it that makes us strangers?
What is it about our love that it holds
so clearly in the past: words
I can see but cannot read,
a child's small death.

Why do they hold us,
why do they tear at the heart?
Where is the stone I'll never see
again, the man I was?

I think of the twisted trail
a friend's dragged body made
when he was drunk with ice
or the hand of a man curled to a fist
in the dust below the trim saws
which the doctors didn't want
and which I carried home
my eyes listing in the cold
the broken fingernails, the silver ring.

Prospect of dream, mirror of water
sheltered in rock, thin shadows
dropped into sleep to hold the fragments
I remember. I think of the past,
how it lives in still images:
the paper seen in passing years ago
when I was still a child
whose writing I can never decipher
try as I might in the recurring sleep

of its being. What is it that holds
the fragments, the women
dressed in their long black
like swans born in furnaces
whose song surrounded me,
the men passing among themselves
the pale red wine in a shack torn down
years ago and a still child, white,
upon an immaculate kitchen table.

Winterkill

I know in the coldest corner of the land
my death is written with the same hand
that holds this skinning knife.
The arm that folds the green skin back
and nails it to the wall to heal
in the long slow grief of the wind
wants only a coat to wear.

The dead care for me as snow
cares for the sea or sand
cares for the stone that was a mother.
There is no other than myself to blame
for grief. I live because I must.

The trail is worn too deep for loss
and time that is spent in time
cannot be trusted to serenity.
The green skin folds and freezes
in the wind. A winterkill.
The truth of love is in the colour
of these hills: a man's cold breath,
the brittle death of trees inside a fire
and the howls of the animals
as they leave behind nothing of their passing.

I Am Tired of Your Politics

"be political, impersonal with passion"

—Dorothy Livesay

Let us remove our vanities
bring our dreams and end
even this with an embrace.
The bitch is old. She sleeps
in the sun with her head
heavy on her paws. The birds
conclude that noise
is an uncertain violence.
We must not hide
our innocence, the distant
singing we call love.

Lady, I am baffled
by your care. The mind is
always a dull thunder.
Shall we make politics
out of love? The bitch
is old. She sleeps in the sun,
decently, with a gift
for silence.

Shall we sing other than
our lives? Peace, wisdom,
excellence in the small
affairs of the heart?
But it is not only an old dog
we speak of nor the quiet
of the birds who grace

her age with their flight.
Listen, once when I was
young, I knew a woman
natural as beauty, brave
with all the mysteries
she was born to.
Let us not pity her.
The sad compassions
are of little use.
She left her love
in a thousand beds
until she lost her mind
and fell into the
dream called death.

Let us respect her now,
give her at least the desire
that she could be in the sun
with her hurt head resting
on her pale white hands.
The will is not holy.
One moves in stillness.
Look, even the birds
are decently silent
while she sleeps.

The Return
For Lorna

The beautiful, the males have returned
after a winter colder than a century of ice.
They pick their way among rotting drifts
in search of worms still buried deep
and sleeping stones below them.
I walk into their arrival
knowing everywhere I am not
it is spring and women
dressed in nothing but sun
are whispering the memory of colour.
Breasts red and beautiful
the isolate males begin again
while somewhere in a place called south
grey lovers invent themselves
and turn towards ice
each one bearing in her beak
a twist of dream.

Marmot
For Rudy Wiebe

Tall sentinel among the growing stones
you break this day into all
the pieces of silence. I
could have wished to be less of an enemy
but that is the dreamer singing again.
Pour out my blood on the hills.
Fear is no longer part of me.

I have walked among your stones.
I am one of the living
driven into exile.

Chinook

Beneath the tree, glutted on winter
apples, seven sparrows lie
drunk, beating small wings on snow
as if they could fly into it
and make of ice an element as free as air.

The Garden (1980)

praise the idea
the disordered care
so the stone

you have placed
for beauty continues
with a studied delight

as if a god
had dropped it.
arrange, arrange

plant within
the casual border
your desire.

this is the web
and the ritual of
the web.

what discipline obtains
what way shall you stand
so your eye observes

nothing? the sand
raked into a sea
and the sea

an illusion of sand.
this garden, sprung
from a desire

for order, remains
a scream. it wants
you to want the

storm. it prepares
for rage, the sudden
irrevocable flood.

If My People Remove from Love

If my people remove from love
turn from the certain mouth
I cannot relieve them
cannot shift the wave whose fall is swift

If I am finished with their fear
their falsity   their disdain
who is to say that song
is so clumsy its sound is less than love

If at the far place the moment
is met with a pure desire
its delicacy is in the hand
whose moving moves upon my thigh   your breast

And if out of their remove we live
among their shame there is still
the fall of your hair and your eyes
upon me are not less are more and are not death

Buffalo Stones

This river was a wall to the wandering buffalo
who drifted here in the last of summers
before turning back to graze their way south
into the American guns and the hunters
who shipped their tongues to the east.
On the brooding hills above the blue
great stones remain. Around their base
wallows curve in deep depressions.
Above them marsh hawks wheel.

But forget the hunters and their steel,
the old ones who wish
the animals' return to these wide plains,
the farmers who turn the rare

skull to sky with their deep plows.
The bones are long since shipped to Minneapolis,
a dream of charcoal stolen from the sun.

Above this river a child slides a stone
and does not know his long smooth falling
is a history of death, his breath
a breaking that the wind will steal.
But I, who wish to speak with history,
will sing of this though kingbirds cry
and coyotes move like ghosts
across the rolling grasslands.

There is nothing to atone; there is
only a dreaming, a child climbing,
and a man above a river who still feels
the heart's revenge, the grieving and the earth
falling like a smooth stone into darkness.

Skull

With my love, the mountains
far away and the wind
eating everything
in its hot mouth.

The river drifts us
deeper into silence.
Two herons rise.
The river moves.

There is nothing
everywhere. The small
patience of cactus
lifting from the dry

earth we found
after the storm
after we followed
the golden antelope

into the hills.
There is only a
drifting. We find
our way to the stone

where buffalo
circled endlessly
before man came
to change their name

to silence. What
is it we wished?
I only know
when we descended

out of the far hills
to the desolate beach
where the carved sand
curves to sky

I found a skull
scraped by wind
into a thinking
beyond death.

I did not know
its name, wished it
covered again in fur
or feathers

so I could speak
its life. Now
it sits below
the cactus

we brought home
nameless, small,
a silent
white in the window.

The Succulent

Dawn surrounds the pallid succulent
I bought in Safeway. Everything
green was on sale, from trees to cactus.
Plants without flowers went for nothing.
What was left moved toward Sunday and
the nuisance ground. Native to the sun
and southern deserts, it leans now,
slowly, with great patience, toward
the light in my northern window.

I have taken pains to water it
and leave it so its life is undisturbed,
have given it what love I have
when no one is around to make me strange.

Only fools talk to plants
in south Saskatchewan. But what can I tell
this pale succulent that strains
toward the sun. How can I say
the bright desert it imagines
is only snow, cold and bitter in the dawn.

The Wind

Open prairie and dreams come thin as grass in wind,
a blade that cuts the mind behind the eyes.
Hawks rest on wind and gulls float everywhere,
flying without direction, even at nightfall,
when a man could follow, thinking they are a sign,
and drown in a landscape no higher than his boots.
Such a man thinks the snow a death. He dreams
of walking into cold; prays for a storm
he can find peace in. But he never dies.
Only a woman walks into wind.
She is the one who will never return.
She knows the waste of sand, the dust,
the spines of cactus caught in flesh.
She is the thought that leaves the breast,
the long wind crying and the dream of rest.

Indian Tent Rings

For Northrop Frye

I

There is nothing here of use, only the spare
grasses bent to wind. Cattle wander through
this place, faces bred to dullness,
mouths vague machines of flesh, cropping
the thin spears. Dust, dirt, hard grasses,
desiccated moss; the stunned explosions
of lichen moving slow as startled novas
on the rocks.
        Look at these low hills.
This earth has never known a plow
yet isolated ranchers love this place.
In sleek trucks they cruise for coyotes
to run down or antelope to push
beyond the limits of blood
until they fall against the walls of wire.

II

I am left with stone rings,
the one image I can endure.
They grow on the slow hills
as if a living dust had been ground into them
making proud flesh. Or rise slowly out of time
like teeth in the mouth of a dead man
that push through brown leather lips
until they consume their own mask.

III

A man and woman walk these hills. I see them,
small against the cold falling from the north.

Their eyes have praised the natural disorder
of ravines, the rare stands of stunted poplar,
the quick hurt of dawn. It is accident
they find themselves far from their city
and they are not sure of what they believe.
Their history is the mortuary house at Leubingen,
the rocks of Stonehenge, the grave circle at Mycenae.

The circles lie like crucibles on the land,
and silent in the central ring, the woman squats,
her small face turned from wind. She wants
to have been here since the sun was born.
Below her, on the slopes, the man is
searching for an arrowhead, a scraper,
some sign to prove he was here.
                         Europe
is a place they've never seen but they
believe it more than they believe this place.
It is like, they say. But like what?
What holds them here?
A betrayal of concern? The flaw of freedom?
It is enough they are here, the woman
caught in the circle and the man
circling below her, his eyes
trying to find a thing more than an idea,
a bit of pebble carved into himself.

Drought 1980

The unsold milk cow falls to the hammer
as the last hog screams himself to a pickup,
pulled by the measured cursing of a man.
A yellow dog circles and barks at a truck
piled high with implements. Dry grass breaks
under its tires as it creaks to the correction line.
A woman slams the screen door and lists her losses:
the spoons, the cups, the names of plastic flowers.
The land, split by the sun, turns to ash
and is spilled by the wind into sky
making at dawn a wound more beautiful
than the night that lies ahead.
The dawn lies ahead.
The leaving.
Strange names are whispered:
Calgary, Vancouver, Okanagan.
They roll on the children's lips, on the back porch
where the yellow dog clicks nails on wood,
in bedrooms where the fear cannot be seen, in shade,
in every darkness where the sun cannot be found.

The Killing Table

*I follow the natural grain, letting the knife
find its way through the many hidden openings.
The blade of the knife has no thickness. That
which has no thickness has plenty of room to
pass through these spaces.*

—Chuang Tzu

The mind is pierced, my knife
slips up inside the throat,
cuts the carotids, the blood sudden,
hot as memory and the hanged bird
beats itself with wings
and flies to death.
The red, like a stream of piss,
steams and bubbles in the blood
that came before. That's nine, I mutter,
and throw the carcass in the box
with his dead brothers.

I have been killing cockerels
this morning. The living swarm
around my feet like white reptiles
pecking at the blots of flown blood
and trying to fly into the dead-box.
Surrounded by cries,
I curse and kick them away,
bear the new dead to the barn.
There is still the cleaning to come.
I slam the barn door and lean back
against their clamour. Into hot
water the dead ones go. Their feathers

strip away like leaves in wind.
My return is known. They have waited
at the door they cannot enter.
At the killing table
feathers whirl as I lower the bucket
to earth. A storm of wings build
a mountain of birds as they fight
to bury themselves in the still-warm blood.
I turn away, knowing the bucket is
already empty. They run beside me.
From breast to comb they are stained red.
Blinded, half-congealed,
they stumble, fall, rise again
pecking each other wildly,
no longer sure who is alive
and who is dead.

Monarch I

Half-pet, half-wildness, Monarch leads
his thirteen hens in search of food.
Range birds, they return to the pen
only for sleep. He guides them
through the day, one eye upon the sky
for the falling hawk, the other on the earth
for weasel, marten, coyote, fox.
He hates their wandering.
His beak drives them from the brush
where they've gone to lay, their clucks
his torment. They fly from their beds
in squawking clusters. Only the brooding
ones are left alone. He knows the mother's

eye. It is his only fear.
When they are lost he scratches at the dirt
and calls out *food*. They run from everywhere,
push him away and peck at the nothing there.
During the sun he mounts them one by one,
his hard black beak holding their heads
as his spurs rake their sides. The soft
flesh tears. The hens brace stiff wings
against the ground and hold him there.
When he is done, some wounded, some surprised,
they flip the tangle of their tails,
rub beaks to stone and cluck contentedly.

Then darkness moves among the trees
and shadows stretch like necks into the grass.
He drives them from their graves of dust
to the safety of the pen. Drinking and scratching
they search for parasites among their feathers.
The preening over, they rise on ruffled wings,
settle above his head. In the bramble thickets
three brooding hens are left. Theirs is
a single eye. He does not go to them.
Their warning chirr keeps him far away.

He counts the rest and gives one final crow,
then satisfied and finally tired,
lifts to his isolate perch among them.
Claws locked, the hens pull night
into their breasts. They sleep a flying dream.
Monarch's red eyes close, they open, search
the gathered dark for weasel sound or fox,
then close like wounds upon a restless sleep.

Monarch II

The strange rooster, splattered black
and barred like a rock beneath the sea,
perches on his rotting log and watches
Monarch and his hens. His is the waiting
learned in isolation. He has flown
from somewhere far away, a cast-out bird.
For weeks he's stalked the margins
of this world. There is hell to pay
in the yard. Monarch rages at his hens,
drives them in explosions toward their pen
and punishes each one who dares to wander.
Hour on hour he rises to his height
and feathers, startled, white,
stick from his curved hard neck
as he crows his pride.

The barred bird rips at his fallen log
throwing bits of splintered wood behind him.
At last his challenge comes.
He crows a single cry
and runs a circling dance
toward the cluttering hens.
Monarch cuts him off.

They curve around each other slowly,
claw the earth with talons, tear
up bits of moss with cutting beaks
and crow and crow again.
Their spurs are living knives.
Blades hard as bone
and sharpened to black points

they angle inwards,
the killing stroke
a perfect falling spear.

The hens curl feathers, preen
and raise their tails
to the fighting cocks.
Black eyes blink.
They peck each other in descending order.
The least of them, a hen with feathers gone,
turns upon herself and pecks her legs.
Their clucking is a whisper, not a shriek.

The roosters leap.
Wings beat the air.
They fall.
The barred bird slips on grass.
Monarch lifts and with one pass
drives his spur into the other's breast.
Blood bubbles from the beak.
His lung is pierced.
He jerks but Monarch's spur
is caught between his ribs.
He pulls, then flops away.
Monarch rides him to his death.

His crowing stuns the air.
The hens flutter, wings
cowled and tails held high.
Monarch stabs at the barred bird
then stalks toward the garden
where young worms have risen after rain.

Weasel

Thin as death,
the dark brown weasel slides
like smoke through night's hard silence.
The worlds of the small are still. He glides
beneath the chicken house. Bird life
above him sleeps in feathers as he creeps
among the stones, small nose testing every board
for opening, a hole small as an eye, a fallen knot,
a crack where time has broken through.
His sharp teeth chatter.
Again and again he quests the darkness
below the sleeping birds. A mouse freezes,
small mouth caught by silence in the wood.
His life is quick. He slips into his hole.
Thin as death, the dark brown weasel slides
like smoke. His needles worry wood.
The night is long.
Above him bird blood beats.

Monarch III

Tendons ripped in his right foot
Monarch thumps awkwardly across thin straw.
The toes are curled beneath and the hard claws
cut into his calluses. The night is gone
and the first raw light has broken
making what remains of dark a crystal cave.
A hard red hand stuffs bodies in a bag.
He tries to peck at it.

A rough boot kicks him back.
The woman leaves, cursing her lost eggs.
Hens forage in the yard for maggots.
The swift teeth of the weasel are not there,
the crippling cut,
the falling,
the surprise.
He has no memory—for him there is no past,
only an eternal raging present. He
cannot remember the sharp tongue
as it lapped, the flapping
hens who bounced against the walls,
the sudden light, the man and the gun
as it exploded near him. He tries to crow
and falls upon his side. His nerves scream
enemy. The hens are wandering, far away
in the secret world of brush. Balancing
with his wings, he clumps toward the door.
The tiny stumps of brain along his spine
rebel against him. His eye
catches the shredded body of the weasel
where it hangs a warning by the door.
He pecks at it,
then rages to the yard
where he stumbles,
falling among stones.

Monarch IV

Monarch hobbles in the rain.
His foot is swollen twice its size and pain
dances like a nest of lice inside him.
The hours have driven him once more
into the yard where he has tried to find
his hens. The brooders in the caragana hedge
ruff their feathers as he staggers past
and pull their eggs into their breasts.
The unclean bird they see is a broken thing
with twisted grimy feathers and a comb
whose paleness sings of death. A hen stalks by.
She's laid her morning egg and now relieved
of birth wanders in search of dust. Nagging
mites have crawled into her crissum.

She stops by Monarch, holding him there,
and like a falling lance she cuts his comb.
She clucks her special cry.
The other hens come striding through the grass
like reptiles from a past almost forgotten.
The rooster croaks.
If he could dream he'd dream of mounting her.
Upon his comb the blood spot sits,
a small red brain, an insect of desire
come out of him. Beaks slash.
Half-quizzical, half-bored, they walk around him,
then drift away in search of food or dust.

The Mother

You wander a long time in search of her.
Her claws have made an opening in earth
and now she crouches there,
her unborn lives around her.

        She has pulled the pure white feathers
        and from her naked breast
        hang startled rubies.

She is the incubating thing
and hour on hour she rolls
the perfect spheres with her beak
cutting inscriptions on the shells.

        Inside, in darkness, bodies jell.
        Their opaque eyes absorb the runes
she scratches in their sky.

The Golden Hills

And they took me to a bar in the deep valley
long after the sun had deserted the golden hills
and I went with them through the dark streets
where old men slept in their dreams and children
dreamed and women turned slow in their sleep
and there the band played songs I had not heard
since I was a child and some I had never heard
they were so old and some that were known
only in that place and I was bright among them
though they were strangers and did not know me

and she was beautiful, the woman I had come
for over a thousand miles through the sun
and the night and the wind and the blue
reaching of trees in the high mountains
and the endless flat plains with nothing
but grass and the high wheeling birds, she
was beautiful, full of what I had not known
and I drank there and I danced there
wildly with her and she danced with me
and she looked at no other man but me
until the shadows were a tangle of strings
and the band became lost in their music
and the music was wild in my mind and wild
was our dancing with each other
while the strangers cried aloud
                    and
I tell you this though you will not believe
me seeing me here still young
that once I went among strangers
and danced and she was of a beauty
but do not ask me why I left that place
and do not ask me

There Is a Time

There is a time when the world is hard,
the winters cold and a woman
sits before a door, watching through wood
for the arrival of a man. Perhaps a child is ill
and it is not winter after all. Perhaps
the dust settles in a child's breath,

a breath so fragile it barely exists.
Tuberculosis or pneumonia. Perhaps
these words place her there, these words
naming the disease and still not curing it.

Maybe it is not the man she waits for.
We want it to be someone. We want
someone to relieve this hour. On the next farm
the nearest woman to the woman is also sitting
in dust or cold and watching a door. She is no help.
So let it be the man. He is in the barn
watching the breathing of his horses.
They are slow and beautiful,
their breath almost freezing in perfect clouds.
Their harness hanging down from the stalls
gleams, although old and worn. He is old and worn.
The woman is waiting behind the door
but he is afraid to go there because of her eyes
and the child who is dying.

There is a time when it is like this,
When the hours are this cold, when the hours
are no longer than a bit of dust in an eye,
a frozen cloud of breath, a single splinter in a door
large enough to be a life it is so small and perfect.
Perhaps there are soldiers coming from far away,
their buttons dull with dust or bright with cold,
though we cannot imagine why they would come here,
or a storm rolling down from the North
like a millwheel into their lives.

Perhaps it is winter.
There is snow. Or it could be dust.

Maybe there is no child, no man, no woman
and the words we imagined have not been invented
to name the disease there is no child to catch.
Maybe the names were there in a time before them
and they have been forgotten. For now let them die
as we think of them and after they are dead
we will imagine them alive again,
the barn, the breath, the woman, the door.

Luna Moth

It was the dream of a room I lived in,
not the real. Nothing had prepared me
for the scream of the cot, the broken
door and walls so thin you could hear
the scalene voices of the rats.
I remember almost nothing from that time;
the steel cot and the rats,
the grey bulb hanging like a sun gone out,
the shredded roses on the walls
and the old woman living next to me.

Nights when the damp was heavy in our rooms
she'd walk the worn hall carpet
as if it led somewhere
but at the stairwell leading into night
she'd turn and walk the blue threads back.
Her skin was thin as glass.
Once she asked me in but I was tired;
no, that's not true. She was old, and I
could smell a kind of death in her.
I knew enough to be afraid of that.

One night she called me to her room
and pointed to her window. Trapped
between the storm and summer panes
a luna moth struggled in the night,
its thin wings leaving on the glass
a fragile dust. She was too old to open it.
Yellow paint had sealed the seams.
I don't remember how I did it now,
only that it finally opened and the moth
who should have flown just sat there
small against the twisting city lights.

There is love to discuss and the pale dignity
the old grow into, sometimes called wisdom
by the young, though they would call it desire
knowing more of pain, but I was young
and for the first time on the street alone.
The rain came down, a mist of falling sky.
I looked out at the city and the lives
that everywhere were sleeping. She stood
behind me shaking, her eyes like small
blue animals caught in a sudden cold
and searching for a place to rest, to hide.

The moth, not knowing it was free, sat
bruised against the glass. The woman
thanked me for my trouble and I left.
I packed my duffle then and headed north
but I remember looking back, the yellow light,
the roses on her walls and her grey face
thin against the window and the moth
between us like an arrowhead
pointed at a moon it couldn't reach.

A Red Bird Bearing on His Back an Empty Cup
For Lorna

It was almost night when I asked the land
to hold in the folds of her bright skin
my body, save me from the wind. But I
have asked for abstinence before. The sun
broke against the land, its death
a witness to the thing I found:
a red bird bearing on his back an empty cup.
His eyes were blind. This is not fear.
I have spoken of prophecy before.
Silence is not the end.

I was walking the long hills in search
of forgiveness. I found the red bird
though all the signs warned me to be gone.
There was a rising moon. It was then
I disturbed your troubled sleep.
And then the grey dog, thin, and you
beside me, sick, grieving for innocence.
The dog carried with him the foreleg
of a deer; the hoof, the flesh still
hanging from the bone, the tired flesh.

Forgive me, I am almost old.
I was dreaming of my father in the garden
when winter was upon us, his rueful laugh.
The years have been long for us too, and winter.
It was finding the blind bird and his cup.
His burden seemed a consolation. He was why
I lifted you from sleep and led you
through the fences and scrub willow.

Perhaps there is a perfect detachment.
God knows, I want to believe in things.

I will list here what occurred: the bird
bearing on his back an empty cup, the dog,
the foreleg of the deer, your sleeping
and your rising, the pain I feel
when you are sick to death, my father,
all the things that swing into the mind
when I am tired of praise. It will always be now
when you read this poem. It will be new
and you and the nights and the long day gone.
Perhaps to name is excellence enough.

I will not speak again of death, though
I want death. There are many ceremonies.
I have not come through but there is
a quietness. It is not for nothing we love.
Even though winter is upon us and all
the signs warned me to be gone, though
my trespass will be called to account,
it is no matter. We are here to praise
the occurrences, the moment when a red bird
bears upon his back for us an empty cup.

The Weight

Part I   Redneck

i

sometimes called redneck
        (though in my dictionary *Britannica World Language*
           for Empire not included as
           beneath contempt: so in this place

one who does not know what a suntan is
as he who goes out in the sun
and is marked there as one
the sun has given tongue to
        (the dog springing on the doe's sweet scent
          giving tongue   and running to earth
which is duty
not to deny
         the neck burned
eyes buried   calling the dead to come
        alive again
           once more
              the sprung
measure

marked cleanly
the land giving up to him who is willing
to be burned by the sun's sure stroke
as that man   old *Jack Lane*
1921
    each spring how far back
planting   (*the Venus of Willendorf*

making / taking
        his measure
                it is time
                      (O double-horned *Venus*
                      and *Mars* mad moving

and at night
would go out into the field alone
this kind of penance.
holding phallus in hand and
spread his seed there   (what flame to open here

        his body naked   an impure white
        as of a growing thing left under a stone
        but for forearms and neck
        his breast a dark V pointing down

face upwards upwards into her pale belly
waxing   as at the stars the same
that flung milk
        allowing his body
to hurl itself without seeing into night
his howl
      upward
         the formal desire
seed placed
      with ritual
on the land
      a pale pool
as *Jack*
said
his mother's secret
by the moon
      a good year to come

ii

one thousand five hundred plains grizzly killed
for what in the *Cypress Hills* (?)
                          from the French cyprès
                     but of spruce and pine made
so *Marty   I am reminded*
           I am not at home
           here where I live
           only at hazard

his fierce hiatus
1877 plus
three years to kill and gone
     rode down on horses in high summer so
                                   the hides
           useless (it was not commerce drove them
                but that space was better made empty
     (the lodgepole pine
will not open unless to fire
unwilling to release
the seed unless born to flame
                          the fires of '79/'80
opened them
                and wanting the land for eden   and all
what else with the buffalo dead? the wild
called by man in this place mis / placed
not knowing eden if they tripped on it
they wanted nothing
but not (as that *american* said
     the land was ours before we were the land's
save us from such romance
                it was by this dream of paradise

they scorned
    such to be pitied now
            nothing to write of

and in the pines
silence does not reign
            (there was a tourist from *new hampshire* once
            one of those who travelled thinking
            they know   and she
                        talked of liberation
            (at least she did not speak of freedom
            not knowing the difference

it's so quiet here
you can't hear anything

her ears could not hear
the languages surrounding her
the wildness singing

            (*Boone?* she asked
            O that Boone! (in disgust westering from *kentucky*
            a *Fraser* a *Mackenzie*
            she would not know them
            their discoveries not
            a subject of her people

everywhere the mushrooms thrusting
after a rare rain
but she would not eat of them
poison she said
            and talked instead of shamans and *Angkor Wat*
                        the *Indians* by god
Indians!

and I had placed before her a rare feast
(the moon would not kill
though the moths fly to her
            and instead searched
            with the dead for grubs   the sweet berries
            the mushrooms thrusting
as in 1200 BC
singing   *In the wilds there is a dead doe*
                   In white rushes she is wrapped

iii

it will be time enough to sing
                        we have barely entered here
                        naked with our seed
the veil not torn
though we worry it
with our breath
Jack Lane said his people entered
            this continent later than most
but not as late as some
                        on the goode ship *Expectations*
                        out of *Portsmouth Harbour*
                        landfall in *Jamestown, Virginia*
                        the year 1630/32?
circa some / time
                        and then after a great deal of
                        property rather than happiness
                        as the *Declaration* was to have read
                        but *Jefferson* knew one revolution
                        was enough for one nation / his
                        (*Burr* maligned and *Hamilton* on the ridge
by *Loyalist* desire
driven north (the many driven south / loyal to anarchy

that the world be ordered
believing still in ritual
        (Joe Fafard saying the queen is just folks
        but she was sundered from them
        and is still *Queen* there / *Virginia*
more than just the self (liberation?   come on!
a riff-raff wanting profit for the self
an exclusive   a private taking
     I said the hell with them all
told a lady older than lace in *Boston* 1966
who called me (chidingly in bad humour
a barbarian
for she saw me a stubble-jumper with shit on his boots
shit!   better on the boots
a daughter of the revolution   ,DAR
well   *Washington* burned
and that shut her up
   (the trees were random and she could not stand them so
her egg would not open in hell or thicket
the seed gone north to order
        (in the museums now the buffalo chips
        by these we warmed ourselves
        the bones long since shipped to
        Minneapolis the tongues eaten
       (the horned beast
       encircled and
       no virgins anywhere

let alone a fire on the prairie
the mountains either
        to be
      on the prairie / *in* the mountains
from the mountains she comes

her hair on fire
out west and beyond

                    no wonder *Bowering*   *Jabez*

     (I too'd be cursed if I'd that heritor
        no gods before him he could hear
the same
             and him the barbaric yawp *Jabez* I mean

or a seed catalogue / what order in desire
              the beautiful they wanted
              an English garden
watch out *Ontario*
 we have left that place   behind
to find a world of which you know nothing
we may not go back / *to the country of our defeat Al*
god knows there is little left of this now old

(grizzly in 1979 ate her breasts off and the soft
 belly stripped her intestines out and ate those
 left her in the bush covered with warm leaves
 intending to come back after the sun
 eased the tension in her meat
 she slept where he was wont to walk of a morning

(followed her wounded up a gully grizzly sow
the *American* three hundred dollars for the head
from *Chicago* or was it *Fort Benton*
      (whiskey back south
      Walsh off to *Wood Mountain*
          (where *Suknaski* would later sing)
          to a man he would send to death
      out of love *Sitting Bull*

---

wanting order in the land
1951
the trophy kind (as Teddy Roosevelt
        damn their ilk
but with money to pay
told him to stay on that ridge and shoot
when I spooked her   *damn his hide*
(shot a *sharptail* cause he was bored with waiting)
all of ten minutes and me moving carefully
if you know what I mean
till I shot her in the mouth
my rifle fourteen inches down her throat
she was trying to eat her way through steel to me
but I crawled up that slope and kept on shooting
at him   till he begged me to stop

what made me stop was the ants on my intestines
I couldn't concentrate

(1961 finding that boy west of *Avola*
Everything eaten but the feet (he had good boots
And the head (he had a good hat

as you might say   *a redneck's dance*
   seen by some as hesitant
but only a careful stepping
        one did not step willingly into shit
        or on a rattlesnake (as *Belford* said
        get a good outfit
        he swings his lantern
        knows where he is going
(killed all them grizzly on the ranch
  there're none left now

but if only one'd come back
I'd feed him just to keep him alive
it's not the same around here anymore
(and I never hunted again
 and still don't like *americans*
 when they shoot a bear
 it's like they was shooting him
 in the back, you know

I guess so   or that bear in the cookhouse 1962
         at *Mad River* with *Winning Chow*
         late of Hong Kong
but that for another time

we kept on moving till
all there was was another damned ocean
so we decided to make our final stand
right
     here   1100 BC
               on the mountains there are fine trees:
               this is chestnut and that is plum;
               and now, that is torn up and this is cut—
               I wonder what crime they have committed?

iv

as the sound from a fiddle's bow strokes lightly
on the strings
               Morrissette on the lawn playing
               to the children and *Suknaski*
               whirling *Lorna* up the street
(and she said: *if they didn't know us before*
                 they know us now

as this is a kind of new love
                    a long way between fires

and as awkward still to say we are here
                                        where
to be loyal
is to have order
the sense of it   a lesson in desire

but in *The Green Home* with my great-uncle *Jack Lane*
Cranbrook deep in the mountains

what year would that have been?

there weren't very many roads   he answered
at least none going anywhere   he added
                              so I would understand
                              the discipline
to make a long story short
we sat at the table at dawn
my mother would've cleaned the whole house by then
(house?
floors so you could eat off them
the porridge sitting cold in front of us
but not eating until he rose
as he rose each day   plaintive / plaint
                                 the bow moves
                                 across the flower
into the room
she not complaining (
to the table and spat into each bowl
we sat with our hands on our laps
heads down

and ate what he had done
                                    just outside Pincher Creek
                    1899
                                    in the foothills
                    mountains so close
                    you could make out the trees
                                            if you'd an eye
                        sharp enough (keen sighted
            foot loose the hills
but my sister
            what was her name?

it doesn't matter now what her name was or is
it's what I'm saying that counts
                                    (without number
going on fifteen
lifted her hands one morning   she had pretty hands

(when she came from *Hamilton Ontario*
  she brought a kitten   all she was allowed
  and we waited a winter somewhere near *Maple Creek*
  and she had to keep hiding that kitten all winter
  in that hole in the ground from him who saw it
  as food — the hole covered with the hides
  of the dead horses we ate all those months:
  him saying: *here kitty, here kitty*

covered her bowl not wanting it anymore her hands
splayed out like this
so his spittle landed on the skin

he had three whips
            one: a quirt for the white stallion

(short and to the point
two: a bullwhip for the stock
(coiled black on the wall
three: a rawhide whip
(kept alive in the rain-barrel
he knew their purpose
so
took her to the barn and tied her
hanging from the rafter where he hung the pigs
and stripped her to nothing   the rawhide falling
around her in clean bloodlines   the flesh   lifting
soft to his touch until his arms were tired

(could clip off the head of a *russian thistle*
 at twenty feet practised it every day
 even in winter said he could cut
 the first flake falling
 into three pieces before it hit the ground

and then

waited at the table with hands still folded
he came back in then we ate our food
the spittle a pale pool
and when he was full
went back out to the barn
where she hanged waiting for his touch
and worked her over for another half an hour
there   he said   *there*
not in anger you know
but as to a young contrary heifer
with patience

in one slow tone

we took her down when he was gone
to *Fort Macleod* on that white stallion

(syphilitic I always knew from that whore
Short-Change Lane he was called from the days
on the ridge near *Hamilton Ontario* where he cheated
anyone he could   till he was run out
the neighbour shooting at him in the field
for raping his woman

kept my sister two months in the back room with
the preserves until she healed enough
no scar anywhere you could see
dresses down to her ankles buttoned up to her neck
and she never married
nor did I
she got religion and married no one by god
that sonufabitch

Jesus   you wanted to know
          something of your history
          eh?

v

the lyric pain
       terror in the mind.   *of this and*
          less we speak
pursued
        but McKinnon you kept the grief alive
recognizing nothing around him

having never returned
as *Kroetsch* begins the long road home
    (I cannot do what you do / cannot risk it
        so the formal quest
            it is no wonder   there are those
                  who came here by choice between
dis / orders
            as rhetoric is *skill*
            in the use of language
            but a *textbook treating of discourse*
            especially written discourse
            (the rhetoric of Frye's image
      in the text the grief is not lost

the dance begins here
a formal complaint   the bow drawn across the mind
    the lyric tunnel hidden from those
        who cannot risk from fear

the rawhide whip in his hand held
writing on her flesh his love for order

Lane
but that old bugger after he lost the ranch
to gambling and women and the white stallion
in a corral somewhere else
because of *three sixes* as against a *flush*
                (mark you well
took himself into the hills and
shot a bitch wolf in the haunch deliberately
till she went back to her den
her milk mixed with blood
then finished her off
but the pups is what he wanted

locked them in the small barn beyond the house
(house?
and raised them caged
was going to exhibit them back in *Ontario*

                        (and then south to where
                        Virginia? and then
                        how far to *Willendorf?*
make back all he had lost

by wagon back through all that space to *Hamilton*
in 1906 or thereabouts
but their howling drew the wild ones
down from the hills and the ranchers
who had taken his ranch the old bugger said
(lost by cards and drink
taken from him what was his by right of occupation
(those fine wires stretched with teeth
standing there watching beyond
      by others ridden
               his land as his woman
threw meat through the hole in the wall

but the ranchers rode in one day
and he was too far away from his *Winchester*
told me to get it

I just stood there

they roped him fifty feet from the house
and tied him to a wagon wheel
               a wheel's iron ring
               tightening around the brain
shot all three of his wolves

masked men and angry at him
they'd been losing beef you see
rode out cursing him and his seed forever
my sister praying in the dirt near the back door
and me
and mother she was almost dead by then
started in on those floors again

they said: *that was enough of that*

he never got over it and that cage
he'd built on the old wagon sat there
till he died and *Ontario* never did see those wolves

        (that he reached deeper than he knew
        to where the song begins and ends

I still got that rawhide whip

here   you hold it

sister used to visit up until she died
and she'd take it out of the box
and hold it in her hands and pray
I never knew for what

and that was your blood
of you and by you and for you
and I never married
knowing what I know I end
                right
                    here

Part II The Dance

i

Maple Creek Olde Tyme Players
the oldest now eighty
the youngest looking forward to seventy
and no one who can play the strains
of the olde airs
of music   but they are
                            firm in their resolve
that I believed they brought out of their bows
a reticence   a music wanted carefully
by the rest
            in the way bones become gentle
                    and not to be risked foolishly

            (the young outside on the lawn
            drowning this music out with an other
            listening to *Nashville*—where's *Nashville?*
            the nightline Tin Pan Alley moved to *Omaha*
            Moose Jaw Swift Current Maple Creek

    but enough of that
enough
            I went crazy with the *two-step*
    thirty years of forgetting
tangled in the strain to have it right

A Circle Two-Step
                changing partners
    quickly without meditation
    as the line must come in the poem   thus!

sure then it was of so deep a past
to mix the blood and break the music
         into a perfect ordering   our turning we
and I said: *I have forgotten how*
and she said: *don't you worry now sonny*
         you are very close   a spry lady
(must have been eighty years old
her feet light
as a doe on dew
         knew then in any other time we
         would have mated
         the concern not
that there be a husband   but that
the blood be kept true
the best dancers mating
in the night
     in the pines
         the gift being the child
of the dance
       and therefore hers
         men on the outside
         women on the inside
        change
    whose face is mine?
      this first one
        the dance is one

A Barn Dance
    this is how we worshipped
      each movement animal
        by its measure an invocation
            imitation
    that there be health in the land

and for those who inhabit it
who give us our strength
                    as the *foxtrot*
        (the dance of the wild
                    animals as we know them
            far and beyond the running dogs
(*pallid the leash men*
                    and not in this life run ever to earth
            but of the sky
so the formal grace of   gone now
as the animals are gone their spirits no longer
worth imitating   their souls beyond invocation
but for *Maple Creek*
the young not knowing
in their desire to end it all here
they believe   (a world where all birds come
                    wrapped in Cellophane
                    as we were hungry on that play farm
                    in upstate *New York* liberal Zen
                    the blizzard of '71
                    the chickens happy pets but hunger
                    made them see them true
                    and I brought in two tough birds
                    (the chosen killer but not by lot
                    clean kills both
                    but their revulsion!
they were
              as they said wanting
                        to find
themselves
              who were lost

What was it like in the olden days?
not by god profane
but pagan   yes
            it has not lived in their hearts
and will not live again in my life

the heart's revenge pumping
black over the block
the keen edge of the axe   (berserker given to blood
falling to a perfect measure   (kendo warrior
by one who is willing to kill
kept intact
by the keen notes of the *Olde Tyme Players*
each sound stroked upon us
our blood
            dancing

ii

by the moon
        a doe
                    in soft moonlight
hesitant as she saw me
and I moved to her
a music between us

as she lightly grazed
her mouth soft on the phallus
pale light
            I called to her
                    doe
and danced
knowing she

The Collected Poems of Patrick Lane

was the moon's light
                    the grove
the mistletoe golden on the boughs
and she
grazing upon the sudden mushroom's thrust
she when I danced to her
(with grace allowing
found the mushroom's lip
still damp from her tongue

and ate of her   sweet night
        in the lodgepole pines
the air heavy with dew
the air

iii

theirs not to be taken lightly
each player is too old
                    know they hold upon their bows
        more than just resin
hold the dance

so my body kept wanting
to let go into any kind of anarchy
not wanting their discipline
and they looked down on me with eyes
saying
                we bear the weight
                            here
the public hears
and we must not shame ourselves before them
our robes are not stained red in the agora

we have come
         willingly to play
for you
         she said

a *waltz*   )the dancers a sedate circling
                     having found their partners
                     arm by arm
                  not holding
              a formal desire
           the woman's arm
        resting on her man's
     she gave him to lead
  and not to be taken
                  lightly
and this be ritual
the dance
           just after the *French Minuet*
circling
upon themselves
one couple crying as they whirled so slowly
around the floor
an *Olde Tyme Dance*
in *The Cypress Hills*

and it was an ancient woman called
                        in the centre
           she

and around her the old men with fiddles and bows
waiting for her

to say

      play
      a *Seven-Step*

and the moon everywhere in the pines

Part III The Offence

Io: *And what was the offence*
    Of which this is the punishment?
Prometheus: *It is enough that I have told you*
         A clear story so far.

My friends, each time I see you, you are
Looking worse. I take it as an omen
When you say you are just barely making it.

yes, Belford, as we all must hesitate to break
the undisciplined spirit
tell them only there is a dark
but in spirit re-forming
until they are no longer
but the music will have verity
                 do you give ear
       it was no eden then or now
     but that we made it so
   this space inhabited
          with dancers
it is only we have stopped listening
there being little enough to say
the grizzlies dead
         and that man still
            tied to the wheel

mandala of the real
spirochaetes whirling
in a brain gone bad
what is remembered
is a foolish act
their dream
where it met the territories
The Cypress Hills   a good place for lodgepoles
where else on these lands where a tent can find
support a good place to find your spirit
the last ground of the buffalo
bewildered / mazed / sequestered
what is your first face?

a circle of more than just wagons
holding them by their bones
I keep it
on my desk
(the stone)   the whiskey traders
up from *Fort Benton*
and then *Walsh*

Jack Lane not far behind
if winter comes can spring

the ways of speech made plains

Cortez brought more than death
to *Tenochtitlan* his welcome
so the horses
met the peoples
at the precise
moment   the peoples met their deaths

look at it this way
the names of the stones are simple
do not change when you talk to them
but from the back of a horse
you can barely hear them

the CPR had a farm
big as all outdoors

The Iron Horse

you gotta keep moving
you can't stand still
if the skeeters don't get you
then the blackflies will

O westron winde

at times
at all times
spoken so slowly
and with such a careful stepping
and not this formal discourse
I have come to only out of grief

to move you was harder than you knew
you preferred another ecstasy
loved the horse the moment

and better'n ridin' a grizzly
for what d'you do
when you get off, eh?
that tyger burning bright
watered down with
anything but whiskey
a trader's delight

twenty miles to water

thirty miles to wood
goodbye homestead
I'm leaving you for good

one buffalo robe
ten days for a woman
to chew into shape
with her mouth
speaking into skin
for your body
        a robe

                traded for
                one-half a cup
                of whiskey (?)

what did you say?
            the offence

           she called me to dance
           and I no longer remembered
the steps

The Forbidden City

Within the city there is a city that is forbidden.
In it there is a garden with
contorted stones and miniature mountains,
tiny exquisite temples and waterfalls
splashing into pools where ancient fish still swim.
On warm nights when the cherry trees bloom
the old ones dance with their concubines
and some with their eunuchs and all are beautiful
in their delicate silks and embroidered robes.

Golden fish rise in the ponds like jewels
and temple bells ring softly in the dew.
Poems are written as the amber wine is poured
and their gaiety is like green jade,
their laughter smooth as ivory,
as they wander among the new palaces and tombs
rising around them like moons in the pale light.

Lotus

Lotus, delicate as shy laughter,
float in the pond at the ruined palace.
A girl in a thin blue shift, cool in the day,
reads English by the trunk of a willow.
Branches drift in deep water.
There is a chance, if she learns the new
language before the end of summer, she
will be chosen for the university in Beijing.
On the stone bridge, strangers, their faces
white as rare jade, point at the fallen
stones, the worn heads of dragons. They
come from a country that has no past
and they are awed by the wreckage of years.
The bridge they walk upon once carried
the concubine of a prince. She was young
and beautiful in her white silks the one
night he called for her. After that, she
languished in the House of Women.
A lotus, pink as a child's mouth,
opens. The girl by the pond is so still
the strangers on the bridge do not see her

and do not hear as she carefully repeats
their words over and over under her breath.

Tour Bus

The day is heavy with heat and the fields,
thick with green rice, bend under the sun.
We follow a truck through the red dust
on our way to the Great Wall. A train,
slow and heavy with freight from central China,
labours through a crossing, and the young men
who laughed in the back of the truck
as the wind whipped their smooth black hair
sit talking in their sweat. One of them
finds a cicada among the empty boxes.
He lifts it out and holds it by the wings.

We wait, visitors in our air-conditioned bus,
listening to our guide tell us of the workers
who died constructing the Great Wall.
For every stone in the wall there is a body.
The long train passes into the west.
The lean young man reaches over the edge
and drops the cicada in front of a tire.
They laugh as the truck moves over its body.
The wind begins to whip their hair.
Fields pass, replaced by stunted trees.
Someone in our van points at the far mountains.

Her Laughter

The day is beautiful, and beyond
light catches the ripe fruit of the trees
above the paddies and the patient men
who guide their bullocks through the mud.

Trucks lumber past the melon vendors
and children. The harvest has been good.
All the oracles were correct and the people
smile at the day and the year to come.

A grandfather sits playing with a child.
She laughs as she runs through his hands.
He could catch her but what for? She is
young and her laughter is good in the sun.

The Great Wall

There is a moment on the wall when a man looks out
over the far horizon and wonders when
they will come. He does not know who they are.
The wall was built many years ago, long
before he was born and before his father was
born. All his life has been spent
repairing the wall, replacing the fallen
stones, clearing away the tough grass
that grows like fingers in the masonry.

Inside the wall the land is the same
as outside and once, when he was confused

by the hot wind, he could not remember
which side of the wall he lived on and he
has never forgotten the doubt of that day.
He has seen no one but his family for years.
They were given this work by someone
a long time ago or so his father said
but who it was he did not remember.
It was before his time.

But there comes a moment, there always does,
when a man stops his work, lays down his tools,
looks out over the dry brown distance
and wonders when they will come, the ones
the wall is meant for. At that moment
he sees between earth and sky
a cloud of dust like the drifting spores
of a puffball exploded by a foot.

He knows there is nothing to do but wait,
nothing he can do but stand on the wall. Everything
is in order, the wall as perfect as a man
can make it. It does not occur to him
the cloud might be only a cloud of dust,
something the wind has raised out of nothing
and which will return to nothing. For a moment
he wonders what will happen when they come.
Will they honour him for his work, the hours
and years he has spent? But which side
of the wall do they come from?
No one has ever told him what would happen.

He will have to tell his son, he thinks,
his wife. He wishes his father were alive

to see them coming, but he is not,
and his son, who has already learned
the secrets of stone, is asleep.
It is a day to remember.
In all his life he has never been more
afraid, he has never been happier.

Commune Girl

It is evening and the geese are lost in their feathers.
Crane flies flutter in the glow of the lamp. Tired,
the woman weaves paper thread through the last firecrackers.
There are almost enough. Market day in Huang-chou.

In a voice dry as chaff from winnowed rice
she sings "The Girl by Green River" quietly
so her husband and sons, tired from driving
the bullocks through the new fields, do not waken.

A young voice joins her from the corner of the room.
Her daughter, because of the moon
and the warm night, is restless and cannot sleep.
Already she is thinking of a man.

Silk Factory

The factory is warm and the lines of machines
clatter as shuttles carry thread
through the weave of dragon and phoenix.
White brocade falls from the looms
and the red silk and the white. A weaver girl
laughs at a young man and he trips on nothing.
When she moves he cannot see where he is going.
Grey with silk dust, windows rattle
and the glass is frosted with snow.
The bitterness of Ch'en T'ao is long ago
and the shuttles are no longer lumps of ice.
Still, the brocade the weaver girl makes
is not for her, and the young man, though
he labours for many years, will never buy
the white silk she works so hard to weave.

Mountain

High on a mountain above a palace
sits a temple, small in the sun. There
Chiang Kai-shek was captured. It was night
and the Red Army surprised him as he slept.
He leapt from a window, trying to escape,
and ran the narrow path to the mountain,
alone and nowhere to go.

At times all history comes down to this:
a small man, running in his pyjamas,
desperate, fearing he will die

or, worse, be chained as a vassal
to an empire far to the west and live
his last days on an island in the sun.

The Dream of the Red Chamber

I cannot find the symbol of the crane on the silver
ink boxes. Tarnished with dust they lie among
the scarred jade bats and scattered lions.
On the walls hang dresses from the Ch'ing.
Their stitching reveals the faded
dance of chrysanthemums. I search for the ancient
in the clutter of dynasties. An old woman
walks with slowness among the curios.
Her feet are bound. They are the last illusion
in a world that no longer believes such pain is
beautiful. What I want to take back from China
is found only in my dream of the red chamber.
Ashamed, I walk into the crowds on the street
where young women, bright as birds,
run laughing among the wu t'ung trees.

Conversation with a Huang-Chou Poet

I fought the Japanese here and here
they killed my mother and my youngest son.
There in the mountains, where the green
meets that line of clouds, we fought
their army with rifles
we won from the dead.

The Japanese were quartered on this street.
They controlled the towns and thought
they'd won the war, but we controlled
the real China from the jungle
and in the bamboo groves and hills
where we sat around the small fires
making poems
and cleaning our new rifles.

Over the Slow Rivers

Sing swallows, small warriors in the empires
of the branches. The trees will not tire of you
and the bridges over the slow rivers
will shelter your nests as the winds
carry you in the bright battles of air.

Sing to me of the tireless, the endless,
the coming and the going that are leaves:
sing the female and the male of things
among the empires of the air, bright warriors,
none as swift as you in the blue worlds.

For Adele and Ding Ling

Our train winds beside the Pearl River and the hills.
My new friend tells of the time when she was young
and waited at the border, wanting to enter China,
to see Ding Ling. Thirty years have passed since then.

Her strong hands hold the bag containing her mother's
dolls, the one thing she brought to show the Chinese.
Of all our gifts, hers was best.

Even the men, so polite and reserved, laughed as she told
the stories of her mother's art. *For the children,*
she would say. The women circled her like flowers,
and Ding Ling. She is quiet as we near the border.

China is already far away. If it is true that for each
gift you leave behind, you carry something away,
then, of all of us, she is the richest.

In the Shadows

At bright tables in the bars
smooth bodies of young girls
move in quick circles of light.
They laugh as young men lean into their arms.
It is the shadows I want.
The ones who sit in corners
blue light brushing the lines from their eyes.
They do not smile.
Time has taken their hours away.
Their hands rest on yellow cloth, patient and waiting.

All Our Leavings

In untidy rooms we touch each other
slowly in brown air. Each of us has done this
many times, the line of a thigh, the curve
below a breast, buttocks, fingernails and lips.
Our mouths open and close.
Moving in the old ways we relearn our hours.
The small cry and the silence.
Seeing each other again, if we see each other again,
in the street, the doorways, or the bars,
we will, without knowing,
not know who we are.

From *A Linen Crow, a Caftan Magpie*

Remember the heart. Fog on the still river. First frost.
Passion. Flowers. The love of cities in old windows.

The painting is a dead eye. A window goes nowhere.
This one is alive. This one has a chance to live. This one.

Look in or out. Beauty is starved and love is afraid.
Dead children. The night in mothers. Remembered delight.

The heart is an argument with darkness. Moon sliver.
Dead eye. The room rings. I do not answer it again.

· · ·

The Collected Poems of Patrick Lane

Magpie, magpie, do not take a lower branch than this.
Last home I dreamed I was night. Poverty and song.

Autumn. The crabapple drops its small and bitter fruit.
The old attend to their gardens. Under the earth. Love.

The ones who are lost sing longer than the ones who are alone.
Blind at birth, I want you back.

Stay with me, carrion bird.
I am thinking of last leaves. The beauty of beginning.

    • • •

I tried to imagine a linen crow, a cattan magpie.
I believe I believe.

The love of the naive. That awkward integrity.
Searching for complaint, complaining.

She holds the needle but sews no stitch in time.
Undo the night.

Blue lines.
I know too many things. Everything broken.

    • • •

The mole's cry as he sleeps. Velvet death.
We rest in desolation, the mind creeping.

Remember the ridiculous.
The lenient master starves beauty.

Desolate. Desolate. The day and the day and the day.
Remember the heart. Little mole.

Last leaves. First frost.
I am the awaking. Your long cry of love.

      • • •

The throttle of pigeons in winter. Eave song.
Now we are anyone. This coming to love.

Our eyes. See. See. The myriad.
Crazed gold like insects. Waiting.

Mad images. Secular despair.
Dreams of pages. It is too cold for night.

When did I look out the window last?
Reproach. Flight in the leaves. First snow.

      • • •

We did not leave the garden. We were left.
Bewildered. Forsaken.

And you, sweet enemy.
How you left us to die and die.

The snake has only one skin. Take it off.
When she eats you she does not ask your name.

Keep your apples and roses.
East of Eden, the only desert is the mind. Thinking.

    • • •

A bad line, breaking wrong, hurts the eye.
How much worse the ear?

A mouth in a tree cries forgive, forgive.
Like a body fallen on a bed. A white bed. A body.

Forgive me.
I was going nowhere and going anyway.

The eyes that name you have no tongue.
Old roads. The arrival in time. Witnesses.

    • • •

Life slides from the bone cage.
Only the rare eagle, the coyote, the enemy called man.

The answer to the answer. The wind knows where.
Eat the soft shell of the womb. Stormy waters.

The horizon turns to your eye.
Relief. It is this moment she remembers.

Wet sack on snow. Birth, you are a winter away.
Binding. She sings her seed to stand. Come, follow me.

    • • •

Who will explain the bones?
The porcupine challenges your passing.

West of the west is the last thing you want.
Old sailor. Meet me again when I am hungry.

Step aside. Politeness has nothing to do with it.
The doe breaks through to clear water.

Words come slowly. Or not at all. Old buck hides.
Goshun painted the young willows. This way. Now!

. . .

To make of nothing a tradition.
The pure.

The undisciplined think chaos order.
Fear and fragments.

Even the wolf's eye sees magpie's beak.
The anvil protests the hammer's dance.

Return.
The flower unfolds without you.

. . .

All that is left. Last names. Morning.
Blood ties. Saturn's breakfast.

He said.
The dead. I don't know why I'm alive.

The body also moves, incomparable, describing peace.
We have forgotten how to be strangers.

Parables smaller than a story.
Keep me awake. Let the blood sing. Last names. Morning.

. . .

Let the women have it. Empty tombs.
I grow wings. Outcast at last.

The living end of death. Faith in flowers.
The withered root. Without love, let it go.

So I have held you and holding, hold myself.
Beyond narcissism. Famine and death.

Little nuthatch, you hang in cold, busy.
I wear my words among strangers. Trust no one. Keep it.

. . .

An egg will not float in open water.
Life clusters on the margins. Marsh grass. Look out!

So you don't want a saint.
Enough of old men climbing mountains to drink tea.

The bird flies back for birth.
Teach me the stars. The way to summer.

Hesitant. The hidden languages.
You aren't going to trick me. Not this fool.

. . .

Love again. A dictionary of symbols.
Your body in the night is blue ivory.

A key. A knife. A stone.
Crows. Greed kills when you are young. Go hungry.

Fly me to the ruins. This is love. Runed.
Mockery. Meaning.

Rip out my tongue. My mouth can't mind.
Hold me. Hold me. Inside I am still young.

. . .

O let the last bird fly.
The way is made for him. White rushes.

Or leaving.
Full of doubt, this absence holds me.

Without love, let it go.
The shadows of the last geese cross my mind.

This holds me. Small beaks.
Shadows in the bark of old trees. Wings.

. . .

Women walk to the sea. Prosperous and obedient.
Their sweet indignity. Happy among stones.

Everything is island. Symbol of failure and hope.
Violence, they say, as if the word could ruin them.

Their prayer. A fish strangling on air. A drowned man.
Love or die. Or walk among gulls. The sea greets you.

Among stones. Caress yourself. The only thing is you.
This is the oldest song.

     • • •

Go back.
In the old city a young city burns.

This life vanishes. We take it with us in a cup.
Flight.

Far to the south they are killing patience.
Perfectly. The horse with rubber heels is a heart.

Listen to the pavement. The beating of hooves.
They are coming. Lie down among stones.

     • • •

Adorned. The weight of beauty. Willow leaves and almonds.
She decorates her world. But she sings alone.

Beauty. The patience of the dancer in the stone.
Still life.

The web in the garden. Little maker.
The moon hangs in a silver bag.

Meticulous craft. Immense time.
The correct wine has nothing to do with glass.

. . .

The natural man.
Fish a little. Hunt a little. Blow your head off.

You are naked when I find you.
There is grace in coyote's kill. He eats as well as he can.

As Buson said: *Pretty clever, eh?*
There is a bank on both sides of the river. Paddle fast!

Or take silence.
Ah, slow, slow. The alphabet began with the moon.

. . .

Pleasure. Success. Order.
Wisdom is laughter at the end.

The hardest to forgive is a friend.
Trust. Honour. As you go.

Don't be sorry. Art is short. Life is long.
Here. You pull the wagon.

Go. Move your mountain. Turn around.
Behind you is a mountain. Move it again.

    • • •

There are no last lines.
The trout in winter consumes himself. No waste.

The answer is not an answer. It refuses faith.
How we search for what is already known. Leaf. Stone.

Blood on my tongue.
But to rise with the wind. That ecstasy.

As the line moves. The leap!
Thrashing there.

    • • •

Patience.
Every battle of the warrior is with confused noise.

There are measures. They have weight. Great and small.
Rest now.

A linen crow. A caftan magpie. Sorrow and song.
The tree bends under its fruit.

The wait of time.
He who appears before you now is the toad of this thicket.

Blanc de Blanc

When morning arrived it arrived without refusal.
It arrived with the urgency of the squirrel
who has seen his hours withering, the days
grown short and the night hours cool. It arrived
with the drum that is the heart beating its way
out of dreams, with the white flesh rising
and the mind far away and the squirrel's chatter.
Pine cones danced their death on the roof
and mushrooms lifted their pale white meat
and offered themselves to the tooth. Your body
lifted from morning as if from moss, as if the earth
had made you out of pure light, out of the moon
and the cool shadows. Everywhere small music sang.
The loon cried out the end of night,
the squirrel raged at shadows, and leaves,
tired of the sky, whispered to each other
stories of earth. I watched you, naked,
rise into morning and I wanted you with me,
flesh with flesh. I did not want the wind
and the sun falling into the south and the squirrel
and the loon and the many willing deaths that are
things giving themselves back to time. But your body
as you left was another language. *Blanc de blanc,*
a stranger's words for which I had no rhyme.

Echoes

The voices I want to remember
are like wanting to know what is inside
a light bulb when it is burned out.
The glass is grey like an ancient egg
found in a country far away from the heart.
Wanting is what we say when we're alone.
The light of a star just after it is nova,
the bright wings of light in the Far North,
the dance small creatures make as they fly,
when no one is watching. That is where
meaning goes when it is tired of trying.

It is the same place a child's eyes fly to
when he points a flashlight into the night
and wonders where the light goes
when he turns it off. Faster than light.

Throwing the voice is not the same.
Your name always comes back to you.
It returns like a wounded dog to its master.
Like a dog with his face torn off, like an animal
who tried to eat himself and discovered pain.
That is the voice you want to remember
That is why you follow the fireflies into the forest,
deeper and deeper, your eyes wanting to know
what it is to burn with such cold fire.

Nunc Dimittis
For Mary Drover

It is morning and I am kneeling
in the garden watching the green
bodies lift into light.
One week ago the tomatoes froze
and now I am astonished at the tentative
green reaching from the blackened stems.
Ours is a cold country.
There are certain griefs: the dry rivers of Spain,
the pain I saw on the face of a child in Rome,
my home, my friend
who has just lost her breast
and whose body has become so numinous I can see through her
to the wall and the Chinese print of Shuan Jua
carrying the light. Last night Vermeer's *Head Of a Girl*
turned toward me wanting
someone to explain why love has made her afraid.
There was nothing I could say.
In three months winter begins again.

White Lions in the Afternoon

The mushroom if left long enough will leave
its mark, a blue flower sudden as night
upon white paper. The beautiful endures.
There are white lions in the afternoon
just as there are scars that roll across the wrists
of small awkward children. They are the same
as the bright burnt hole in an eye

that has looked too long at the sun.
Something at the end of the mind
cries out. That is when the pain comes,
motiveless, with a pure efficiency.
We spend the end of our lives
calling down upon ourselves the images:
the fragile mushroom lifting pale flesh
out of the memory of rain, the scar
strung like a bangle upon a delicate wrist,
a hole in an eye. They are why we sleep
and why upon waking, bewildered by the day,
the white lions rise with us in the sun
and move with great patience toward the mind.

La Gioconda

Why we attach roses to our skin is why
we run with innocence when we can no longer
be trusted. It is beauty we want, thinking it
alive. And Buonarroti loved when alone
to shape bodies out of clay. If we know why
da Vinci carried her smile with him
all the way to the room in Paris
then we know why
the young woman in the bar trembles
when the man with narrow hands takes
his lighter and burns the golden hairs
that grow from her rose tattoo.

The Cheating Heart

Bright darkness coming, the sister of my friend
singing Hank Williams, loneliness and the night
when crickets break inside their wings for love.
That mad crying everywhere. The ruin
that was my friend's home, the city begun
among hills that were a wilderness to me.
How, when you are young, tragedy is always taken
wrong, getting it that way, laughing because
I was young, understanding nothing.
How I saw his sister across the bonfire,
her white face laughing, the darkness beyond.
My friend for the last time beside me.
The unspeakable beauty of our bodies
singing in our flesh long before manhood made us
ashamed. How I loved him. Summer and betrayal.
The crickets in their madness. The cheating heart.
The sister singing far from the fire alone
whom I went to also singing. And returned with,
the fire finally coals, the potatoes we threw in
bursting, the white flesh exploding
that I would not know again, living as I do
far from childhood, her song in the darkness,
the way I turned from him to her white breasts,
the fire blazing.

Dominion Day Dance

The night is summer
and the hour is heavy with air that moves
like a slow mouth in the leaves of the chestnut,
the branches of the elms.
A boy dances in their shadows.
Across the street in the Legion Hall
music falls upon the dancers.
As the boy moves he imagines
a girl whose breasts
are small perfect pains on her chest
and he wants to touch them.
He has sworn tonight to dance
with a girl who is beautiful.
He does not know his desire
to never be alone again
is the beginning of loneliness.
It is a new kind of fear.
It has entered him like a cage enters
an animal, this thing his body does
moving in awkward grace
with nothing in its arms.

Brothers
For John

We were brothers long before we were men,
small, tough because the days kept hurting us,
days when a word like *beauty* had to be learned,
our mother making us spell it over and over

until it seemed the word lost meaning
and was only punishment. It was before I had glasses.
I didn't know I was almost blind, and didn't know
what I saw I didn't see. Years later, looking
at Van Gogh's wonderful cypress tree,
that blue pain twisting like a heart into the stars,
I saw my original world, everything out of focus
and understood that even small birds die and mountains
burn when a child wants them to. Whenever I smell
fresh bread I remember us climbing out the window
at dawn and running across the alley in our pyjamas
to steal bread from the bakery, that warm yeast
lifting us from sleep as it cooled in the last air.

Sometimes when I'm afraid I walk into the hills
where the trees are. Stunted desert pines
the world leaves alive because they're useless.
The earth is made of terrible stones and sand.
There is no rain. *Sustain* our mother might have said
and we would spell it together, our voices
singing. I remember how it took a day to reach you
riding the miles north into your madness, thinking
you were dead. It was like listening to a song
from the war and suddenly knowing there were men
who stumbled into death singing it, desert men
who didn't believe their eyes, the sudden silence
in that strange country the end of their lives.

It's why a pine tree in the hills can heal me,
why when I hold you in my arms after singing
the old songs, I begin to understand how words are made,
the awkward letters at the beginning of *beauty*,
the way sound holds inside the word *sustain,*

---

the rain that only deserts know, living things
in a place they are far from, or two children
standing in the dust, their mouths breaking open
the hot white heart, leaving behind them
the crusts of bread for birds.

The Woman with the Horses

The woman with the horses
when the light is almost gone from the fields
and the doves have begun to mourn
and the clouds wait in the many myriad shapes
that are the secret language of the young
when they are lonely
and of lovers when they are far from each other
and of the evening
when the blackbirds descend
and the woman
with the horses in the field
when you are driving
west.

Harvest

The delicate dried seeds found in the tomb at Thebes
and her in the field picking the stalks of grain
saying, *it is time*. It was time in the same way
the earth preserves a leaf or man a relic. The seeds,
in it. As his seed was in her and her leaving.

He lay in the small room thinking of a snake
he saw in childhood writhing as it left its skin.
He killed it, thinking it in pain.
Birth.
Innocence must pay, the memory being in the mind.
Plague and lamentation and the ancient seeds
found in the tomb at Thebes. Watching her go
feeling nothing, how it felt to feel nothing,
the hidden harmony, the way things move
through things, divinity escaping notice.
Her in the field picking the oats and barley,
her hands saying, *this, this, this,* and *this.*
Pregnant and leaving and him feeling nothing.
Her saying *oats, barley, body, spring,* and *death*
as the grain flowed out across the Mediterranean
and whips rose and fell upon the masons and the slaves
and the people prayed and the Nile rose again,
the waters rising over the waste of far Egypt;
Antony,
the fleet burning, Cleopatra's dry breasts,
nipples rouged, the snake raised up in praise,
him naked, lying in his room, the seed entombed
and the sound roaring in his mind, the terrible
Thebes, Thebes, Thebes, Thebes, Thebes!
and the harvest, the body turned to stone.

The Happy Little Towns

Walking the muddy road past the swamp
I thought the butterflies a gift I couldn't bear,
there in the sun pulling light into their wings,

drinking sweet water with their tongues.
I was so young I thought I was a man
and that little town a place where a life could be
made, that things like bears or ravens
or the body of a woman were sufficient to themselves
and without guile. That the man walking beside me
had a boot full of blood was nothing more
than the end of a day. A man who had opened
his body with an axe. It could have easily been
a boy with an eye scooped out, or a woman
bleeding into diapers for a month, afraid
to tell her man she'd lost his child.

That was the year my wife slept with my best friend.
I could tell her now the summer was oblivion,
that the blood gone from a body cannot be
given back, the wound opening like a mouth
without forgiveness. The inside of the body
when it first feels air feels only noise, as the
butterfly when it first crawls out of itself
feels only wonder and never eats again. I remember
the brightness of the days as my hands healed
the many injuries, the hours alone. It wasn't sadness
or self-pity, only oblivion, the kind a boy feels
when he is made into a man, wanting only to be
held, for the first time in his life without love.

The wreckage of that world stayed wreckage, though
we tried to build it back. The steady years of trying,
her taking the flowers I picked in the fields
and placing them in a jar where we watched them die.
What I remember most is that injured man who,
with the dignity of the very poor, told me he was

sorry to bother me, as if his wound could have waited
for a better time to happen; my hands putting him
back together, the stitches climbing up his leg
like small black insects I created out of nothing,
the curved steel needle entering his pale flesh,
pulling behind it a thread thin as a butterfly's
tongue, him saying he was sorry, and me knowing
for the first time in my life what that must mean.

Variations

For Doug Jones

1.

In your garden, the wild,
the flowers fading, your cabin
still not built and the far
smoke of first fires
hangs above your lake.
It is cold here too
my friend. The leaves fall
fast and the prairie
from my window does not move.

2.

And in love, your lady
moves through her hours.
The trees drop last leaves,
cry out
we are naked, naked,

their voices fading
as sap sinks into earth.
Love is what the almost dead
depend on, what they turn to
in their last beds.
They cry out, we are
naked, we are naked,
give us at the last
at least love. The last
hour when we desire most,
falling as we do
into sleep,
into the blue worlds.

3.

A cricket on a grey rock
climbs to silence. Last songs
and the deer, remembering
winter, are still
for one moment in your garden.

4.

The delicate eye extends
with grace. The song
does not falter, moves
upon stone and water,
moves as the magpie moves
when he is not busy at death,
alone
and bright against the sky.

5.

The language defeats
and the centuries of faith
ignore me. I cannot find
a word that will justify the word
will. Still, this poem,
this crude curio, this
imitation of destiny
will suffice.

6.

It is like a woman on a narrow path
with three dogs and a child.
In the moment of doubt
she works with the leashed ones
and the child is left to wander.

7.

The flesh has its own song
to sing. I will
becomes I know not
what to do. But to allow the line its length,
to let it fly
to the far edge
knowing its return will sustain
the breath. This is enough.

8.

In less than four months
the sun will begin
to move north again.
In this country we call
that image hope and the fog
rests upon the water. The sun
cannot burn it away.

9.

It is dawn and your poems
have moved me to poems.
To improvise as the leaf
in its falling. That music.
The return to simple things,
to a garden, to a last drink
at night and in the morning
the tentative, the body's act
in the act of its being
a body.

Dostoevsky

1.

A dead mouse on a forest path, ants and flies
sharing the feast. He can understand that.
He can understand the young crows
stumbling in the branches of a tree,
feathers not ready for flight. Bewildered,

innocent, the young do not know fear. This
makes him afraid, makes him want
to catch one, to slit its tongue
so it will speak in the language of crows,
the language of translation, the first chapter
of *Crime and Punishment*, the last chapter
of *The Idiot*. He knows he is mad. He does not
need the crescent moon to tell him this.
He does not need to hide in the trees,
a pale criminal watching the beautiful
young monk in the monastery garden
take a single strawberry from the field
and eat it very slowly as he walks to vespers.
Can a woman write about a man?
A man a woman?
Tristan and Isolde. There are too many
things in his mind. Who is Dostoevsky?
He wants to answer that. He is in retreat
playing Patience. It is a solitary game
played only in retreat, everything ordained,
everything in the turn of a card. The monk is
a crow in his black gown. Dostoevsky.

2.

A young man who is a dealer of *chemin de fer*
is rooted in the body of a German dowager.
He lifts a heavy breast covered in sweat
and puts it in his mouth. *Amor. Eros.*
His lips are the skin of a dead mouse.
He does not know why this has occurred
to him. He is thinking of Dostoevsky
and he knows nothing can be redeemed by this
image. Christ, he thinks, they must have smelled

at the gaming tables, their bodies unwashed,
drenched in perfume and pearls. Dostoevsky
gambling with the rich dowagers at a spa
in Germany, losing everything and wanting
to lose again. The game is *chemin de fer.*
It is the nineteenth century after Christ.
Prince Myshkin is singing.

3.

When he was a small boy he sat on the floor
gazing at the crotch of his mother's friend.
She was talking with his mother of the heat
and she opened her legs, her dress a blue flower
draped across her knees. Tea and matrimonial cake.
He thought an animal was biting her.
Sweat and gambling at a spa in Germany.
To turn great beauty into loss, to lose
it all on the turn of a card. Dostoevsky.
He thought an animal was biting her.
She smiled down at him knowing that pearls
were not drops of dew, were not the milky
semen floating in the menstrual sea.
Manichaean heresies. The blood and body
of Christ. A monk eating a strawberry.

4.

In Germany the dowagers wear pearls
if they are rich and fat and German
and they are gambling in a casino
during the season in the nineteenth century.
Raskolnikov is sweating in his room.
Natasha is about to laugh.
An animal eats her.

5.

He is playing a game called Patience
and he does not want to think.
Everything hurts him.
The young monk walking to vespers,
a strawberry in his mouth. A dead mouse.
Crows singing Russian songs.
She eats matrimonial cake knowing
a child is looking up her dress.
Is that why she parts her legs?
Or is it just the heat?
Meanwhile the game is Patience
as the monks sing in high clear voices
the *Salve Regina* in the last hour,
vespers over and the compline begun.
Crows stumble in the trees
while their mother screams
and Dostoevsky thrashes in his room,
his wife forcing a stick into his mouth
to stop him from biting off his tongue.

The Beauty

This too, the beauty
of the antelope in snow.
Is it enough to say we will
imagine this and nothing more?

Who understands that, failing
falters at the song.
But still we sing.
That is beauty.

But it is not an answer
any more than the antelope
most slender of beasts
most beautiful

will tell us why they go
going nowhere
and going there
perfectly in the snow.

Night

In the bright room where Albinoni's adagio
plays its endless variations, my friends,
the few who know what silence is
and know this music is the pain
Alden Nowlan felt as he stumbled toward death
alone, blundering against the walls, I keep
the ivory *netsuke* and the fragment of blue
tile from the baths of Caracalla.
When I tell them of the musk of the flower
that bloomed for one short night in summer
they understand. The cactus sings to me.
I have these things to share. The ephemeral
moves among us, delicate as Cavafy's phrase:
like music that extinguishes far-off night.
I think of that phrase in my study, how
it moves among the things that are mine:
the scarred jade lion I bought for nothing in Xian,
the photograph of my father, the quiet one taken
when he was young in Europe in 1943,

and my poems, the broken ones that will never
be seen. These I keep for myself. They are
the other silence, the one that sings to me
when my friends are gone and the night
moves with great slowness in my hands.

THE NINETIES

Winter

1

The generosity of snow, the way it forgives
transgression, filling in the many betrayals
and leaving the world
exactly as it was. Imagine a man
walking endlessly and finding his tracks,
knowing he has gone in a circle. Imagine
his disappointment. See how he strikes out again
in a new direction, hoping this way
will lead him out. Imagine how much
happier he will be this time with the wind
all around him, the wind filling in his tracks.

He is thinking of that man,
of what keeps him going.
The thought of snow,
small white grains sifting
into the holes where his feet went,
filling things in,
leaving no room for despair.

2

In the album he holds in his thin hands
are the thousand photographs he has made of winter.
Each one is perfectly exposed, each one a pure
white with sometimes only the barest of shadows;
a fleeting, ephemeral grey that betrays
the image of who or what it was he took.
It pleases him to go through it slowly and remember.

3

It will be winter when they come.
He will sit with his back to the high window
and imagine their tracks in the snow, the circles
and arabesques, the sudden turns, the fallen angels.
He will follow them to the end of their tracks.
He hopes it will not be where the ice ends.
He hopes it will be in the centre
where they have mounded the snow.

When he arrives he will wait for a storm.
Surrounded by crystals
he will peer down their breathing hole
smelling the sweet simplicity of their mouths
deep in the blue cavern where they sleep
and then
he will take his spear
and thrust it through fold after fold of snow
holding it there while they twist
just below him in the cold.

4

He is thinking of the end of *Oedipus,*
not the beginning, not the part
where Oedipus chooses by giving the answer
to the beast at the Gate of Thebes.
No, it is the end he likes. The part
just after he puts out his eyes
and stands, suddenly
in that certain darkness, decided.

It is not a story of winter
but of the sun, the ceaseless
perfection of the Aegean.

How different it would be
had it taken place here, he thinks.
Here the critical moment
would be putting the eyes back
in their sockets, that first shock
exactly the same as in the other story
only the beginning would have
to be different, all the roles
reversed.

5

The sound of winter is made up of all
the things not there. That is what *north* means,
to remember by forgetting everything. It is
precisely the same as someone
knocking on the door with a tentative fist.
It is delicate, muffled by leather and wool,
a muted sound he does not hear, perfectly.

6

The guests have arrived at last. The old
woman in rags who pushes a steel cage
filled with her life, and the man with dogs,
the two pit bulls who whine with eagerness
at the end of their tethers. The young boy
with the burns on his face and shoulders
stands by the piano where the girl with no legs
plays early Mozart, one of the pieces
full of promise composed when he was still
a child. There is wine and fruit and fine brandy.
Everything is ready to begin.

The host is sitting in his study, staring
at a painting from the Ming Dynasty.
Soon he will go down the long white stairs
and join them, but for now he is simply happy,
the painting one of winter, so much
like the porcelain of the period, pale,
with only the faintest of green
buried beneath the pure hard surface.

7

It is the bare bone of winter
he holds in his hand, a wisp of ice
slender as a fifteenth-century Spanish knife
fashioned in Cordova. A woman's knife
to be hidden in a sleeve when meeting
a false lover. It is delicately curved,
a small floating rib, just right
to slip into the heart as they embrace.
He looks at the thing in his hand
as it transforms itself, changing,
melting into a thin pool of water. He is
almost afraid to return it to its element.

8

The second riddle is more difficult.
The answer to the first riddle was *snow*.
Not the soft snow of early winter, but
the coarse granular snow that sweeps
with the wind in the blizzards of January.
The kind that leaves the skin
scored with myriad tiny cuts.
The answer to the second riddle
could be *snow* as well. He

repeats the enigma to himself,
pondering the last couplet:
*The absence of colour
is the colour of blue.*

For a moment he wonders if the answer is *love*.
Perhaps it is *ice*.
Or it could be *cold*, that simple word
for which there are a thousand meanings,
all of them correct.

9

Each day the time grows less, the hours
shorter by a few minutes, the sun
farther away. He remembers the Inca,
the way they would tie
a rope to the sun and hitch it to stone
out of fear it would never return.
How strange to think of their songs,
the supplications, the hearts torn out,
the blood on the altars. What wonder
must they have known as they lay
their bodies on stone? How simple
their desire, the priests chanting,
the sun drifting farther and farther
north. But not now. For him it is winter
and for them the sun is returning.
He sees them singing on the terraces
as they plant the young corn,
their children waiting for the season
when they are chosen, the one that begins
when everything starts to end.

How beautiful, he thinks, gazing
from his window at the night, this darkness
gathering in the blue snow.

10
Standing under the dark spruce trees,
their branches bent under the weight of snow,
he watches the people enter the Sacred Heart
just before midnight, just before mass
when they celebrate the birth, the
beginning of light, the promise
things will get better. He likes
to listen to their singing, the voices
of the young children, and the women.
What he likes most is to watch
them as they leave and enter
the storm that has risen while they prayed.
How they pull their coats
tight around them, the mothers
sheltering their children, the fathers
staring at the night just before
leading them away. The small
moment of doubt in their eyes.
He likes to stare at the priest
standing behind them, the one
who touches with great gentleness
the choir boys in the sanctuary.
The priest is full of hope and fear,
knowing they are leaving with his words
in their minds: All that singing
and still no end in sight.

11

He reaches down and strokes the white fur.
Each day the animal grows larger. He wonders
at the cells multiplying beside him,
duplicating and reduplicating themselves
without end. Somewhere in the animal heart
there is a single cell which has begun
it all. He wonders what it looks like now,
grown grotesque with the myriad others
surrounding it, weighing it down,
their impossible crying for more.

If that is the first cell, he thinks,
then what is the last? He reaches out,
pulls one hair from the animal's throat.
He breaks off the base where it is still
a pure white and swallows it.
This is what it is like,
all these choices without refusal,
only waiting to see if you are right.
He feels the animal beside him, its heaviness.
He thinks: *Later when it tries to remember*
I will point to the snow.

12

The magpies wait in the bare tree.
They cry out for the dead.

There is no food
in this place where nothing moves.

This is what he likes. All this hunger
and nowhere to hide.

13

There is a brief thaw and now
everything is frozen. Outside
ptarmigan wander ceaselessly
trying to find a way back
to where they believe
there is release from cold.
Beneath them their white sisters
struggle under the clear crust.
In the rare moments
when they are still
they are mirrors of each other,
each of them dying, each of them
wanting the other's dilemma,
believing the cries of the others
are lies, something done
only to torment them.

14

The moon arrives just before the clouds,
hard and bright in the sky. The hunger moon.

So much time. So little patience.
The snowy owl sleeps on his pole in the garden.

15

Fragility and nowhere to go.
So many questions. Like
where do the snakes go?
What he wants is
stillness, absolute zero
when everything becomes
the same, perfectly still,

waiting. Fragility, like
the snakes know as
temperatures fall, their
bodies getting colder
and colder. So many questions,
as in *what?* or *where?*
Or resemblance, that word
like making it all possible,
fragility and snakes,
the night dragging on.

16

Everything moves without change. The trees
without leaves dance sadly, allowing
nothing to get in their way. Not sorrow,
not snow under snow, but a slow forgetting.
The old moon sleeps with the young moon in her arms.
Words like that are like reaching out
in the darkness, wanting
to sleep and not being able to. Reaching out
to find nothing at the end of the hand but cold.
Wondering at flesh, its need, as the trees
who do not remember leaves, dance sadly
with a steady dumb grief, their dark moving
a monotonous music in the snowy night.

17

The stones in the thin winter months
melt what little snow stays on their backs,
melt and pull the spare water beneath them
where it freezes, lifting them
higher where the wind cuts them,
reducing them to dust, a single mote of which

has blown into his eye, blinding him,
making him see through the sudden tears
a world made for one moment entirely of water.

18
Naked in the empty room
the young girl offers herself. Such a forlorn gift,
such a hopeless dance; so incomplete
with only innocence to offer. Her love, so awkward
without wantonness, leaves him
with two possibilities: *transgression* or *transformation*.
A simple defeat.
How he makes himself holy in order to suffer loss.
If there is anything in him
resembling love
it is for the two white pom-poms on her socks
which is all she wears on this cold floor
as she moves around him,
so much like the snows of early fall.

19
His tears quickly freeze, forming
delicate icicles on the pale hairs of his lip.
If he stands perfectly still in the wind
he can breathe their small impossible music.

20
Winter is not Colville, not that violent sentiment
without feeling, control without grief.
He is not how we imagine it. We are not
his model of intolerance, that accuracy
which is performance designed to instruct.
Imagine the space in falling snow

left behind by a woman
when she is walking through a storm.
We think it chaos,
but it is only presence reduced to intrusion.
Another order, which is what he praises.
It is soapstone before the carver
lifts his chisel, the form before form,
desolation without regret. Propriety
in a space made alien by the thought.
The answer to the question:
But what does it mean?
The old Eskimo laughing at such a strange request.

21

To be under ice in the dark is just
one more way to believe, as a fish must who leaps
from water in the wrong season, suddenly
finding no way out. To relinquish movement.
That kind of decorum, the one
without imagination,
the one the Japanese have, their tradition being
the repetitive, the struggle to do something
so perfect no one will ever know.

Kamikaze.

No wonder he loved their deaths in the war.
All that duty turned into loss. No wonder
he wonders at his garden as the wind
carves it into the shapes
that do not matter, a kind of chaos,
perfection
being the one thing the wind does not know,

just as ice does not know it is only in the eye of a fish
another form of sky.

22

There is almost no air left
in the white balloon blowing across the snow.
It is wrinkled and barely lifts from the drifts.
If you could read the writing on its side
it would say: *Save the Whales,*
a temporary greed he loves,
the wish to preserve without regret.
He loves it in the way he loves
those old poems about Byzantium,
cages full of gilded mechanical birds,
that impossible dream of beauty,
while everything blows away.

23

He imagines a horse walking in snow,
consuming time
on the perimeter, going from post to post
wondering if the wire
will have fallen this time around.
That is what patience is, dumb beasts
repeating the random, going
in the direction of the greatest resistance
without even hope to guide them. It is why
he has to imagine magpies on the fence posts,
hungry, knowing the flesh is
its own cage, insisting on it, demanding
a solution to all this dumb dreaming.

24

Just as a woman when she is brooding upon solitude
turns to winter as a metaphor for loss,
so stories are made up of missing parts
which is where all the terror comes from
the child pleading for just a little more
before it is time to be left alone in the night
with that shape behind the door. It is someone
leaving, someone calling out, as if the words,
Go to sleep, were an answer,
as if a child and a woman in separate rooms
were exactly the same, both of them waiting
for whatever is going to be inevitable.

25

The hoarfrost on the trees is a beauty
fog leaves when it is at last consumed
by cold, obscurity transformed into light,
the bright world the heart knows upon waking.
How little it remembers of night, the fallen
animal singing as the wheels broke its flesh
on a road whose one colour was white, there being
no hesitation after the act, but to be driven
down that road believing in destiny, the confluence
of lives, animals crossing in the night.
Or the dream he remembers of his hands,
their touching innocence
knowing what they held as it cried
would never forget.
That is what is in the word *never*.
Transgression because beauty loves itself too much.
Transformation because there is nothing else to do
after the crime is committed
but shine.

26

A kind of fragile wanting as the body is
when it is too old to move without pain, desire
when the other is long gone. It is relief
from song, the same that lovers know
when they are born again, belief
when the spirit is at last made flesh.
It is the *after* as song is after singing
when the tongue makes other sound. It is
the wanting the old remember that the young
do not know, the outcry
as someone we do not know
moves toward us, the mouth making
a sound we've never heard before
wide open, taking it all in.

27

When the wind blows it blows without regret,
invisible as the lean heart telling riddles
in the dark. It is tradition,
dumb form waiting to be filled up.
Look at the way he shovels the snow
knowing behind him the wind begins again
to worship the empty. See where he finds a leaf,
the beautiful veins, desiccated, worn fragile
as a ring upon the hand of a woman
who has turned it into a fine lament.
Everything is so thin, a leaf, a thought:
that moment in Kings when the woman lies with the leper
and he is not made whole. Everything
a kind of famine. Everything
diseased.

28

He lies with her in bed, the moonlight
falling through the window. It falls
upon all fours, stunned by its arrival in a place
alien to the idea of light, hunched there in a square
upon the floor. The woman beside him dreams anything,
revenge, the sound of ice in the wind, mercy,
that most intangible of songs. The picture
she has in her mind is of children
building a man out of snow.

The light trembles
as he stands to pull the curtain.
He knows passion is only distance. That is how
she described it when she described the picture
in her mind. Her version was of time,
children in a chinook, watching what had been made
melt into nothing at all, the wind
destroying everything the cold made possible.

29

There are boxes over the roses and delphiniums,
plants too tender to survive in this brutal cold.
This is the place of nurturing, the rose
because it resembles the unfolding we call love,
delphiniums because of the temple in the rock
and the oracle singing her enigmas
as she tricked men into giving up their treasure
only to find death. How they struggled to arrive
at this place, prostrating themselves, unwilling
to believe in betrayal, giving themselves to it
in the certainty there was only one answer.
That is why he moves the boxes slightly as he passes,

the living things in his garden believing
his touch is the beginning of warmth, the moment
of fecundity, the wanton madness of birth;
in this season of cold a possible temptation,
the somnolent world so willing
to believe in destiny, so willing
to believe in a beginning that has no end.

30

The brightness around him in the garden
where he stands with his hands outstretched
to the sparrows. They descend to the rich grain
he holds, quarrelling among his fingers, pecking each
other, especially the crippled one who lifts away
from their beaks and flutters in the air
just above their greed. The cold
climbs into her as they drive her into the trees.

This is what God must have felt
on the eighth day, he thinks, cruelty
everywhere around him, the omnipotence of knowing,
feeding even the least of his creatures, listening
to a bird as it dies
give itself to song in a garden
he has made out of snow.

31

What the child finds in snow is what a ship finds
in the sea, a wake left behind, a froth
that sinks back into itself, everyone else
waiting for the return, the full hold,
the grain come again, the hosannas
which are prayers to plenty. The child knows

nothing of this. He has been sent out to play
and has discovered misery.

He is learning that the footsteps he finds in snow
are his and his alone. How sweet his lament,
this silence in the negative world of cold.
It is a kind of perfect mutiny, everyone waiting
and him knowing there will be no return.
If he were a priest he would say: ·
This is the end of the first lesson.

32

He has already decided on the North.
He will die only when everyone else is suffering
the simple deprivations in the season
where the weak have no place.
That is when he will walk away from them into the snow
with nothing but a look of clarity
on his thin ascetic face.

This is what they will remember.

This is what they will carve
in the months when the moon
is named *starvation*, named *suffering*.
All those ghosts climbing out of their heads
when the food is gone, wondering
why the stone changes into the shapes
their hands make, white creatures that live
only now at the end of things.

33

The brightness which is the light seen from a tomb
and which is what the dead see when they gaze
with their marble eyes from the dark rooms they are
laid in. This is a whole city this snow.

34

If the word *companion* is made out of the idea of bread,
the ritual of sharing, the gift given
when there is only enough for one, is *absence*
the idea of cold? Is the space in the room
where the tree was decorated for worship
only a configuration, a chemical
map in the mind, something there that is not?

No wonder Cassandra came from a warm place.

No wonder no one believed her.

35

One is about the man who walks out into the storm
and is never seen again. We all know that one.
It is the story about grief and music,
where all the dancing is an escape
from virtue, everyone shaken by a higher crime,
the emptiness that follows completion,
the one the body knows
in the formal gentleness of suffering, everything gone,
everything forgiven in the land East of Eden.

Then there is the other story, the one
where the man enters out of the storm,
ice melting from his beard, his huge hands

moving over the fire, the fear of what will follow,
the women quiet, filling his cup and bowl
with all the food there is in hope it will be
enough, in hope he will be satisfied only with that,
and knowing he won't, knowing
this is the part of the story the reader will call
the middle, and hoping for an alternative, another
beginning, and ending it
before the mind reaches the end
with everyone crying out, everyone
saying things like: *Lie down in sorrow!*
Or: *This is the burden of Babylon!*

There is another story, there always is.
The one about . . .
Of course, of course.
How cold it is with only a lamp in this small room.

36

He has arrived at a possible solution.
He will create himself in the image of a woman.
He decides upon his sister. She
is the only one who can guarantee a future
precise as the past.

He sees himself inside a body that resembles
his own, the forms of himself progressively
weaker and weaker, each version fading
into a line of translations
that are always the same text.

What a world where everything is itself.
He writes: *Dear Sister,* knowing

she knows their flesh is a repetition
of their flesh, as all snowflakes are
immaculate variations of the one original snowflake,
a shape taking shape in the cold night.
He signs his letter: *love.*

37

There are many possibilities and all of them
are endings. Each one is parallel
to the other, each one a fidelity,
a pleasure that closes the eyes
when the blood rushes away from the senses
to digest whatever has been eaten. Look
how the branches shake in the trees as the wind
rises out of the west, driving the warm air before it.
See how the snow is released from tension
only to find another, a shape it didn't know
it was. Look at the child in the gutter
making the corner of First and Twenty-Sixth
the confluence of the White Nile and the Blue.
See how he takes a stick and changes
the directions forever. Can you hear the people
starving to death on the Delta? Can you
see the bloated bodies as the vultures land
upon them, the featherless necks
entering their anuses, the beaks tearing
the delicate flesh? How powerful the boy is
as he watches the temples empty, the priests
lamenting this end that is of all endings
one they never imagined. How painful spring is.
How impossible this snow.

38

The scavengers have arrived
at last, the crows, returned,
having feasted on the remains
of animals he has only read
about in *Life*, the naked
opossum, the gila monster,
jewelled with poison, the
sidewinder and the mockingbird.

They are here for the season
of birth, and the snow, knowing
desire, releases the bodies
it has preserved for them in ice.

The yearlings bend forward in praise,
their black wings spread in obeisance.
The older males
climb upon them
spraying glaucous seed into their bodies
as the females circle the sky.

These are the bright cries
he hears, the abrupt terror
of greed in the moment of innocence,
a light turned off, a curtain
drawn against the bright
sickness of the sun.

39

In the North where everything that is ancient
is only in the mind, he creates his own lost city
and dresses it in flesh. It walks away from the sun

toward a frozen sea in whose name
all the letters are silent, the *a* in beauty,
the *e* in love, the *w* in snow.

40

She is a northern woman, barely more
than a child, one who has walked through the drifts
to find her dream vision. Her eyes are
covered by a blade of bone, a thin slit
cut in it so the light does not blind her.
The man she has found is not one of the four
possibilities: father, brother, lover, son.
He is the dream man, given to her by the snow.

He has wandered far from the sea,
his crew dead, his ship broken in the ice.
If there were someone there to translate his song
it would start with the words: *At last.*
But only she is there.
As he sings she cuts off his fingers,
only these small bones and the twenty-six
teeth for her necklace.

They will be her medicine, something
to shake over the bellies of women
in childbirth, the heads of men
who have returned empty from hunting,
their minds become snow.

How like a real man he is, she thinks.
How real this dream, the blood on the ice.
How thin he is, how much like the snow is his flesh.

41

Being on a journey without knowing
you are on a journey is to understand grace,
which is what he is doing
with the glass globe full of snow.
In it a small child is perpetually going nowhere,
one foot permanently anchored to the ice,
the other out there trying to go.
When spring comes it will be all that is
left of what he wants to remember of winter:
piety, because everything is weary in the rain.
A certain grief, that is what he will have.
That is what is in there, the furious snow
swirling whenever he shakes it.

42

It comes after the return after
everything has been won and the body
feasts. It comes just after that.
That is what the story is all about,
the crashing through the door,
the shouts, the lamentation after
when the hero leaves all his dead behind
to find anything that terrible.

43

He remembers the wagon, the old
man with tired eyes, his thin horse dragging
cold through the summer days. The ice pick
and the tongs. That clear cold jewel
swinging from the arm of the iceman.
Memory. The mouth sucking with the greed
that is a child in the far past, a child

who is imagining the man he will be,
a sharp lean hero, immaculate and alone.
Already he is practising his cool walk,
hands in pockets, his cold eyes
staring through all the pain there is
at nothing. The iceman in the heat
clicking his tongs, the old horse
leaning into the leather and the chains,
the small boy watching, in his hand
a piece of ice.

44

The body of the woman in snow, naked
and drunk. Her falling, blonde and young
into the drifts. How he carried her back
cradled in his arms, saying everything
would be all right, that love and loneliness
are lies. Remembering how he hesitated
and simply stared at her.
Remembering that.

45

The man without a name who reversed his snowshoes
and walked forward, head down, shoulders hunched.
The man who climbed the mountains
in the heart of winter, crossing the pass,
heading west into the snow.

The one they followed.

The many trails he made, each one
a perfect map, a calligraphy
for those who pursued him.

His turning upon himself,
an animal born into his own making,
crossing and recrossing his tracks.

This way, this way, they would shout.

Him walking, head down, shoulders hunched, moving
toward his own quick death, his breath
breaking sharp and hard,
entering,
leaving.

The Far Field

We drove for more than an hour, my father's hands
on the truck's wheel, taking us farther and farther
into the hills, both of us watching
the sagebrush and spare pines drift
past, both of us silent. He did not know
what to do with me. I think he thought of
my death, as a man will whose son has chosen
to destroy. I think that's why he drove
so long, afraid to stop for fear
of what he'd do. My mother had cried
when we left, her hands over her mouth,
saying through her splayed fingers
my father's name, speaking
that word as if it were a question. I
sat there peaceful with him,
knowing for these hours he was wholly mine.

He stripped me naked in the last hour of day
and made me stand with my back to him, my bare
feet in the dust, my back and buttocks to him,
a naked boy, hands braced upon the hood,
staring across the metal at the hills.

I remember the limb of the tree falling
upon me, the sound of the white wood crying
as it hurt the air, and the flesh of my body
rising to him as I fell to the ground and rose
only to fall again. I don't remember pain,
remember only what a body feels
when it is beaten, the way it resists
and fails, and the sound of my flesh.

I rose a last time, my father dropping
the limb of the tree beside me.
I stood there in my bones wanting it not to be
over, wanting what had happened to continue, to go
on and on forever, my father's hands on me.

It was as if to be broken was love, as if
the beating was a kind of holding, a man
lifting a child in his huge hands and throwing him
high in the air, the child's wild laughter
as he fell a question spoken into both their lives,
the blood they shared pounding in their chests.

The Killer

I have spent too many of my years in you,
have sat inside your body in the bars
while you drank your solitary beers,
their wet circles somehow making sense to me,
the way they almost touched each other
as you lifted the glass to your lips
and drank. I have risen with you
and gone to your truck where the Winchester
rested in its rack and driven through
the country, down the dusty roads,
past the creeks and willows
where grouse and pheasants find their lives
in the quiet thickets. I have stopped
with you and waited for nothing.
I have stepped from the truck
and stood in the gravel, have reached down
for the stone and picked it up and hurled it
at nothing. I have gotten back into the truck
and driven into town past the many friends
and enemies and stopped. I have taken
the rifle from its rack and aimed it
through the window and pressed the trigger,
felt that soft blow in the shoulder
as the rifle recoiled.
                    I have travelled through
the air, through a window, through a wall,
and through my father's chest into his heart, and
I have stayed, a small thing lodged there,
and felt the blood that made me
heave into silence. I have spent most of my life
with you, you whose name I do not know,

you who drove away, leaving
my body inside that heart
lifting up the many pieces, unable
to put any of them together, surrounded
by my father's blood, and wanting
not to be there, wanting only
to be with you, riding quietly
into whatever it was you knew.

Father

My father with his bright burst heart, the bullet
exploding in him like some gift the wind had given him,
fell from the sky he'd climbed to, the blood
rushing into him from his startled flesh
so that I imagine his heart a broken sail,
the centre suddenly torn and the strong wind rushing
through him, his blood taking him nowhere
at last, his body a whole vessel.

Who will I be,
I who am now as old as his death,
I who have never been a father to my own
lost children, who have left them
to shift in their worlds, their faces shining
in the bewilderment of their lives?

I have turned in my flesh,
rising to the night and the light of the candles
and stood among shadows that are only the stunned
wandering of moths, their burning wings thin sails

in the flickering light. It is here in the shadows
I try to imagine myself young again, a man
who can lift his father from the sky,
take him down and hold him in my arms,
hold him against my mouth,
and with one free hand, stroke his wet red hair
away from his forehead and tell him it is all
right, that I have him, that the bullet
that screamed through the air toward him
was only the wind.
                    It did not want his death,
was only a bit of wind in the wrong place
tearing him apart. I want then the whole sails of his heart
beating against my chest. I want him smiling
up at me and saying something I can hear at last
instead of this silence, the sound of his voice,
my own children far away rocking in their lives,
his body next to mine, both of us still alive
and not falling, not falling,
the hurt heart dead at last.

Fathers and Sons

I will walk across the long slow grass
where the desert sun waits among the stones
and reach down into the heavy earth
and lift your body back into the day.
My hands will swim down through the clay
like white fish who wander in the pools
of underground caves and they will find you
where you lie in the century of your sleep.

My arms will be as huge as the roots of trees,
my shoulders leaves, my hands as delicate
as the wings of fish in white water.
When I find you I will lift you out
into the sun and hold you
the way a son must who is now
as old as you were when you died.
I will lift you in my arms and bear you back.

My breath will blow away the earth
from your eyes and my lips will touch
your lips. They will say the years have been
long. They will speak into your flesh
the word *love* over and over,
as if it was the first word of the whole
earth. I will dance with you and you
will be as a small child asleep in my arms
as I say to the sun, bless this man who died.

I will hold you then, your hurt mouth curled
into my chest, and take your lost flesh
into me, make of you myself, and when you are
bone of my bone, and blood of my blood,
I will walk you into the hills and sit
alone with you and neither of us
will be ashamed. My hand and your hand.

I will take those two hands and hold them
together, palm against palm, and lift them
and say, this is praise, this is the holding
that is father and son. This I promise you
as I wanted to have promised in the days
of our silence, the nights of our sleeping.

Wait for me. I am coming across the grass
and through the stones. The eyes
of the animals and birds are upon me.
I am walking with my strength.
See, I am almost there.
If you listen you can hear me.
My mouth is open and I am singing.

She

I have no god but you. Inside
your dress, your dry breasts
lie flat against your chest. They are
the first full moons of my earliest night. Inside you
I heard the great drum of your womb
beating and beating its slow measure,
as my hands like the small buds of the jacaranda
reached through the living air for
the murmur of your flesh.

I have no god but you. The immaculate
moment slips away into all the things that are
lost. I see you everywhere. You are the old
faces on buses, the women with their eyes
fixed on a place beyond tears. You are
the women who stand beneath willows
on the far side of the river, who lie in the many
cramped rooms, all of your bodies beyond
tides and darkness.

I have no god but you. I fear
the words that mean nothing, the words

that are the cries of the son, the words
a woman calls birth and bereavement,
crying out as a whole body swam out of you,
my hands moving like silver salmon
into the pure pale air.

I have no god. But you?
When you gather yourself into silence
and the women chant as they prepare you
for your death, and the men have fallen
to their knees with their last gifts,
will you find me among the strangers
and bring my hands to your breasts?
Will you sing the last song,
the one that begins with the word *yes*?
Will you ask me if I've travelled far?
Or will you say: *I don't know this one.*
What is his name?

The Birth of Narrative

The boy's father killing the cat in the garage,
swinging the two-by-four through the air,
the cat leaping, trying to escape,
and the boy's seventeen-year-old wife standing there
pregnant, crying, telling him to stop, and the father,
having begun all of it and now somehow trapped,
starting to cry too, still swinging that board,
the cat leaping, the boy somewhere else working,
pulling, I think, green lumber off a chain,
waiting until he could come home to the story.

Precision

The party was almost over. One of the guests, an older man no one knew who had lost the wig that had curled over his eyes, danced naked in the largest room. His body was strange, the legs too short and his torso too long as if he had wanted to stay a child and refused to grow The women encouraged him, laughing at the grey pubic hair, his lank penis and his arms as he staggered before them, his face slack and featureless. When he finally fell two women pulled him to the door and rolled him outside. Someone would fight soon. Someone in a moment would stumble in from outside, his cheek torn, the flesh hanging in a flap from his chin. A woman would wrap a pillowcase around his face and leave him to bleed in the bathtub. The men in the basement would begin arguing about who got the only pistol and who had to make do with knives. The one who had to leave would go, but not quite yet. First the argument had to start, the fight over the girl with red hair, how to split up what was left. The boy in the corner who would be a writer someday watched everything very closely, the way the woman on the couch breathed, her dark skirt pulled up over her face, the fabric lifting very gently from where her mouth had to be, the way blood mixed with water in the tub, the laughing, the arguments, women screaming, men sullen and cold, the hour moving through its difficulties, the boy not knowing yet, but waiting for something he would later describe when he was much older, his green eyes moving across a hand as it turned into a fist, a dark breast hanging from a torn blouse, a man with only one shoe, someone vomiting, something about to happen in the next hour that would, for the boy in the corner, resolve the immense complexity of this night.

The Attitude of Mourning

He had walked out of the Pitti Palace into the rain, thinking
of that painting of Frans Hals high in the corner
where the light was dimmest, its anonymity intact.
The one of the young girl in the attitude of mourning.
She had reminded him of the vulture he had seen
in South America years ago, the one that huddled
under the geraniums during the rain,
not blinking, its two dark wings
pegged through the cardinal joints to the ground
while everything above it flowered red.
The rain striking its naked head.
But that was years ago when he was young.
Back then he had thought he understood
the magnitude of such an exile.

But this was not Medellin, it was
Florence with all its clarity intact,
its opulence a kind of tired memory, malignant
as light when it struggles with the rain
in the winter of Italy. It is the same
light an apple contains that rots from the inside,
that slow umber growing from the centre
toward the beauty the skin inhabits.

That is what art is, he thought, the perversity
of wanting that, the choosing of innocence
as a model for loss. He imagined the stained hands
of Frans Hals, their sureness as they removed
the young girl's shift, the light
from the northern window, the girl's mother
at the door counting the money
the canvas ready, the brush and the other brushes.

Later that night the palace was what he had wanted,
the walls rotting, the frescoes crumbling. The woman there
was all flesh, someone who simply wanted less.
This century would never paint her.
He looked at her breasts and her long wrists
and understood that pleasure when it becomes cruelty
is inward, a kind of bruise the body grows,
and knew then
he wasn't speaking of her but of himself.

Do you want me to hurt you? he asked.
No, she said, *non c'e necessita,*
her dialect peculiar, so that the host,
the large Englishman with the bare red feet
who had been talking of his mother and her distaste,
how she had told him when he was still a boy
she had slept with his father
only once, unsuccessfully, told me I should ignore her.
She is from Rome, he said. *And they know nothing in Rome.*

Privacies

She was the lover of his friend, a girl
with red hair and a body Renoir might have painted,
small and opulent, a figure Renoir would have placed
to the side as a decoration of the larger event, two men
talking perhaps about art while the woman lay on the lawn,
naked, waiting for something to happen.

That night when his friend was teaching
he had made love to her

---

and after, she asked him not to tell, as if betrayal
were made easier with promises. *He is*
taking me away to Montreal, she said. Later
when his friend came home
they had all sat together on the bed and drunk wine,
her watching as his friend and he laughed at the bad poems
of their enemies, his friend's last year at the university,
Montreal, and beyond that Jerusalem. Earlier his friend
had told him he would not take her with him.

He watched her touching his friend, her lover,
her small hand resting lightly on his shoulder, the look
in her eyes which his friend mistook for love.
Her artful modesty. His friend's indifference.
He thought of them later when they would be alone
together, their privacy, the touching.
For a moment, in the middle of their lives,
he was strangely happy with his burden.

The Book of Knowledge

He had been reading volume seven of *The Book of Knowledge*
and he got to thinking about those fakirs,
the difference between one nail and a thousand,
so he had taken his mother's sewing basket
and slowly, with what he thought then was patience,
took her needles and shaking only a little,
pushed them slowly through the skin
of his left arm, in and then out, the nine needles
resting there in a row, the flesh white and hard.
There was very little blood.

He pulled his sleeve over them
and went down to breakfast, his father quiet
as he drank his coffee, his sister watchful,
his brothers arguing over the last bits of meat.
Each time he lifted his fork
he could feel the fabric of his sleeve
catch at the needles, his flesh moving.
Sitting there he realized for the first time
how dangerous he was.

Fragility

She came from Normandy, one of those
villages on the lower Seine
where they make the good Calvados, the kind
you can only find there. She was very small.
He remembers that, the bones of her feet
fragile in his hands. They met
in Cuzco, the city of cut stone,
and parted in the Cartagena before
the tourists came, the one where,
if you closed your eyes and smelled it
you could remember Drake and his plundering,
his queen and glory. She had red hair
and that fair clear skin you can see through
at night in the last of the candles.

The Firebreather

In memory of Marcel Horne

She took him to the shed in the field behind the house.
For six days he sat there naked in the darkness without food
while the water he was allowed went slowly bad
in the New Mexico heat. On the last day the gypsy woman
came in and told him she was tired of his impatience.
She began to talk of her day, the morning in the market,
her husband's drinking, her daughter's whoring
after a Mexican businessman who sold melons in Texas.
While she spoke she began to light wooden matches,
striking them on a flat stone she held in her lap.
She sat very close to him and as each match flared
she would hold it to his skin, sticking it there,
the match burning, the smell of his own flesh.
He looked at his arms and chest, the way
the match would sometimes burn all the way
to the end and not fall off, the match curling,
those black stems sticking from him like fragile quills.
This went on for a long time until he no longer remembered
what he was there for, the sweat from his face and shoulders
running down his body, that sweet salt touching his wounds.
Then she opened his mouth, burning his tongue and lips.
The pain you feel is the pain of the outward, she said.
Later I will teach you the other pain.
When you have learned that you will be ready
to breathe fire.

Balance

He watched the horses come, huge in the afternoon,
their rubber hooves a dull sound under the screaming,
the riders swinging clubs to the right and left.
As he watched he saw a woman with a child go down
under a black horse, the horse careful not to step on her
as the rider leaned like a polo player
and struck her across the shoulders as she fell.
The horse and rider looked like they had practised this
a long time, the rider balanced perfectly,
the horse moving as if without effort, though
he could see the great muscles moving under its hide,
the crowd splintering into the many
narrow streets that led from the Avenida del Sol.
He had always remembered that, the horse's gentleness,
so strange in a body that large, the rider's steady grace,
and the woman
rising after they passed over, the look on her face,
the baby crying, the street almost empty, people
stepping from doorways to sit at the tables again,
the waiters bringing wine and beer.

Stylites

Most of the women had gone to bed, some of them alone
and some of them with the men they had chosen
or the women. He was very drunk and very happy
and he had not wanted anyone.
The woman his friend had travelled there for
had taken a soldier instead, saying, he likes

to dress up in my clothes. When she had gone
and only a few men were left drinking
he climbed up to where his friend was
among the beams and rafters
high above the floor. His friend
didn't know how he had got there.
He was afraid of heights.
They had sat there together
looking out at the far night,
the drunken voices of the last men below
rising to them on the clear cool air,
taking a drink, taking another one.
They talked quietly about the food
he would need, the ropes
he had to have to tie himself with
in order to sleep, how long
he intended to stay there, the night,
and the many nights to come.

Detail

The room was thirty inches by thirty inches
and there was a light in a small wire cage
in the ceiling above him.
He could stand but he could not sit
and after a week his legs began to swell.
The wood of the narrow door was a pale yellow.
It was a kind of wood he'd never seen before.
There was almost no grain, the thin striations
on the narrow boards almost invisible,
varying only slightly. He spent his days

tracing the patterns, following them
the same way the saw had followed the wood
into the heart, cutting
a little deeper each time. He knew
he would tell this story years later
and when he did this would be the place
where his listeners would shake their heads,
understanding the attention to such detail,
his legs swelling, the light,
and the thin cage of wire
he kept trying but couldn't reach.

Grief

He sat at the foot of the low bed and watched her cry.
It was not like Rome burning and it was not
like the spare fires he had built
when he was alone in the wilderness,
the ones he sat away from, the ones he put out
when he was tired of watching.
Her grief was of another kind, an event
that was merely ornament, a thing
that perishes as it is made, as a performance
in a northern town perishes line by line
with no one to remember it, something less than art
as time is less than merit. He had made her love him.

She hadn't wanted to. He had shaped her love
by shaping himself, giving himself to her
in the exactness of her integrity, becoming
her, and so, becoming less, their time

together an intimacy which was only imitation.
Sitting there he felt the same
as when he was a child and dressed
in his mother's clothes, his posturing
in front of her mirror, the inaccuracy
of that kind of dance.

He understood his gluttony, the wanting more,
his greed for her loss, the pain
she seemed to love more than him.
She did not tell him to go away, and
she did not call out to him.
What he had was what an observer has,
the man who gazes alone from a private box
protected by velvet curtains, a glass of good wine beside him,
the play going on and him with no rights, one way
or another, the man who watches with detachment
as a critic does, having no stake in the event.

La Scala

Ready to go to her then, saying he was sorry
and almost believing it, saying it again
as if it were a song a baritone sings
during an opera in a provincial town
while the tenor and soprano watch from the wings
just before entering for the finale, the moment
just after the tragedy, and always during the third
or fourth performance when all the singers
are at last sure of the version
they have settled for, the reviews in,

the songs always in another language
which is never translated and
which the singers had to memorize,
their precise imitation making it
another kind of beauty, and going to her
singing it, singing it.

Impression

Imagine a man who remembers. Imagine
a man who has left his country forever, a man
his friends helped over the mountains say, or over
the northern deserts, a man who his friends knew
would be arrested, tortured, made to tell all
his secrets. Imagine this man years later
remembering her, thinking of their nights
together, the smell of her flesh
on his hands, her dark hair
above him, her back arching, the way
her breasts would rise, shuddering
as small golden fish do when they lift
their bodies into the sun.
She is the one he is remembering now,
the one they caught three days later.
Imagine him thinking of her, remembering,
his mind going around and around, her breasts,
the corner of that last street he saw,
the blind man who sold pineapple there,
the one people used to stand and watch,
the sharpness of his knife, the way
he would cut the pineapples perfectly,

each slice precisely the same as the last,
the one who never hurt himself
seeing that in his mind, the van, the noise,
him on the floor under the rags and papers,
shaking, going somewhere,
the mountains say, or the desert.

The Image

Now that he was older
the artists had begun to paint him, and the photographers,
the clever ones with their miniature machines came
and arranged him in gardens and poolrooms, bars and verandas,
to capture the images of who he was, who they thought
he had been. Most of the artists were his age
but some were younger, beautiful young men,
and women with large hands, their hair pulled back
tight, their clothes unruly. He liked them the best.
He liked the way they would walk around him
after spending days and nights with his books,
his poems, the way they would stop and stare
while they painted him, all his words in their minds,
all the suffering intact, precise and imaginable.

Short Story

And then there was Billy, the quiet kid from Salmon Arm, Jesus, everybody liked Billy, who loved her so badly. He kept saying it: *I love her, God, I love her*, over coffee at the Coldwater Hotel, her in the bar, the baby crying. She was Nicola Indian, long gone down that road, and then Billy, after the strike and no money, the months of standing through the long winter of '56 while trucks and scabs rolled by, the RCMP young and tough from places like Hamilton and St. John, went home and sat up all one night and in the morning took the baby by the heels and smashed it against the wall, and Rose, the Indian girl, the wife, came to our house, and said: *That Billy, that Billy*, and had a cup of tea and then went down to the Nicola River and this barely spring, ice still holding in the log jams, took off every stitch of clothes and floated all the way to Spence's Bridge. I think it was Cole Robinson found her, he'd been short-logging there, and when he asked her what the hell she was doing naked in the creek, said nothing, said: *That Billy, that Billy*.

The Garden (1992)

From his window he looks down on the winter garden.
The rocks he carried across a mountain range
and the great plains rest in the arrangement of snow.
Beneath the spare limbs of the forsythia
the Japanese lantern glows in the thin sun, its patina
slowly moving toward the colour
which will make it finally beautiful,
something that will occur long after he is dead.

Sitting there he thinks of his first wife and wonders
what it is she knows now. He remembers just after
the divorce, her telling him how
she had slept with all of his friends.
Over the years. It was not
a confession, it was a sharing, as if their past
needed that kind of clarity. He hadn't known that, but
he laughed with her anyway. So they had sat there
on the couch in the room he had once inhabited with her,
all the things surrounding him what he would once have
called his belongings. He thinks he remembers his children
playing somewhere in the house but he's not sure.

The sun at the horizon moves and the garden changes,
the shapes under the snow assuming light. He thinks
that he will put a candle in the lantern
so he can watch it at night, the shadows
wavering in the cold, the stones around it
like white animals come to worship something
they have never seen before, a light in the darkness,
their bodies surrounding it in wonder, all of them,
as if they were alive, saying they would never forget it
and believing they were telling themselves
if only for this one night the truth.

The Children

The children are singing.
Hear them as they rise out of the deep hollows,
the tangles of wildwood and wandering vines.
They are lifting from the shadows

where the black creek water flows
over mud and stones. They have left behind
the green whip of a snake
thrown like a necklace into the trees,
and the body of a turtle, heavy,
buried beneath stones. The birds
are silent behind them. The paths
are still, waiting for the quiet ones,
the red face of the fox,
the thin touch of the raccoon
as she lifts her paws from their hiding.
The children are returning.
You cannot see their faces or their hands,
not yet. There are only their voices
rising from the tangle of vines,
the wet of black water.
Listen. There is nothing
to be afraid of now. Nothing.
The children are singing the old songs,
their hands empty, their small sharp eyes
alive.

The Meadow

The day in the meadow when he reached for her
and pulled her down into the wild grass
their cries were animals singing
so that the hawk circling far above them,
hungry, her young like soft explosions
on the nest, flew on, forgetting what she saw.
How they lay there in their limbs

laughing at the world they had begun
not knowing the words they would use
when the injuries began,
the betrayals,
the other bodies they would touch
imagining desire was to be cold
and perfectly alone. And then the confessions,
their hands finding each other awkwardly,
promising themselves it would never happen again
and almost believing it
as they said the word *love* over and over,
as if that hawk circling in the sky above their meadow
had stopped and held there above the humans
saying to herself
of all things surely these will live.

Gifts

Who are you? Are you
the one who opened your blouse and gave me
in both your hands your breasts, holding them out to me
while my wife in the dark living room
knelt on the blue carpet?
If you are the one, I remember wanting
not to be with you, but to be
with her, watching while someone's hand
moved in her thick dark hair.
Where have you gone?
What gifts have I refused?
Why do I remember now only the carpet
and the narrow feet of my wife
white against that heavy blue?

Orpheus
For Leonard Cohen

He is mostly laughter and willingly,
thinking of all those years of music
and the tears given to the wind, struggling

back up through all that silence, a second death
a cruelty he began to understand. To flee
from women, knowing only the trees and stones

could hear his song. This was the mystery
men turned to, a giving up to grief,
a going into song without complaint, for what

else but love had brought him here
to this place of birds and serpents? But to see
such death, and for what? To speak at last

in a voice that touched no one, the women
with their rakes and hoes hacking him to death
for whom the trees let fall their leaves?

And then to have his song lie beached on Lesbos
with Bacchus squatting on his head, cacophony and din
and nothing more? But these are only questions.

He should have known love would bring him this,
and of course the greed of women, their desire,
thinking death a suitable revenge upon neglect.

Orpheus who sang man's mysteries and died for it.
You too who dance upon the beach, you who have never
listened, listen now: the leaves fall without you

and the birds sing in the stream where your head lies.
Make your lament. It is only noise.
The whole world does not hear you.

So We Come

We have come to this
with what gifts we have, holding to
the terror we know and trust, the memory of things

we reach for, all our dreams,
the shaking drift of wings across our minds
when we are lost in sleep. There is no image

as we lift out of the dark
drowning, our whole bodies holding us there
in our beds, screaming. As I hold you

rocking you there in the dark, your hair wet
and your eyes staring. The horse that rides your night
rides mine as you slip back to silence,

your body still. This moment
when I want for you what little can be given,
when the night is huge

and a bird in some far tree cries out
because a shadow moved. My hand upon your breast,
the distant sound of breathing

in the street below, the night horse running through us
in the dark we made
giving as we have ourselves to dreams.

Dinner

I would like to have dinner with the man
who didn't follow Christ, the one who,
when Jesus said: *Follow me and I
will make you fishers of men,* decided
to go fishing instead, getting in his boat,
pushing out from shore, his nets clean
and repaired, thinking I will have to work
even harder now in order to feed
everyone left behind. I would like
to sit on the beach with him
in front of a careful fire,
his wife and children asleep,
sharing a glass of wine, both of us
telling stories about what we'd done
with our lives, the ones we caught,
the ones that got away.

The Desert

How beautiful to rest in such light
a fire brings to the night, a beetle
clambering from beneath a stone, a cactus
moving its green paw to hold the flower

it will grow from its flesh,
a jackpine's roots
so deep
they have found the water that will make the wind
come alive in dry branches,
a hand that keeps to the small, one stick
and then another, laid on a careful fire,
gladness,
the beetle staggering as it carries its shoulders over stones,
the cactus above it dreaming the flower
who will bring out of night
the sensual starving moths
their wings on my eyes the only sound
you can see in this spare land.

The Pool

We grace our days with what thanks
there is, laughing at the hummingbird
who bathes on deep water, his orchid body
moving on the surface of the pool.
Where to go but down into such deeps
this thimbled bird makes play of,
his small wings flaring like love
in his joy, or watching you in the bath
when you are alone, your hand touching
your breast as a flower might touch you
or a leaf in the fall, falling as your hand
falls, a single wing above such depths.

There Are Holes We Leave Behind Us

There is a spider basket in the old lantern.
Such small mysteries
we are heir to, this bassinette in the wind.
If you breathe on them they scatter
down the ladders they make out of their lives.
Such a huddling, this holding of spiders
in the beginning of the ordinary day.

These Ones

I think of the ones thrown out of their lives
like stones flung on water, each leap somehow lower
until they sink under their own flying, nothing
left behind. There are lakes so clear the eyes burn,
that deepness flaring so you think you could
swim down to where the blue begins.
I think a sinking stone moves as Nijinsky
moved in his last years,
all memory, each step a shadow
he felt in his thin legs
as he stumbled in front of the mirrors.
What the body forgets is
what memory is, but like Trakl's tiny aster,
it makes nothing possible.
Yet something is there inside that blue.
Something hides in the cupped bones of the skull.
It peers out from those holes, afraid
to move, somewhere in the clarity
a creature it always knew was there
in such clear waters.

Balsam Root

I don't remember her name, think now
it might have been some kind of flower,
brown like balsam root before it breaks
into that yellow spring is, a single heave
that turns a desert into bloom. Like that,
brown, when she came to me up-country,
her small breasts high and white
so that I saw them not a part of her
and thought they'd burn in such harsh light.
I had gone into those hills
to live away from things, a bed alone
under ponderosa pine, the stars
as they were before the cities put them out.
She came walking barefoot on the shale,
some man's daughter, fierce in her choice.
When I washed her in the flume after love,
she touched the blood as it mixed
with the cold come down from snow
and tasted herself. It was a time
when a man gone into hiding
could think a girl turned into woman
wouldn't know to take that much.
This is me, she said.
She said it like young balsam root
before it breaks to colour. She said it
like yellow would say when it dreams
itself yellow, before it is a flower,
all root and flesh in the dry earth.

Stars

Those lights in the sky.
Little butterflies of the night,
little dreamers. Each time my lover
rises to walk in the early garden
I watch her from the window.
I cannot take my eyes from her.
See how she leans inside the dawn,
the cherry blossoms on her shoulders
as she touches the cat
who follows her everywhere, wanting
only to be with her
among the dark mosses.
How much light there is
in the high window of night.
How I wait, knowing, for now
she comes to me,
her small feet wet with dew,
white as stars
in these last hours.

Palms

There are those so stunned by beauty
they lay down their hands and cry
for fallen angels, cry for the ice
that makes the petals fall in early spring.
How we love the heart when it breaks in us.
I think of your palms, the lines
that tell me you will go on forever.

I imagine you on the hills you call home,
some prairie where crocus rise
in the last snow. You are in a place
where you touch the last of winter
making a blue as sudden as a flower
in your hand. Little bones,
how hard the night
when you are far away. The angels here
are only owls. When they leave me
they leave their wings in snow.

Naramata

She has the full breasts of a woman,
a yellow the colour of stone
when it is first quarried, startled
by the air that touches it. She reaches out
and takes a flake of ice from my glass
and rubs it against a nipple, the flesh
rising to the cold. There is in her
what desire is, a kind of wanting
that does not disturb, provocation
as spare as pleasure. She makes me
think about the temple I visited today
and the old woman in the garden there.
A spider had built its web in the mouth
of the bronze bell and the woman
who had to strike the bell
at a certain hour went to the kitchen
and captured a wasp. She carried it
in the cage of her one good hand,

whispering to it the high whine that is
the song of wasps. She released it past the web
at the precise moment of striking, the wasp
trapped now within the bell. I loved
the sound, so small among stones
and bamboo, the wasp trying to find a way
out, its hard body striking the bronze,
the spider tensing its long legs.
There is in every ritual necessity
which moves us to delight.
It is why I love the clear water
moving very slowly down this woman's
curved belly, drying there in the heat.
She is waiting and she does not move,
her nipples still hard, her eyes
all willow leaves and almonds
as the wind rises from the river
into the temple sound of early morning.

The Artist

These are the shapes he wants, the map of
the wilderness he searches in, the driftwood
he finds shaped into the beasts
that are his dreams, the broken
weathered to resemblance by some wind
inside his mind, the imagined mountain
in the stone he climbs,
the peace he feels before descent.

Knotted Water

She never returned from that rain, knotted water
like a wound that would not heal. She had gone
to the baby after making love with him
by the broken window. How small death is.
When it was a week old he had kissed it
between the legs, saying he wanted to be the first man
to do that. At three weeks it was dead.
He took it from her, the three of them whirling
inside a room as small as water. Her arms then,
empty, thrashed in the air like blades of flesh.
Desert moon, how far we live from such days!
There were the thin rains and her going into them
much as a body will when it wants to drown,
those arms like sweeping blades
and the many pieces of sky in that bright flail.

Wisteria

You say *wisteria* and something plunders you,
a mouth heavy with blue
as if it had spent the morning eating grapes
or the heavy black cherries of childhood you picked
wild in the alien orchards of the desert hills. Words
come flowering, myriad
as if they grew in clusters on your tongue, as if
you were speaking to the grandmother
you never knew who sat
strapped in a chair for the last years of her life
asking for fruit from a tree that wasn't there.

Hers was a kind of frailty, tough and trembling,
like a scant branch you think if you take
will break. She wanted
fruit for the pies they wouldn't let her make.

A trembling, as wisteria, or hands when you are still
a child that reach farther than they can to plunder
a distant branch of its first fruit. Still,
inside that old woman I never knew was a stone
as there was inside my mother. *Cherries*,
she would cry, *cherries*, and I would go to her
if I could, my mouth a rich purple,
and speak to her of the hills
and the solitary lark beyond the wisteria
real as the knife she holds as she peels
the skin I wear like a shroud, whispering
through whatever blood there is:
you must eat child, you must eat.

Held Water

I have discovered I cannot bear to be
with people anymore. Even the querulous love of old friends
defeats me and I turn away, my face staring
at the hard sleet
scraping at what little is left of the trees
in early spring. The bellied pods of the wisteria hold
my face, upside down
in minute mirrors of held water. Ice falls from the eaves.
The telephone rings and like a monk I chant to myself
the many names of whatever gods I can find

in the temple bells of the hidden voices. I know
under the rotting snow there are small flowers
like insistent girls giggling in narrow attic beds,
and yes,
I know the flowers are not girls, just as
I know what resemblance there is
is lost in the ordinary crying
we think we will release and don't.
The furred pods of the wisteria crack open
dropping the mirrors from their blue hands.
Ice slides from the roof and for a moment the air is torn.
If I wasn't afraid
I could play back the sounds of my friends,
the measure of their voices
almost steady in the hard wind out of the North.
Little flawed bells.
If I didn't hear them I could almost listen.

The Hiding Place

How carefully you have hidden it away
and so long ago. What a perfect hiding
place for such a small thing, out there
in the open where everyone can see it
among the spoons and coffee cups,
the sparrow's feathers, the poppy seeds.
All these years and you have never told anyone
where it is. Try to remember.
It is such a little thing out there
among the bright shells and the pennies.

The White Box

In the white box
you keep hidden away
a white salamander
waits with a flame
in his small hands.

How bright the fire!
How long his breath
has kept it alive!
But the box is closed.
Why do you keep it closed?

Without Innocence

In the centre of the night lake,
only my head above water

and letting the air out
of my body, slowly, the water

rising past my mouth and eyes,
and me sinking with that darkness,

thinking how I have never
done that until now.

Carousel

The horse not ridden on the midway, the one
who runs alone in the circle of the dance,
mothers and fathers standing by their children
as they go round and round, holding on to what
at that moment is most precious to them,
trust and fear, a kind of crazed happiness
on all their faces. The painted horse
goes into that darkness where all circles go.
There is such strain in that painted mouth
as it cries itself back into the light, this horse
who plunges riderless,
rising and falling upon the silver stake
that holds it in its round,
the children screaming, the madness going on.

The Changing Room

In the changing room our naked bodies moved
from our dark cubicles to stand in a circle
around a rusted grate where the slippery water
heavy with sweat and steam sank into a hole.
On the other side of the wall we heard
the girls, their screams, their crazy laughter,
the high wild madness of summer at the lake.
Listening, we passed among ourselves the picture
of a woman on her knees holding a man in her mouth.
Her eyes were closed. I remember that, remember
thinking it was what she held that made her blind,
remember the look on the man's soft face,

a flat pale stare that made him somehow missing
as if at the centre of himself he wasn't there.
I knew even then there was a holiness to it
and would have called it *icon* had I known the word.
As the picture moved among us we circled
the heavy grate, our bodies hunched
emptying ourselves in that white silence.

We changed then and ran into the light,
banging against the girls who came out
from the other side. I wondered
if the girls had a picture, the man in it
blind as the woman was in ours? Would he be
on his knees and if he was what of a woman's
did he hold in his heavy mouth?
As the bodies of my friends
scattered across the sand, I climbed under the pier
where Margery stood in her cotton dress.
We undressed on the dark sand and stared
at each other. I used to dream her on her knees,
holding me in her mouth. I imagined
the look of the standing man, practised
his vacant stare as my body poured into her.

When we were dressed I walked her through the alleys
and stood with her under the elms at her mother's shack,
our bodies almost touching, our secrets safe, staring
beyond ourselves at what I thought must be the same
imagining: each of us on our knees, each of us
holding each other in our mouths, though what I held
in mine I didn't know, and with her eyes an emptiness,
I heard her mother calling her to home,
knew my own was somewhere calling me,

and ran with the last light back to my flesh,
my supper waiting, my mother at the stove, my father
silent, all of us eating the food that she had made.

Cougar

The cougar before she falls from her high limb
holds for one moment the ponderosa pine, her back
arched, her tail so still the forest stops.
There are silences to learn,
each one an invocation: the one that follows
a father's rage at a child, a woman's rage at man,
a child's tears — you watch as if the sound
was a language you must learn. But a cougar's falling?
Nothing is so quiet. Even the wind stops to listen.
Beetles, busy at death, lift up their jointed legs,
whiskey jacks slide quietly away, and ravens appear
as if they had been made from the air.
It is to watch a thing whose only gift is death
give to herself, feeling the explosion in her heart
a thing she has made and not the men below
and not the dogs as they watch her falling
through the limbs and then erupting into sound,
their hard mouths biting what is already dead.
It is the boy on a horse so old it will not run,
a boy who watches, not understanding the men
who, when she falls, shoot their rifles at the sun,
as if with such exultance
they could bring a darkness into the world.

Lion Creek

It is water so clear the mind shudders
when the whole body lies down among lilies
and pushes the face into the memory of ice.
It is to open the eyes in such water,
and watch the salmon, tails rotting,
fins fallen off, move across bright gravel.
It is the female lying on her side to scour a bed,
the bright eggs squirting out of her, bits of her tail
breaking off in the clear current,
as the male, fierce, his hooked beak
and scabrous sides, beats the gravel
above, driving a cloud of dust to mask her laying
from the scavengers, and then to slip through water
beside her to spill his milt, that white cloud flowing
upon her while trout and kokanee shudder in like sharks,
their bellies so swollen they can swallow nothing,
only bite at the eggs until, rent by their teeth,
they burst like planets in the tumbling current.
It is to open the mouth and taste their dying.
It is to hold the breath until the face lifts out
and pulls the whole sky into the lungs.
And it is to walk the sands of Lion Creek and sit
with the dead, the bodies rotting, everywhere around you,
the bears so greedy and full they ignore you, grizzlies,
black and brown. It is to be young. It is to see
that huge death, to sit on the long sands of Lion Creek
and watch the salmon beach themselves as whales do,
their bodies shivering, relieved at last of their burden,
the smell of their birth stream everywhere around them.

Far North

For Ken and Alice

Waking into that blue which is the death of stars
by the margin of a lake so far away there is no trail
but for the wandering tracks the animals have made
to salt lick, meadow, crush of early berries,
trees where the stretched claws of bears
have left their mark higher than I can reach, I open
my eyes to the dawn and breathe the light.
It is my third week alone and I have gone past being
lost, knowing all water leads home, the spring
that turns into creek, into river. The mountains
heave beyond the trees. I lie in the bed of my own
making, the fire of night gone out. The ashes do not move
nor do I as I stare into what stands above me,
a moose, its soft nose wet, its rack
reaching across the sky it is so wide. For a moment
he stares down from the opening light of the world,
then steps over me, going on into the trees.
I am in a place far from myself
this fall morning, gone deep in solitude.
It is enough to lie on the sand beside this lake
and allow the drops of water on my face to dry,
the ones that fell from the moose's belly
when he stepped so carefully over a creature
he had never seen before, afraid
that he might waken it, an animal
who had not yet risen from its sleep
into the quiet grace of the light.

Lost and Found

Twenty-one feathers in the blue jar
and you still can't fly.
Thirteen bones in the white saucer
and you still can't walk.
Three bells in a drawer,
a berry in a snail shell,
a doll's head in the window.
If it was spring you could watch
the apple tree grow, but
it is winter and it is always
winter. How hard it is
to save everything.
Stop losing things, you cry,
but they keep dropping
from the hands of the fir trees,
from the pockets of the little boys.

The Calf

In the orchard they had tied the calf between two trees
and, because they wanted to please, knowing
he was from the town and knew about books and songs
they offered her to him first.
He didn't understand and refused, standing there
awkward in his town shoes and ironed pants.
The boys laughed at him then and dropped their jeans,
taking turns, one hand gripping the curved
bone of her hip, the other holding in a fist
her tail to the side, their white buttocks

pumping in the sun. When they were done they were angry
though he wasn't sure at what or whom. Perhaps they thought
he had disdained the gift, or disdained them.

They turned from him then,
going through the apple trees to the fields,
their narrow backs changing from shadow into light.
Alone, walking back to the farm, he was afraid,
the trees heavy with green fruit in the heat,
the swollen grass breaking with pollen
against his legs, covering him with dust.

Later the last of summer would give him Emma's breasts
in the snake-grass meadows below the swimming hole
and in the deserted barn, Irene's mouth, wet and warm,
but he thinks now only of the boys
and their offering, how he had failed
something or someone, the boys moving slowly, shuffling
sullen away from him.
                    The calf had snuffled the thick grass,
still tied, and when he released her thinking she would run,
she didn't move away, instead
bunted him softly, the hair around her budding
horns curled and white
where he placed his hands, he thought then
to hold her away, holding her in the way
light is held when it does not come from the sun.

The First Time

The first time
I saw a chicken
run headless
across the yard

I wanted
to do it too

I wanted
to kill something
so perfectly
it would live

Cali

That woman with a dead child on her back,
the wound still in its small face, the blood
brittle on the corner of her dress,
and the flies. She said nothing to me, nothing
to anyone. I remember asking the man at the table
who she was. He pushed his rifle to the side
so the waiter could put the glasses and beer
down on the wooden boards. Who knows? he said.
She has walked by here each hour since morning,
each time with the same child. I think perhaps
she is crazy now. Who knows?
He hesitated a moment and drank some beer,
then leaned toward me in what I know now
is the conspiracy of men. You know, he said,
she's driving me a little crazy too.

Chiapas

Past the hard stones, the packed clay
where the earth is worn away by heavy feet
that scraped there in the night to find relief
from the hours of day, the cries of women,
their lament as they huddle
in their rooms of crockery and clay, a child
hanging from a breast, another curled at their feet,
wrapped in rag cotton, breathing from its mouth

Past the scarred green leaves of cactus,
the dust-ridden stems of plants that've lost
their leaves to hands and hooves and teeth,
the staggering lines of ants who sail
like ships into the dark, the leaves they carry
trembling underground past stones
whose sound is the silence stones know

Past splintered windows where beetles
clatter their thick shells to a stoop
where, kneeling on a rag, a child
combs her hair for lice, the blood
between her thighs dark as earth,
still, the mother gone for water,
the father gone to the light you go towards

Past the doorway you do not stop at, knowing
who is there, pariah dogs rushing
at your boots, their broken muzzles searching
the beaten clay for whatever might have fallen,
cringing, yellow, their fur scored, matted, torn,
they follow you as the old men follow,
begging, their mouths dark holes

Past the old man on the three-legged stool
who shoves his bowl at you, and past the old woman
whose tattoos run from her ankles to her eyes,
a whirl, a rising, whorled and whimpering,
testament to the hours of blood and beauty,
her back laid bare so the gods of night can breathe,
between her knees a bottle and a beetle on a string
who runs from breast to elbow, wrist to withered hand

Past the whine, the night, the cries, the earth
ground clean, a desert place, the far cantina's
hot light, and deep the sound, the muttered
voices mumbling, drunk, a screaming parrot, the pulque,
the cerveza, whiskey, wine, the flowers in the hair
of the woman who wanted you last night, her thighs,
mouth, hands, her feet, her back, all
you wanted in your drunkenness, some coins

Past the men who lean upon the tables,
the heavy muscles, arms ending in fists
around their bottles, to the bar
where you are waiting, the sweat
drying as it leaks from your skin, the light
blond hairs curled over like fallen ferns,
your mouth closed, hair still wet from turning
in the day's hot sleep that wasn't sleep again,
to the place that is your place,
the one they have made for you
in this village where your hands reach out
and trying one more time, refuse to shake

Señor Señor a young pimp whispers, his sister in the shadow
by the door, her eyes half-closed, her small mouth swollen,

and you, as you always do, say nothing,
look at the iguana who watches you, the still one
made from stone, the chain around his leg nailed to the bar,
and finally safe, you lift what is left to you and drink
the first long drink of night, staring past everything
you've passed at the mirror above the iguana
where the one you want to die stares back at you
looking like the man you used to be when you were young
in the mountains of Chiapas years ago.

China White

He sat in the small room thinking of geraniums,
that crowded red as close to blood
as any flower is. It was after Archie offered her
to him, saying, *Anything you want,*
and her on the bed, nodding off, the exact particular
in her mind a shell she might ride on without menace.
Her blonde hair was another kind of light.
When he declined, Archie covered her again, his hand
hesitating just a moment as the blanket fell, a quietness
he tried to understand. All this for some China white.
Sometimes you can't imagine what it's like, given
such magic as occurs in time. What is in his mind
are geraniums, those bloody flowers
rising from their arms into the last syringe,
and the ones his mother grew so many years ago
beside the stones covered in red lichens.
Such textures as there are in the many
gardens we make from ourselves. Then, leaving,
going out into whatever beauty he can find.

Too Spare, Too Fierce

When the dawn is large enough
you will go out into that stiff blue and find a cat's paw
in the bird bath, a gift from the crow to morning.
There was a moment last night when you started walking
the iron rail in your bare feet on the bridge above the river
and you believed you wouldn't fall. Now, this morning,
you shake so badly you can't hold the glass,
lowering your face to it, your tongue
a thick grey muscle trying to drown.
Outside, mosquito larvae dance
among the claws and the little red cords
where the birds come to bathe. Old crow,
I will come as soon as I can.

Musical Phrase (fragment)

and the body full of whiskey and cocaine
swaying in the dark and the dark,
pissing on the devil moon,
the wind
cold on skin
that sang once of beauty
awkwardly,
misshapen,
a dwarf who danced for kings
knowing beneath that shining
their shared disease, the grace
gone now, the roses
cut back and banked with leaves

against the cold,
naked
and the stars

That Blue Overcoming

It was almost morning
and he was left with the struggle
light has with darkness,
that blue overcoming
when everything starts to live.

He had sat on the stone
he had moved for beauty,
the one that had lost
the moss that had made it
into a mountain.

He talked to the cedar,
the old one of the forest.
It was after he killed
the dove who had mourned
in the slow evening. He knew

he had done a great wrong,
that soft body in his hand,
the wretchedness, the
certainty of that grief.
That was why he was

there, watching the light,
knowing he must leave,
seeing the forest come alive
again, that great blue growing
and him with no way in.

Silence (1995)

It is night and the new moon
reaches through the branches of the elms.
Today I planted the potatoes in the spring earth
and tonight we fought
over my silence, you calling me a hermit, me
saying nothing. Two thousand miles away
the grass begins to grow on my father's grave,
my brother's. And my mother burns
the few letters that might have explained who she was.
In another week the elms will leaf and I
will have to go far to see the night.
Under the earth the harvest prepares itself,
the eyes of the potatoes sending out roots,
the long tendrils of the dark.
My mother's silence, my father's murder,
my brother's death. These are what
I think of under the moon. They are not
a sadness, though you in your anger
think it so. It was your eyes I was afraid of,
their sudden flowering, and what was behind them,
my body no longer wanting anything
but peace, the quiet I have searched for, the moon,
my shovel still in the earth, dead wood, iron.

The Story in His Bones

In memory of Howard O'Hagan

He sits in the room of autumn
lost in the struggle of words, trying to believe
they will redeem, if not himself, then someone
lonelier, some woman wanting what little there is
of love, a child, some man, perhaps himself, who stares
through his fingers and finds them making a church,
a steeple, and repeats the old song of childhood,
ending it with the cry: *And there are the people.*

The fire begins to die
and he rises and places on the embers
wood, vine maple, whose leaves in autumn
always promise glory and turn brown
before the blaze of colour can appear
that could bring back that earlier forest
when someone looked amazed into the dark
and did not know himself. Gone now
except on isolated farms or in old poems
where taciturn, reluctant men built walls
against their lives, tearing down the dark,
turning the land into a story to be told.
His room surrounds the place where words
begin, the fire which batters back the cold.

Inert, the log remains a dark thing on the coals,
and the man watches what he believes is death, the cold
come creeping as if the northern bear, old polar animal,
has come at last to claim him, standing web-footed
upon the snow, swaying there.
The bear is what the man calls from himself,

a great white animal who is the story
in his bones, the one he tells himself
in a room where the fire dies.

He waits then for the muffle of paws on ice
and, staring, sees the maple burst to flame,
the slow accretion of the years when it
pulled into itself all that the earth had offered
and blazes, and it is as if the man
has turned to flame, his flesh leaping into fire.

He turns then to the hands he holds, each finger
locked together, and opens them to his eyes, the myriad
beings lifting there, such praise as what he knew
when his mother held him in the bowl
of her blue bones. Beside him, the huge animal,
its white fur radiant, murmurs to the man
what the far wind knows that falls
out of the North: *consumed, consumed,*
his white head weaving words out of the light.

Snow falls upon snow, the maple burns, and somewhere
where the forest begins, a man
steps into the trees, entering a world,
leaving behind him only a story to be told
around a fire to children who will soon go into dream,
how someday he will return, the one who left,
bearing in his hands a church, beside him
his companion, a white bear who will give to those
who weave above the flames in their last hours
a story whose very name is without fear.

Moths

The air breathes like a tree just before dawn
and my hands that rested on your body
when they held your sleeping, move away from me,
and fly like moths with only night
to guide them, go with their wings to the sea.
Who I am falls behind and all I can see
are the dead who have gathered here to free
this hour from the many hours.

Pale moths, soft birds of the night,

move among their grey faces, touch
their small shy feet, cleanse what must be
cleansed in this dark where the dead have come
for blessing. Touch their lips
with your wings so they may sing.
Be to them what the heart is when it sleeps.

Kingfisher

A full white moon at break of day above the loons.
No rain. That eye upon the western hills.
The heron waits the tide upon a rocking boat and I
think of the kingfisher who died the first day.
That sign.
Blue feathers in my hand and the crows above me in the pine
speaking of this solitude and that.
In the tidal reach the loons throw silver fish in the air
and catch them, laughing.

Here, perhaps, here.
White moon. The tide. The fisher king.
All things receding.
Praise.

The Neurotic Poet

He looked up *neurotic* in the dictionary
and there was a moment when he felt affirmed,
that having a *morbid nature or tendency*
was all right, and then, because he tended
toward being absolutely sure, looked up *morbid*
and read, *taking an excessive interest in matters*
of a gruesome or unwholesome nature, and thought
that definition excessive and unwholesome
at best, but, just to be sure of his affirmation,
shaken a bit now by a book full of words about words
and not necessarily to be trusted, looked up
unwholesome and felt the editors, Funk and Wagnalls,
were a bit neurotic themselves, given the meaning,
deleterious to physical or mental health,
which made him think of his friend Virgo, and then,
because he felt the desire to look even deeper
into the subject, read *not contributing to moral health;*
pernicious, bad. And it was the word *bad* intrigued him,
remembering how his mother would say things to him
when he was a child and was caught dismembering a bird,
or burning little Purdy's fingers with a torch.

Stop being bad, his mother would say, so he went there, thinking
this would affirm him if nothing would and read,

Not good in any manner or degree, unpleasant,
disagreeable, injurious, vicious, inadequate,
deficient, incorrect, worthless, and finally,
sick, in poor health, and so began to worry about that,
his possibly having lung cancer or stomach cancer,
a brain tumour, or heart condition, and so began to feel *bad,*
how that word seemed to be at the root of it all, how
merely to have a *tendency* could lead him to such
trouble in his mind, and then he felt, perhaps,
the friend who had said he was *neurotic,* which made him
wonder if he was his friend, and would a *friend*
say such a thing out of friendship or was there
a deeper meaning to the remark, something strange
about the friend who had begun all of this craziness,
had been wrong and it wasn't about being *neurotic,*
but about being *erotic,* and so began again with what he thought
might be a *prurient* or *morbid* interest in such a word,
but went on anyway, sure now he was on the right track,
his hands turning the pages of the dictionary quickly,
hurriedly, and read, *not conforming to rules or standards,*
irregular, eccentric, and realized he was looking at
a different word altogether. *Erratic,* and that was it,
he thought, or could it be *eruct,* which meant to belch,
and thought he had been having a bit of gas lately,
and felt suddenly that he was *in bad health* and did
tend towards a kind of excessive worry about things,
and the word *erotic* jumped out at him and he
felt that his *morbid propensity to love and make love,*
his *uncontrollable sexual desire,* and the resultant
melancholia caused by love, fitted his personality
perfectly and so went forward, sure of the many meanings,
not feeling in any way *neurotic* at all, but then started thinking
about his poems, the one about the boy sticking pins through his arm,

and thought that might be a bit unwholesome,
or the one about the man who breathed fire, how a woman,
a gypsy say, would stick lighted matches against his skin,
and thought that poem was all right and not excessive
in any way, not really, thinking how else would a firebreather
learn his trade, but still, it seemed to him to be about
a kind of *uncontrollable* feeling, and thought a poem about a boy's
first love, a calf say in an orchard, and the boy not wanting
to engage in such a *bestial* act, and knew that was it, that
such a boy could not be construed to be *neurotic* at all,
but merely good, not *bad*, not *inadequate* or *deficient*
in any way, but he knew he had to end up with some kind of love,
some kind of desire, something that would lead to the *melancholia*
caused by love, but where to go once you start, he thought,
and felt *morbidly gloomy and sad*, and slightly *dejected*,
that somehow he was in *low spirits*, and thought
what he needed was some *pensive contemplation*,
some serious and sober reflection, and knew that would be a good thing,
not a *bad* thing, and better than thinking of girls and boys
playing together, perhaps taking off their clothes
and touching each other, their laughing shyly, taking down
their pants, and thought that what he was thinking now was
a kind of *morbid propensity toward love* and, wanting to be good,
wanting only to be good, and sorry now he had burned
little Purdy's fingers with that blowtorch, and sorry, too,
about the bird he had dismembered, let alone the family cat,
Newlove, he put into the freezer that day, and Mother finding it,
yelling at him again, saying he would have to wait
for his father to come home before he'd get it, and wondering
even now if he had misunderstood her in some way,
and thought it was a gift his father was bringing him
and not a *punishment*, all of it bringing out a *tendency*
he knew he'd always had about *excessive* things, and felt

suddenly *inadequate* to the task at hand, a bit *worthless*,
and thought then it was his readers who kept demanding
such *prurient* and *violent* things from him, and who were
Funk and Wagnalls anyway, and what made them think
they were authorities on such a subject as *neurotic*,
two Americans who decided to clear it all up for everyone,
so that no one would ever be confused again by words
and what they meant, and so took out his pinking shears
and began cutting up the pages of the stupid dictionary
he was looking at, saying to himself, *Bad, bad!*

And then began looking around, hoping no one
had seen him do such a thing, cutting up a dictionary,
and began to hide the pieces of paper, but then his companion
of many years suddenly came upstairs and he knew
he wouldn't be able to hide it all from her
so said he had begun to use William Burroughs' technique
of cutting up sentences in order to make a fine poem,
and she asked if he had been drinking again, and
that made him feel *unworthy* and *inadequate*, but not
he felt, *neurotic*, which was the main thing, he thought,
in what he was sure was neither *morbid* nor *excessive*.

Yet there were his friends, and he began to think of them,
how they might be of a *morbid nature* and how they
more than he *took an excessive interest in matters of a gruesome*
or unwholesome nature, Stephen Reid who wrote happy-go-lucky
stories of cops beating up prisoners in dank rooms in the Don Jail
and how his wife, Susan Musgrave, who couldn't possibly be construed to be
neurotic, dressed in leather and studs, skulls and bones,
and how he felt good with her when she was dressed like that,
and the way she beat out the lines of her poems
as if she had a little tiny whip in her hand, and how he liked that

and sometimes late at night thought of her perhaps beating her man
with such a whip, but knew these were *salacious, depraved* thoughts,
or Brett who was definitely *neurotic,* how he had
a strange relationship with a parrot and spent too many hours
in the meadow with the sheep and who knew what he did there,
what *depraved, unwholesome* acts, and how he was nothing like that,
or MAC Farrant who wrote little square things in boxes
and how that was of concern, her preoccupation with boxes,
and then there was Lorna, his partner, and when he said *partner*
it was like Gabby Hayes or something from a movie deep in the past
and hoped she hadn't heard him whispering *Gabby* to her last night,
but her fascination with penises, and how he'd searched through her
Penis Poems in hopes he'd find his own, struck by the size and variety
and how his seemed smaller and tended toward excellence over
size, and how she was a lot like a vegetable in a way, a kind
of squash, Hubbard or some such name, and then
thought of his audiences, the ones he read to at night,
how *they* weren't really contributing to *moral health* either,
how they were somehow *pernicious* and *bad,* and there was
his mother again, but this time she was naked and she had
a little whip and was reading to him a poem about penises
and suddenly he and his friends were tied up in the Don Jail,
and the guards were saying, we're leaving you to these two,
and there were the women, each with a parrot on her shoulder
smiling at us, and somewhere we could hear the bleating of sheep
and everything became dark
and we were watching films of *unspeakable* things,
little Purdy's fingers burning, or a boy opening the freezer
to tell his mother he'd found Newlove after all,
and the night was getting long and he knew he needed
some sober reflection, and that he'd always had *tendencies*
and *morbid* thoughts, and thought he'd go back to the dictionary
if only to double-check the word *neurotic,*

but thought that would be *unwholesome* or *gruesome*
and thought only a truly *neurotic* person would bother
to do such a thing, wondering still, after all this searching,
how the word *eruct* was closest to him in a way he hadn't
fully understood before, a bubble of gas inside him, and how he felt
strangely like releasing it, and the need to read something, anything,
perhaps a poem about a boy sticking pins into himself,
or a boy with a box of wooden matches who wanted to learn
what it would be like to breathe fire.

THE TWENTY-FIRST CENTURY

The Old Ones
For Al Purdy

He thought of the horses in January,
the old ones who had stopped moving
and stood away from the wind
in the bleached coulee above Six Mile Creek,
snow and wind scouring their matted backs
and he wonders now what they dreamed
in the dead cold of that winter years ago.
Were they the horses who had loved
the steady pull of trace and strain, the long
journey in from Six Mile, buckboards
and wagons resting grey under the trees
in late summer, still hitched, standing
in the bare shade without water, waiting?
It was winter when he saw them last,
the old ones in the wind, their great heads
bent to spare grasses in the coulee.
He had watched the wind crawl
through the horses' manes and tails.
Even then he knew he'd seen the last
of their long journey to the town,
the blacksmith shop shut down,
the trees where they were tied
a lot for cars and trucks. The old ones
in their last winter, the ones who loved
the wagons and buckboards,
the steady sound of hooves in the dust,
the men and women and children behind them
talking their way to the stores and bars,
the hitching rails on Main Street, all that time
gone now. Still, they must have dreamed

or maybe it was only him,
balanced on his haunches in a frieze of wild rose
staring down at them and taking his body
among them for a moment,
snow cutting his eyes, the wind not yet
ready to die in those sagebrush hills
where the coulee lay below Six Mile
and the old ones waiting for it to end.

Morpho Butterfly

For Mary

They were not lost. The yellow butterflies who lay
their tongues on the drenched mud of a dirt road
found surcease in their flight. And that is old,
a story I'd have told when I was young.
It's not a deer upon the road, though I have seen
an animal fall into my lights and break
into fur or feathers, and then my stopping,
lifting from the broken grill its death. There is
no single memory. Every image flies
into my mind. So much of time is rest
after long wandering, and the wings that were
as much our bodies as our eyes, grow tired. Once
in my first manhood I stood in the heavy snow
that was a narrow cut of road and found in the broken
ice of a deserted shack a butterfly of iridescent blue.
I tried to breathe it into life, but there is a time
when the fragile falls into our hands and dies.
What high wind from Costa Rica blew such colour
into my hands and why was the breath I lifted

from my body not enough? A century ago
and still I dream of its small hands on me,
the mirrors of its wings. I saw myself
in the fractured glinting as it wavered on my palm.
Christ, it was winter. I was cold. You still
lay in bed with our first son in your arms,
your thin breasts bleeding milk.
I was building a highway in the mountains
so far away from my mind I don't remember it,
think now it was the way a body breaks itself
against what holds it, water falling into a vase
riding itself back to the stillness it was.
Nothing is lost unless we make it so.
I held that startled blue in the northern mountains.
I've held what I have held and every mark
the creatures made upon my flesh is totem
to what others would call scars. How terrible
when the flesh is torn, how beautiful the wings.

The Macaroni Song

I remember macaroni,
the end of the month,
the last week
when there was so little.

I made up
a song for the children.

The Macaroni Song!

Around the table
we would go,
laughing and singing.

Macaroni, Macaroni!

I can't make the song
work now on the page,
just remember, we
laughed so hard.

My wife stood
over the grey metal
where the macaroni boiled.

She never sang the song.
It was always six o'clock.
The children would cry:

Sing the Macaroni Song!

And I would sing.

One night
I stole three tomatoes
from Mister Sagetti's garden
and dropped them
into the curl of water.

My wife.
She loved me.
We worked so hard
to make a life.

Three tomatoes.
I still dream of them.
We were, what you
would call now, poor.

But when we danced
around the table,
my sons and my one
daughter in my hands
and sang the Macaroni
Song, God, in that moment,
we were happy.

And my wife at the grey stove
spooned the pale bare curls
onto each plate
and that one night
the thin threads
of three tomatoes.

I still dream of them.

Mister Sagetti, dead,
wherever you are
I want to say
this poem is for you.
I'm sorry I stole
your tomatoes.
I was poor and I
wanted, for my children,
a little more.

The Bare Plum of Winter Rain

The instrument of your poverty
is an infinite departure, the hawk unseen
until you see him without prey
in the bare plum of winter rain.
He rests inside hunger
and he does not sing today.
How rare the gesture we make
with nothing. It is of the spirit and without
value. The bare plum, the winter rain
and the hawk seeing what you cannot say.
These steady accretions, yet allowing them
to stay as you stay with music after music
plays, and of course there is always,
always hunger, and, of course, poverty,
and the bare plum, empty, and the rain.

Say

I got out of the car and walked into the fog.
She was dead. I felt what I felt
and there was nothing to say to them
except say, *Stay in the car.*
And then we drove another two hours.
The fog was still heavy in the low places
so that you wanted just to fly away.
What else to say?
I don't know if that is a question,
what it feels like to be a body
riding up over the hood

---

and rolling off the windshield.
So the cop said at the end,
What a night, and I agreed,
the kids asleep at last in the back seat,
their mother quiet. But, you know,
just to fly off the high places
when the fog isn't there,
just fly,
one of the kids, I think the oldest one,
saying, *Dad, did you kill her,*
Did you kill her? And just driving,
going on home, going on home.

Other Days

I remember laving her body as she said
over and over the one word, *No,* my hands
moving the cloth over her breasts and belly,
and the blood. I remember how blood,
when it is lifted from a body, becomes
another thing, and pale and pale
is as much thin water as a life. And
at each sound she made, that long *O*
turning around her still face, I said
Yes, as if I understood something
I didn't, the cuts coming clean like mouths
of children when you touch them with a hand,
their lips as bright as wounds, again
that word following hers, and now,
old, I don't remember whose word was last,
only remember her touching me

with the kind of touch the hurt ones use,
half-love and half-forgetting; *you*,
where are you now? And how long
must I hold you in my arms
as I carry you away again, your man
in the kitchen crying, the knife on the floor
waiting for whatever other life it had,
and our words ringing like soft bells
in the night when only the birds are asleep,
lost in the tired wings of that other day.

The Day of the Dead Horse

The day of the dead horse there was no rain.
It was hot on the iron cot, the bend of my body
stained on the stained sheets, the sweat still pooling.
The kids clambered over me
and told me of the horse who got killed by a truck.

They danced me from sleep. Half-strangled
by the sheets I fell onto the scuffed boards.
Mothers send their children to men like me,
strangers who sleep and do not work,
their own men gone into the fields to hurt themselves
with everything the fields do to those
who can't eat what they have grown. Such men
hate themselves with whiskey.
Cross-legged on the ground, the women
watched me as their children swarmed over
my body like small wasps with a need
only the mothers understood.

It was the day of the dead horse and someone,
a man, must cut it before it blows.
The heat turns the overworked heart
into a green wreck, the rot
already singing as the mottled eyes
caught darkness from the sun.
It was a lucky death in that village,
a strange horse wandered down from the hills
and killed by a truck. It was not a horse they knew.
I cut its throat with a knife a woman gave me,
the blade so sharp I thought the edge alive.

Cutting a dead throat is always crazy.
At least the living throat at its last heave
relieves the heart from wanting. A dead throat
is what the poor dream. With my cut the body
held its blood, the heart having blown
itself into the belly. The children
watched as the knife entered flesh.

Remember, I was dry drunk. It's the kind of drunk you have
that waits till you drink again, the kind that eats you,
the skin flowering with seeds that crawl like barley
under your skin. You don't want
a drink, you're only dry, a drink away
from what's been lost.
                    So I cut and cut again, stupid,
looking for blood and not finding it, cutting through
the throat and down into the chest, finding the lungs
and cutting deeper, splitting the chest
and lifting out the exploded heart, the smell of green
around me, flesh when it's gone bad.
How strange to look for blood when it's not there.

It was just a horse on the damned road
killed by a truck. It was a road that went nowhere,
not Damascus, not Ithaca, not anywhere.
South as far as Kamloops, north to Jasper or Prince George.

The kids watched and the women watched.
What lay in the ditch was food.

There are bodies so large only the earth
can hold them. I thought for a dry-drunk hour
I could feed them all with the heat-blown wreck.
I thought the death was mine to give.

I saved just ten pounds carved from the haunch
where the blood flowed least. The rest I left
for the dogs that are always there.
They seem to make us human. All the victims of our sleep.
I sat there by the ditch and thought I could make
out of meat a dream I'd understand.

That night I lay myself
in the dry salt-body of the iron cot,
so tired I couldn't touch myself or touch
another. The children watched their fathers
come in from the fields that were their lives,
and I knew as I lay in the stiff cushion of my sleep
they understood what I had done.
I lay there wishing I might have saved more,
that the knife could have healed the horse enough
to make of his body for all our lives a meal
that might have lasted longer than the one
we were to eat.

And the dogs howled
over the carcass, and the women seared
the bits the meat, and the men ate and fell into their bodies,
and the women wished a world where their men
didn't suffer so and the kids fell into a swoon,
their hunger gone, hiding
around the corner from the flies,
waiting until they too could sleep
in the healed and healing wounds that were to come.

Dance of the Wings

Every year my father nailed hawk wings
to the grey wall of the shed. He'd
sit me down by the chopping block.
My father worked in town.
The farm he'd been driven from
when he was just a boy was only a memory,
something he hated, something he wanted to love,
but he kept inside him what he used to know.
He pulled the small axe from the block,
placed his great thumb on the joint
and spread the wing. The dead hawk
flew in his hand when he brought the small axe down.

Once with a goshawk's wings
he danced in the yard by the well.
He held the wings and circled in a trance.
I thought he flew and flying
was the wind of those dry hills.
After, he nailed the wings to the shed wall

---

alongside the others who were dead.
The rotted ones had fallen away, nails
all you could see of wings
that once were there, hollow bones
like pipes of ice in the wrong season
littering the ground below the creeper.

I loved my father, knew he knew
things I would never know. The foothills,
Blackfoot and Kootenay, drift and far away
beyond the valley we lived in, prairie,
poverty, a boy thrown from his home.
I knew in my father's dance of the wings
he was back inside a century where birds
like hawks were things that had to die.
Rats, mice, cats, and dogs, deer, moose and bear,
fox, lynx, the bobcat, anything he thought wild.

For him there was only the human.

There's a picture somewhere of us
standing by that wall. A man and boy.
It's years ago now. For me a century
that drags behind the century he knew.

But when you see your father dance with wings
when you are just a child, you know something.
redtail, marsh, goshawk, peregrine,
all of those he flew beside. I fly too
but what I know I can't tell my sons.
It's my daughter who's learned
the death inside of life. Like women everywhere
she holds a skull inside her womb.

And the children of my children, well,
maybe if they came they could see me dance
alone in the garden, tranced,
no shotgun, axe, or nail,
no small one reeling on the wind.

The Night of My Conception

The night of my conception I wasn't there.
My father searched among the broken boards
and the dust of the rooms, my mother
behind him, her hand on his heavy back,
her mouth urgent, whispering, *Find him,*
find him. My brothers cried in their cages
behind the wall. I can see my father's hands
now, the swollen fingers as they picked among
small sticks, the fragments left behind
in the shack below the Sullivan Mine,
the silver lying deep and the zinc and lead,
the snow falling and the trees leaning to him
beyond the window as if they could help
in his search *Find him, find him,* my mother
cried, and my father, crying now, lifted grey stones,
dug down into the earth that was their home.
My mother's hair settled on him like sound
settles on the floor of caves. I wanted to help
but there was no time. I lay between
my brothers, my small hands touching
their mouths, the open holes that were their song.
Soon, I said, *soon,* and when they had fallen
into the thin light of their arms

I went to my father and gave myself
into his hands, into the dark
of my mother's only body, long and white.

White Water

I want to write my way out of town.
I want to write all the way to the river
where my brother and I sat on a cold hard day
when we drove Cat on the new highway.
I want to eat the lunch we ate that day,
baloney sandwiches—bread, margarine, and baloney
and cold coffee we'd saved from morning.
I want to leave a crust for the grey jay
who landed on my hard hat.
I want to sit alone on the high cold rocks
and watch my brother where he lay
in the tired loneliness of his bones.
I want to write my way there so I can say
to the rough and tumble of water
two boys who were men sat here,
and while one slept the other watched
a deer come out of the trees
to drink at the white water.
I want to write my way out of town
just for one day. I want to feel the sun
my brother felt, asleep. I want to know
what it was I knew as I gazed
at the delicate mouth of the deer.
To drink at the white water.
I want to write my way.
I want to drink at the white water.

Apples in the Rain

I return from the rain, bearing in my hands
the fallen apples, rusted and tired from their lives
among the branches of the trees I remember
and do not speak of but in song. They are
the ones whose limbs have sung
and singing gave their fruit to me
that I be made whole. Death is never a surprise.
I am surprised by life, and the holes my friends
made in me when they went away are the ways
small creatures find their way back in —
moles and mice, and the cry of the midnight heron.
I believe even in the dark. The gift
I have been given is to see what's left behind,
a hand upon a woman's face, a mouth I touched,
a footprint on a stone. What else but song?
What else to draw me through the rain
only to find a child, apples in his hands,
finding what he can of his own way home.

The Last Day of My Mother

I ask myself what I did on the last day of my mother
and now no longer know, think only of sitting with her
in the mall next to the Home in that last month
and lighting her cigarette, her hands still strong
though they trembled in the way hands do
when they go through an act of remembered delight,
obsession, addiction, her eyes bright as the jewels
my father couldn't give her.

I had pushed the wheelchair into the smoking section,
her urine bag swinging below her, the smell of her
dirty diaper, and when I told her we should go back
to change it, she told me to go on, people moving away
from us, ashamed, embarrassed, then both of us
smoking. The cheap coffee, the smell of her bowels
emptying the tables until we were alone together
as we had always been in our silence.

Tonight I don't know how to take these lines and make them
 poetry, any more than I could change my mother
who still looked upon me as a child, someone
she delivered in the night in the far mountains before the war.
I tried at the end to talk of the past and she admonished me.
*Why do you keep going back to those times? They're dead
and gone. Your father, your brother, all the dead.*
And then, *When we go back we'll play "Spite and Malice."*

But I don't want to turn this into metaphor, that childish card game
I played and lost, the sharp and vicious look she'd get
when she played me to a standstill
and then her glee when I paid her card for card
in nickels, her scraping the coins into the jam jar she kept
by the television where *Jeopardy* blared,
and when I didn't know an answer to some question,
said: *You're not very smart for a poet.*

In the bed beyond her an old woman lay in a coma,
the ward cat sleeping on her chest. Dead in her living body,
she had lain there two years. *That cat won't come to me,*
my mother said, her lipstick ragged on her cheeks and chin,
the last few hairs pulled down in a bang over her forehead.
I counted them one day when she slept and then, ashamed,

cried into my hands. That last day I changed her
diaper, took a cloth and cleansed her thighs and sex,

and thought of the place I'd come from, those legs
spread, her pain, the opening where my eyes first found
what light there is, her quick silence, my first cry.
Now she has grown tired of me, grown tired of us all.
The Black Widow. I called her that for years until
it was a joke between us, her telling me to stop,
both of us finally laughing, thinking of the desert
we had known and the spiders in the basement's heavy dark.

These lines have become a stumbling web as I move now
slowly toward my death. But I don't want to turn this
into a lament. Death is in us, it's how we're born.
She was impossible, implacable,
strong as a desert pine. Old lines, old poems,
her singing them when I was just a child:
By the Nine Gods he swore
That the great house of Tarquin
Should suffer wrong no more.

Now, that's poetry, she'd say, and I can't make it, not like that,
not like the hours of childhood when she sat upon my bed
and put me to sleep with the thousand lines she'd memorized
when she was a girl. I was a child then, as she was still
a child, not safe in her father's arms in a memory I know
nothing of except as story. *You're so gloomy,* she told me
once. *Did nothing happen that wasn't dark?* And then:
What's wrong with you? What's wrong?

Sitting as she slept inside her flesh, reading Dickens
aloud, *The Old Curiosity Shop,* her favourite, the sounds

of that other time, that century slipping through
the smells of the ward, the carping woman in the bed
beside her, the other woman who slept forever with the cat,
and another who rocked her hours alone, no visitors I ever saw,
Dickens taking us all down the lost streets of another time, and
knowing she heard even as she slept, her mouth gaping.

I carry her in my flesh, can smell her if I try. No,
not the diaper, though that's there too, along with powder
and lipstick, and the trace of something I don't understand,
a smell from birth, or maybe from her breasts when I suckled
there. Something, nothing, a remembered thing from when
there were no words and everything was touch and smell.
Perhaps it was her womb I remember, that small salt sea
I grew in like a fish. And there, I've made this into poetry.

What else can I do? She carried me in the clutch
of her blue bones. My father put his ear to her belly
and said he heard me singing. She placed her hands
under that curve and held me before holding.
There's more than just the dark, she'd say, and it was
as if she'd said, *There is no death*, as I write and break
these lines again and again, letting them fall where they lie.

Owl

A saw-whet owl in the garden this morning
coming upon my mother's death in the far city.
We send whatever we can with all the hope
that we be understood. *At every turn
there's always something lovely.* My mother's last words

and that night bird staring out of the dawn,
her small claws clenched around a mouse upon the lawn
and I wondered what she thought. What does an owl see
when she finds you in her eyes? Perhaps a man
in first light wandering among the things
he knows and does not own, a chrysanthemum stone,
the Emperor bamboo, a goldfish hanging in the shadows
below the shadow of a koi, still in the last cold.
The owl had come out of the darkness to rest
among bronze needles and scattered, bitter cones.
Fly away, little one.
I will listen for your wings in the night to come.

In the Small Box, Ashes and an Opal Ring
She Wanted with Her, My Mother, in Her Death

Death is like walking through deep water,
something that resists and gives way
so that to raise your foot, to bend the knee,
to place it forward on the giving sand
is a great effort, the foot placing itself
and the body moving forward, the water
on your chest and belly a wall
that shapes itself, immovable,
as it moves sluggish as quicksilver
in a curve beside and behind you
in whorls that twist themselves
into quiet again, and the foot rises
again, the knee bending, and the arms,
held out of the water, descend
and move forward in fists, and the body

leans into that thick walking, only
the head above it all and the face,
the mouth open, breathing heavily,
the nostrils wide, and the eyes staring
at wherever it is you are trying to go.

That Strawberry Roan

What I want is the horses in the night, the storm
and me, drunk on potato vodka, my friend holding the bottle
to the light, his eyes full of the same squalid clarity,
the two of us stumbling into the wind
and the fire. The horses chased the pasture fence
like fists of love, that kind of yearning, that kind of want.
God, it was holy, and good and pure and right.
I sat with my friend among their thunder
as they raced over us without a touch,
the beat of hooves when they are wild.
It's like the earth knows what a window is
and rides straight through it. God,
when they came around the creek's bend
under the alders and ran through us, their hooves
a smell I carry in my skin, their sweat and fear
what I know of the night, young men,
drunk on their bodies, no woman near us,
bare to the waists, our chests and shoulders
shining in the startled cold of rain. We wanted nothing
but the bottle and our hearts. Horses
who sprang into fire from the sky,
vodka sweet as flight, like the neck we wring
in fury, an animal asleep in our wretched hands.

What else but love and horses
riding over our young skin.

The Ward Cat

The man in the hospital who, late
in the night, the women sick, asleep,
took off his clothes, folding them neatly
and laying them down, the shirt and pants,
the socks and underwear, and the shoes
side by side beside the white chrome chair,
in a room with only a small light
burning above each bed, lifted
the covers and lay down
beside his wife who had not wakened
for two years from the coma, and
placing his arm across her breasts,
his leg upon her leg, closed his eyes,
silent, still, the breathing of his wife,
his arm rising and falling with her life
while the ward cat who would sleep
only with her, watched from
the foot of the bed, one ear forward
and the other
turned to the sounds of the distant city.

The Madboy

Every Sunday the madboy runs
up the street from the Home,
his heavy feet hard on the pavement,
his arms flailing, his blond hair
wild in the sun. He has slipped
from some door or window,
some crack in the wall only he knows
and now is free to run. As he goes
he keeps looking back at his pursuers
who follow him into the light.
In the boy's face is both glee and terror.
He knows they will catch him.
They always do.
If there is fear it is the thought
they won't come after him
and will go on making breakfast,
flipping pancakes and bacon
for the other boys locked
in the bodies of men who crowd
the morning table at the Home
and he will finally make it to the corner
and be free. It is the place he never gets to.
The boy slows as his pursuers come on.
They walk slowly in the morning,
quiet, tired, knowing this is just
the beginning of another day,
and the boy will wait for them just short of where
the road breaks. And now he is happy
as they hold him in their hands.
He laughs at the run he's made again,
his face lifted up into the sun reflects

the knowledge he knows is his,
that for him the only escape is surrender,
that giving himself up is his whole life
and the room they will take him to
is a place where he can hold himself
sure of the great journey he has made,
bound once again by a locked door and the glass
in a window where he can see himself
among the thousand cells of wire embedded there,
knowing in his single mind there is nowhere to go
but into the arms of those who want to hold us.

Rome

There's not enough room in the small world of the heart,
and when the words came he felt almost happy, even
though he knew they were old words from another century,
words coming out of the cornices and cul de sacs of his mind.
There were no bars this side the Tiber. Christ,
you'd think they would have thought of thirsty pilgrims.
He had tried climbing the many steps to St. Peter's
but there was no faith in him and his body, drunk
and shaking, would not go. So, he decided to pray there
on the stones of the square where millions
had prayed before him. He did not trust himself.
An old woman dressed in black stared at him.
She stood in the dismay of someone's death
so he pretended to pray harder, balanced
there on his thin knees, his hands raised up to his face.
But he thought his hands weren't quite right
and he kept adjusting them, moving the fingers

carefully so they would look exactly
like a man who had come to pray at this precise spot,
a spot where, perhaps, his mother had died, or a woman
he had loved for many years had succumbed at last
to the riot in her bones and flesh. He
remembered then a Jew he'd known who swayed
when he was chanting. He began to sway,
thinking if she thought he was a Jew
she would somehow forgive him though
why he didn't know, and he chanted in what he thought
was an unknown tongue, something he had made up,
a child's tongue full of fear and he looked out
from the bruise of his right eye, the one
that sweated blood, at the old woman dressed in black
carrying, he thought but wasn't sure, a broom or spear.
She stood in what seemed to him now early morning
though he knew it was evening and day almost gone,
and she was old and beautiful in the way old women become
when they no longer want men, and a song crept out of him
ludicrous and old from the Salvation Army Sunday School
he'd gone to as a boy. *Climb, climb, up Sunshine Mountain,*
but he couldn't remember the next line so he kept repeating
the words as if they were a prayer or incantation
and for a moment he thought he was on such a mountain,
a mountain made of sunshine he might have climbed
when he was a boy and there were mountains, and the brightness
around his hands was more than he could stand,
his eyes hurting, and when he opened them
into what was left of light, the old woman was gone
and he was alone in the great square.
That was when he thought of the words that had begun
all of this, the words that came before he was on his knees,
and wished he had pen and paper to write them down,

but he didn't so he committed them to memory,
thinking he would write them when he got back
to wherever it was he had come from,
but he couldn't remember where that might be,
somewhere on the other side of the Tiber,
so he said the words carefully to himself
as if by repeating them he would be spared
the ignominy of where he was, knowing
he had pissed his pants and was ashamed and old.
The warmth on his thighs turned cold
against the gabardine. The words he spoke
somehow made sense to him, and he felt
he was in his glory and felt this was the moment
his life had been prepared for, and then there were hoses
sweeping the great square clean and a very old horse
grey and staggering on stiff arthritic legs
near the steps, and he wanted to stay there
until the waters washed over him and he wished
the old woman dressed in black were still there
that perhaps she might then
come over to him and bless or curse him,
the saints nodding above the great square
and the horse lying down now. He knew
he could talk to the horse if he could get to where
it lay in the long shadows but the water sluiced in gouts
across the stones and the day was gone
and the old woman and the horse and the thought
was gone and he was alone with his shaking hands
trying to remember the line that wasn't there.

The Chest

In memoriam: Gwen MacEwen

The lock is heavy, embossed with gold
in a filigree as intricate as the weave of metal
in a Japanese sword-guard from the ninth century.
It hangs from its hasp as silent as a wasp in winter
that waits for the warmth of a hand to wake it.
Dragons and phoenixes guard the corners of the lid.
Their dance is carved, their dance is woven wood.
They stare at a dark sun who never moves
from the centre. It is a closed eye
in a country I can never travel to. Inside
are the masks I made of my life,
each one preserved, each one
waiting to come alive again,
to lift to my face so I can dance.
The steps are intricate, learned
when I was a child and my legs
were light as snow, as quick as ice.
I practised the story of the dance
until it became the eaten sun, the dragon
we call sunset, the phoenix we call dawn.
The chest waits for me.
Find the key, open the lock, lift out the story,
the one that ends with a gilded mask,
begins with a Japanese sword hilt,
a single image that moves me to the hidden,
the reminder of a sword, the hand's guard,
the one who writes me into the violence
of My Lord, You.

The Table

Here we are at the end of day sitting around the fire, keeping as warm as we can, our shoulders almost touching we are so close. It is winter and cold and the animal the men brought home is finally burned. Everyone is tired — the men from their long day hunting in the snow, the animals they missed, arrows broken, an ankle twisted, one of the young men dead, his body far from the fire, lying broken from his fall in the snow — and the women, their bodies tired from the day of children and breasts and milk, and the digging down through snow for crystal berries made of ice and winter. No one thinks of a table. They squat on the earth. Now is the time of food, the time to fill the mouth with frozen berries and charred meat. It is late. The night comes and a girl lies down under skins, her body full of light. She curves her back into the cup of her mother's hip, bellies against the hard muscles of her father's arms. The child dreams. Perhaps it is a table, perhaps a bed filled with the down of birds, perhaps a window with yellow curtains and the image of an animal sleeping there, a lion or bear, a queen or king of beasts. How far away we are now! Think of an impossible table, think how we sit in this child's imagining as we eat our roast beef among candles and napkins, knives and forks, a glass of wine, someone's hand reaching for cranberries, someone's knee touching another knee under the idea we will someday call a table.

Bone China

I thought when I was young
fragile was a woman's bones and flesh,
her life so delicate to touch it was to break.
I imagined it like a teacup.
You know, an old one,

---

bone china, the kind our mothers
wouldn't let us hold.

Beauty (2000)

Once you knew you were beautiful
but you don't know that anymore
which makes you even more beautiful.
The most beautiful women are the ones
who don't know. They are why
men lie down beside them in the strict observance
of grace, wanting to be a part of such forgetting.

Their Bodies Only Bodies

My children lay in the crouch of my belly,
their bodies only bodies, born, I thought,
before they should be born, all head and shoulders,
eyes all salt and dreaming,
so that the first time I touched their mothers
after birth I had to imagine this place of the sea
and, gentle, gentle, the mothers gave themselves to me.
I wake sometimes with memory,
and think a child has struggled into bed
as my small daughter did, who braced
her shoulders on my back and pushed
her mother out of bed. Or my sons'
fat arms and legs that would grow lean
and hard as a man must be when first

he rises into the smell of a woman's thighs.
But it is in the crouch and tremble of my belly
I remember them, my huge body rolling in bed,
and their sleeping over, under and around me,
safe as a child can be
when what is dreaming them
remembers in its story a father's flesh.
And the child when placed
back in bed, rolls into sleep
and the father finds in his arms their mother,
her quiet hands, the shudder of her arms
as she pulls him into her, again,
to that place he came from, crying
into the world the child he was.

The Bright Hours

Whatever changes, changes back to you,
the hours and days, the nights when I'm alone
inside the dark and time is what I knew
when stumbling down the miles of fallen stone

in search of anything but me. Long years ago,
and I still wander there though the tiny wren
who stares at me in the half-glow
of the opening day did not know me then

and wonders only why I stare across
the air at his bright eye. And maybe that
is what I once called loss
thinking myself alone and cold and flat

as any man could be. Now every day
is all I'll ever have, and night
a darkness in the heart so that I pray
for the only sun and the bright

forgiveness of a single bird now gone.
I know the wren dreams morning too.
Where do we go and for how long
and what in our making do we do

when words are all we find?
Yet the wren returns as if he knows
the question on my mind
and sings of stars and crows

to heal this hour I cry.
There is no place to go that is not time
and nothing I can do but touch your eyes
and know that what you see is the hand's climb

through loneliness, this braille of love
where what I touch is the body's sign
and nothing in the night that I can leave
now that your bones lie breaking inside mine.

The Spiders Are Back

The spiders are back. How I love them,
these dream catchers who weave in the night
the nets of morning. I have spent the last days

watching them draw out of themselves
a long story, the circles becoming smaller
and smaller until they rest in the centre
of the day. What makes us turn to such imagining?
The ones I see in spring
among the maidenhair and maple are so small
I don't know they rest on me until
I find them on my hands, sure that where I go
is where their web will be. Then they drop off,
the mothers of the fall to come. But what
do the males do, stuttering dancers,
solitary wanderers, waiting for their time,
thin hunters in the green worlds.

Anyway, a question in the garden today. Love,
their webs are everywhere.
                              Fierce dreamers!

I think of them in my loneliness, and I am lonely,
have been all my life, but though for what or whom
I do not know. Perhaps the spiders know,
their bodies as much emptiness as air.

But, little bones, I broke today in the arc
of such silence I thought the world was made
of web and wandering, walked like a man walks
when he is alone.

Yet such days are pleasure when I bend,
when I take off my glasses,
bring my eyes to the spider
and we stare at each other in the day.
I would show you if you were here.

Blind, I've seen such things!
                    If what we know
is what resembles us, what we know is a garden,
the moment when a spider worries the dead
into a carapace of web, then rests upon
what will become her only self, the eggs
everywhere inside her. Somewhere
her mate hides in the green shadows.
As he waits he plucks a single filament of her web.
He hopes she will still long enough
for him to place his seed in her, then drop
as she turns to consume him.

He falls like a pebble from her jaws, his death
as close as that. Yet what music he made
she made for him. How I loved
him plucking the walking strings, her waiting,
as I wait here, to go, to come back to you.

I Go in with Death

1

I go in with death, knowing nothing
but the heart, the little one that beats,
the one gophers carry in cartilage and bone.
I am meat and I wait for the eating,
some animal like me, gnawing my bones.

It is what keeps me tense, the way
it wants more. Some other thing

---

come to bother me. Hell, a chickadee.
She gives me hell, wearing her feathers
to my slipping on wet stones.
Strange how lonely isn't, bewildered
by love and by regret.
                    And here,
and I can't stop this now, the hawk's wings
on the shed wall. A boy nailing flight to weathered wood.
My father nodded with the kind of *yes*
that came from the practise of years.
The angle of his mouth was the harmony
of goshawk and redtail, the way
their feathers became my hands.
The cry still torments and hurts the hand.

2

A hummingbird wing is what I hid.
I found the clot of colour hanging dead
under the wrong clouds. My father knew
there was something wrong. I
held its sharp wing under my tongue
as I nailed for my father the hawk's wings down.

3

My father was much alone.

4

I nail him here.
I nail his hand and arm
to the planks of my eyes.

They are warning to what
wanders near, someone
who flies, someone
who dies, arms bent,
fingers splayed.

5

Go now, try to give me something more than
the harrier riding his wings through goldenrod,
the gopher running inside its blood. Or my father's
wrist rising with the axe and dropping
steel on the thimble joints of the shoulder,
the wing coming away, still flying.

6

And what am I to make of wings?
Almost to die, beaks and jaws, the men lying down,
their women in the kitchens at the stove
shaking their heads at one more thing dead.
It's the way spilled blood crawls toward flies.
Late in the afternoon a child could stumble
out of the sun with a dead gopher in his hands,
trophy to what he thought he would become.
Stones and withered grass. *Come to me,*
the dead cry, everyone asleep, some man,
old in the night, thinking with regret
of the whisper a snake makes
when you tear its skin off to make
a boot or belt, laughter in gone rooms,
fear, so long ago, the kill of killing,
the shoes I walk in someone's skin,

the pores remembering a single fly,
skin twitching, what my mouth remembers,
two wings resting on my tongue,
the shed wall, grey, south facing,
finding with a boy's small hands
the cartilage at the joints
that took the nails.

How Small Love Is
  For Lorna

You're small, no, say it, short, a woman
who turns the day around, who turns
and turns upon imagined bones. Your flesh
is flesh, as much as the turning
a rose makes when it unfurls the first
pale leaf we call a petal. I am undone
by the small mound you are under a simple sheet.
I touch your feet with my mouth
so you will remember me when you run.
You're round and round again, so many
curves my mind's undone by wandering,
I hold your bones in my hands

Does the word *little* offend you?
I stroked a wasp once into stillness.
You understood. It's why my hands tremble
in the darkness of your hair, the gentle
place the inside of your thigh is, high up,
as much a filly's tenderness, so strong
it could break a man. The curve of your belly

---

you think old. How you let me cup it now.
Your last eggs glisten like forgotten grains
in the sand outside a silo. I've known each one
in the menses of your last blood, tell a story
to the child we never had. It always begins
with *Once upon a time.*
                                There is no once,
there is no time. You are small, admit it,
but like those holes they say there are in space,
you are a stranger kind of star. You are
what I see in the eyes of deer in spring.
Everything I know, reflected.
They shine in light. Dark stars, far spring,
the weight of smallness, how it takes
what I forget and turns who I am
to the opening of rain on old trees.

The Dead of Winter

In the morning light the willow trembles
and mirrors sing. Last night my woman
imagined what a man might be
if he gave up everything. I believe
in simple stories. When we least imagine
there is music. Fragile cups of sound.
Imagine song when a tree is bound in ice.
You know that ice, willow ice in spring,
straw ice. The kind you take apart that sings.

Chickadee

Late night and the moon doesn't answer me.
What if all the stories were there just
to make us fall asleep? What if the night
was a man dreaming himself asleep, and the weave
was a mother's wanting, a half-dream, the kind
that keeps a woman awake in the sullen arch
she calls love and calls down upon herself
the last stars and says to herself:
This is the moon in my belly,
and rocks herself awake with her hand between her thighs?
What if this is the moon, her ass flaring white
in the night I reach for and enter,
and the whole darkness is only wanting?

There was a man who, when I asked him of love
said he wanted every woman he saw
and I said to him, *But that is only desire.*
What of love? And he looked at me long,
standing on the deck among the drift,
the men and women moving through their lives.
Desire is only style, I said. *What of form?*

And turned away
and went to the moon which is *rabbit* here,
and *man* in other tales, and sometimes, *in extremis,*
just the moon. One night a chickadee fell into my lap
and I climbed the tree and put her back
on her perch, she who would admonish me
the next day in the morning delight
of black sunflower seeds, and who, if I asked her of love
would say, in the pursed lips of chickadees, that sweet

slide of lip on lip, the breath inward, calling,
would say, *There are no stories but that*
which held me in the night, fierce fluff of only air,
she who stores everything under the sun
and when the moon calls, calls it the waste of time.

The Garden Temple

> *Tell me every detail of your day—*
> *When do you wake and sleep, what eat and drink?*
> *How spend the interval from dawn to dusk?*
> *What do you work at, read, what do you think?*
> —P.K. Page, "The Answer"

No one comes to this garden. The dawn
moves through the bamboo beside the bridge.
It's quiet here and I'm alone. The small nun
who led me has drifted behind the screen
and I'm quiet as I watch a slender mallard
drift on the pond into first light. She is two birds,
one above and one below. Night and day,
and night was long again. You are far away.
Tell me every detail of your day.

Now more than ever I miss your hands,
your small feet, the slight swell of flesh in the dark,
the breath you hold before crying out.
I'm trying to remember that sound but I don't know
what time it is in the place you are.
The small nun appears and disappears
behind the paper screen. She moves slowly now

The Collected Poems of Patrick Lane

and I can't hear her as I once did. This garden is how she thinks.
When do you wake and sleep, what eat and drink?

Solitude is presence. It is the absence
I live in now. How long have we lived apart?
A week, a month, a year? It all feels the same.
Time doesn't move but for the day and the night
moving like a curtain behind the maples. I imagine your hand
on a yellow curtain by a window in the room
where you sleep. The mallard has slipped into shadow
where eelgrass meets sand below the arbutus.
How spend the interval from dawn to dusk?

I don't know. There are nights I go for long walks
in the narrow, twisting streets and stare
at the bare lights in windows as they flare,
then I come back to my room in the dark
and I sit in the dark for long hours.
How far away. Here there is water and leaves
and I think of your hands and feet, a yellow curtain,
a room of light, or is it dark there now?
What do you work at, read, what do you think?

What Breaks Us

It's night and the hours won't answer me.
I stare through the window. Heavy clouds
have risen from the Pacific and now
throw themselves against the glass mountains
in storm and rain. The slow night
drags me toward morning as if I were a body

pulled raw across wet stones. I am trying
to understand what a man is, trying to find
some goodness at the heart of what I am
but words fail me. They are frail stays to rest
a life upon. A man killed fourteen women.
Is it enough to say just that?
He spared the men. Is it enough
to say *spared, killed.*
Now the world I understood
is gone and nothing is right.
Somewhere I carry in me a killer too.
There's a storm in my hands tonight.
What is it in a man?
What rage, what hate, what hell of thought
can make him murder beauty?
Fourteen women, one and then another.

He spared the men and now
men live with a question.
Here in the night I am trying to find
a clearing in my mind where I can stand.
I never loved killing,
the deer who stood under the apple tree
I shot at twilight years ago,
the bear who dragged his gutshot blood
into a swamp and who I tracked
and finally killed, my hands shaking
at the wrong I had done to the world.
All my dead are many years ago:
my father murdered, my brother
drowned in blood, and friend after friend
long gone. Each leaving took
a piece of me away. I sometimes think

there's nothing left. It's as if I could
stare through my flesh, see through
these hands that cover my eyes. Death
makes us thin. It breaks our fragile bones.

Today at the university I taught a class of writers.
All young women wanting to learn
what a poem is, how to make one.
They want to make things beautiful.
I watch them as they struggle to find a way
to capture what is at the heart of things,
what they know inside, something
made out of words. To imagine
them dead would break me.
They are everything I love.
They place their stories on the page
and though some of their poems are dark
they always bring a light
to heal what might have broken them
when they were only girls: lost love,
lost lives, lost innocence. They are witness
to what they know and they tell us
that we might hear and be made whole at last.

Saying that will get me through the dark.
The storm in me will pass.
The clouds will fall at last and the wind die.
I am a man who's held death in his hands
and I will hold it forever.
The bullet will enter my father's heart
and he will die over and over . . .
my brother too.
But the young women will come again,

proud and tough and clean as quickened light,
delicate as beauty. I will give them what I can.
Only they can drive away what breaks us in our bones.
It's what I pray for here in the night alone.

The Day

Twenty years and today in the garden I knew
the butterfly's flight is as much device as artifice,
the way the erratic serves the creature best, no bird
able to catch such wandering. What to say?
You are far away in retreat at the monastery
and I am imagining you again. The day is quiet
but for the crows who nag the kittens at their play.

The owl has returned. How I love the small bodies
she drops upon the third stone below the fir tree,
the one that slows you. You must look down
to find it and, in that moment, see the maidenhair,
the way it falls beside the emperor bamboo.

I stopped among the ferns and feverfew
and you came back to me like a blow
and I was of two minds, owl and feverfew —
both fierce, both sure, both wanting.

Tomorrow I will be in Japan, a world away.
You will still be in retreat.
I feel a soft bewilderment. It makes me stumble,
unsure of where my feet go or my hands.
The butterfly hangs now from one of the last lilies.

The cats sleep in the shade. The owl sleeps in the fir
and the crows mutter on and on. Strange
how beauty enters me. It rains
tomorrow, cloudy, cold. The butterfly gives up
his wandering. Tomorrow in Kyoto
I will sit below a pine and watch a monk
bend with great patience as he kneels in moss
to pick up one by one the fallen needles.

The Dance

For Sophie

It is as if our hands keep trying to hold
what we cannot have, as if some other child was there
breathing light into the leaves of the madrona, the brittle ones
who die upon themselves, their fruit forgotten
in the fall. Words stumble toward us
like the children we have lost. My friend surrounds the day,
one safety clean as the knife of night he cut himself with
years ago when he carved his flesh into his own hands
for want of love, thinking of all the blood there was,
and taking it, and his child leans into him
with all she is, the girl having forgotten the child
she was, so that looking at her you can hear her dream.
What thou lovest well remains, and I, in the centre
of whatever world there is, watch him take his child
into the velvet sea and dance. Broken stone
is how she touches his arms. That way, startled
by the man she will describe when she is old
and holds him as the sea holds stone, her words
the many arms of herself, remembering everything—

the blood, the stone, the sea, and her body's touch
bright as what remains, as my child's body remembers
the many tongues who speak to me, as she speaks to him,
practising what must be done, this step, then that,
a foot moved and a hand, as the old dancers used to do
when they were in their crazed beds, their bodies
the leaves of the madrona in the fall, something
in the music of their skin remembering the dance.

False Dawn

For Stephen & Susan

We turn to words because there's not much more
to turn to. *I love you* becomes what I used to call
the dark. I prayed this morning. It wasn't much,
just me and the god I understand. The earliest birds
wake me now and I keep getting up into what
others call false dawn. I know it sweeter.
That's the hard part, knowing darkness is there
and singing anyway. Becoming more
becomes less. It's like an origami dove
chased by a flying child, a kind of solitude
so perfect you keep searching even as you know
there is no cure. I think misery is mostly
what we know. Yet there are days I overflow with love.
My friends are so fragile I'm afraid
to take their hands for fear I'll break them.
This morning I set out the early sprinkler
and out of the darkness robins came
and varied thrushes I thought our cats had killed.
The water from our highest mountains turned

and turned above our earth
and all the birds went under that falling
with everything they had.
Maybe that's the measure.
Maybe in the morning light we pray
and rain falls and we lift to its falling
as if we still had feathers, as if with words
we could scrape the sky clean of every kind of pain.

Praise (2000)

I come back to praise, the hummingbird in the rain,
that single knot of colour among the dying
blooms of the geranium, another kind of day,
a woman leaning out a window, naked, her breasts
no longer young, slack with the loss that comes
from a child's suckling. She was staring down
into the flowers she had planted in the window box,
blue lobelia swaying like a kind of sky,
geraniums, the weight of their blooms, like fists
of men who fought with their hands bare,
knuckles rich with blood. She
did not know I was watching, or if she knew,
didn't care. What she wanted was another
kind of praise, the kind where, if she arranged it,
could make the flowers in her mind alive,
like the ones she saw when she was just a girl
and the whole world heat and waiting.
I thought in the thin shade how, if we were lovers,
her breasts might rest upon my palms
or in my mouth, those nipples on my tongue

and feeding there as she leaned and stared
past me at the light in the window and the flowers.
All this, and the hummingbird, the flare
of his feathers vibrating there, his body
bringing back to me her flesh, his tongue
deep in the blossom, that fierce honey
I want to praise, crying out as I do
in the thing I have called memory and trying
to remember, the rain all around me.

The Sound (2000)

The voice you hear is the sound
inside the emptiness of a great bell.
It is just before the monk comes
from the cloisters to stand below
the curved bronze in the silence
far above him waiting.

God Walks Burning Through Me

When I sleep the birds come to the garden
with their gifts of seeds. Out of ice

last year's leaves of grass lift into night.
All my songs have been one song.

The palm of my hand and the sole of my foot
remember everything I have forgotten.

The old lantern by the pond has always been there.
Now is the time to light it.

The Sealing

This is for your eyes alone. I have folded
the paper precisely, one third and then another,
and placed the parchment in its envelope. Here
I place my seal. I heat the honeyed wax and watch it
drip by drip until it forms a liquid pool on the seal
and then I take my hand and make it into a fist
and, standing, press my whole body down
until my house is made here, my seal, my insignia,
my mark, my making. These are my words.
You are the one I have made
them for, in the quiet of my room,
in the dead of night, one word and then another,
and now no one can break it but you.

Small Elegy for New York

A bird sings in the apple tree today
where the fruit hangs heavy in the heat.
The harvest is still weeks away.
He sings to leaves to shelter him,
that there be flowers, nests, and seeds,
that the sky he knows will always be the sky.
In New York far away the great fires burn,
yet what birds sing will stay
the night to come a few more hours.

In the garden I am bound by what I say
as you are bound. I pray for what I know,
that birds must sing among bright leaves,
that apples ripen toward the fall,
that we must hold what we are born
to hold, and all our weariness today
is just a stay against the hours. Prayer
is birdsong in a garden far away
from the play of shadows fire makes.

The silence of the dead is what we own.
It's why we sing. The sky is clear today.
Go on, I hear my father say, my mother too,
and though they rest in quiet graves
I hear them still. The sky is clear today.
The dead sing too in the wreckage and the fires.
We must listen to their song.
The burden is our lives.
We pray because we cannot turn away.

Old Storms

Old storms. Hills holding on to what I remember of them or don't,
        but imagine, so there is only a kind of brief clarity, a stopped
        image, a thing I have made up, appearance being only a
        trout in the hooked talons of an osprey I saw, was it yesterday?
        Flying to a nest made up of sticks and shit, bits of bone, fish
        scales and feathers, a pediment for its young to display their
        naked wings.

The hills, yellow, and the spare grasses riding up to where the lakes
are hidden in the high country, swollen with snow runoff, and
trout, fat in that deeper dark, for how long?

A landlocked lake so that I wondered, fishing, how the trout got there,
and thought an osprey must have dropped one full of eggs a
thousand years ago. How else come to the high country?

Teaching English in Medellin to the boy without eyes who begged for
pennies in the bright square below the cathedral, and the one
with no feet I also taught, how he rode on what we would call
a skateboard, but not, only shaved wood he rode down the
sidewalk, wheels howling, to greet me; legs, yes, but thin and
tapered to a blunt point at what we would call the ankles.

But no feet, and bright, bright he was, moving down the stone steps of
the cathedral as if flung, the board with its wheels hung over
his dark shoulder, and down to the flagstones, onto the board,
his legs hidden again, how he did not want me to see what he
was, that on his board, flying, he was complete and whole.

Or the boy without eyes, begging in the bright sun, whom I also
taught, and who thought a long hour the day I taught him
red. And how I took his hand and led him to his mother's
stove and said, yes, to the heat, the radiant waves, the shape of
fire, and *red*, he said, *red*.

Sometimes a poem is all we can know, part of me struggling to escape
the violence of simple things, and how rare is the speaking
of it, that a blind boy and a boy without feet can be the only
strength there is, to say there is no loss, that all creatures
remember rescue best and not the betrayal that precedes it.

How draw together what can't be drawn, what balance find among
images that have found each other? They are as strangers on
trains and buses, who on a long journey across a continent
become friends and lovers, only to disappear at the end into
the vast chambers of the station, a moment only, creatures
who touch each other in the brief hours and move on.

A girl moves, then gone, a bus coming down from the mountains
into Hope, red hair dishevelled, the two of us under her
blanket, making what love we could. Her laughter, and the
bus moving on to Vancouver, 1959, was it? I don't remember,
remember only her red hair, my hands on her young breasts,
her thighs.

So the osprey moves, a stopped image and yet flowing, fishing perhaps
even now as I write, the cat purring on my lap, those boys
I knew almost thirty-five years ago, now men, somewhere,
with strange words I gave them, dead now in some alley, or
brought down by some *bandito*, or not, perhaps happy driving
a bus down dusty roads, owning a small store, or teaching
their own languages to gringos, the word *rojo*, the word
hombre.

Boys who went on as a poem moves on, somewhere now their being.
They are, as I am, or a lake in the high country, a caught
trout in an osprey's talons, its life what I have tried to speak
of and not, as the fish is not, but for my seeing it in the bright
air, or a girl in a dark bus, rising to me as a fish rises in swift
waters, fierce and wanting, then gone into the night.

As the poem is, the fish now blood and bone, riding a wind, or
perhaps dropping out of a storm toward a place there is no
escape from, but for the falling, a home of sorts among naked,

hungry birds, a lake in the far hills where someone perhaps comes to cast a line out upon the still waters.

Temper

That I remember the old blacksmith tempering iron in dust and fire,
the way a blade or horseshoe struck the water, the blue flare,
a sudden quench marking the iron, an axe head's colour his signature.
Along the blade of the knife he made for me, a whisper moved
as if the sun had breathed on it. He showed me the tempered whorl,
traced the waves of blue and gold with a finger thick as my wrist.
I carried the blade through the sagebrush hills and high above the lakes
stood and saw the smoke from his steady fire, the bellows deep
in the coals, setting in the sky a trade, his great hammer ringing.

I have seen the names of men on swords from the Shogunate,
on wisps of steel from Spain, the far Toledo fire still living there.
That blacksmith stood in fire for me. His hammer rang the folded iron
in layers thin as leaves and now I write the knife that it, long lost,
be not forgotten, that the sun in words he set in iron, that flames
leave as a blade a tempered breath, a blue as cold as the sun,
that a man be sure as the edge all lost knives know,
that a single breath drawn out of fire can be an iron name.

The War (2004)

Afternoon, and the heat upon the table slipped across the Melmac plates
and the steel knives and the butter, melted from the plastic saucer, slipped
to the edge of the scarred pine table and sank to the linoleum. Heat
like the pale water you see on desert roads ahead of you, the shimmer
and the mirage of a lake reflected from the bellies of clouds. You drive
through thirsty, the wheel wet under your palms. Before us water glasses
beaded from the sweat of air when the cold meets it, the homemade beer
thin with foam. He lived above Swan Lake and made pottery there,
celadon and slip glazes drawn from the yellow clay cliffs, temmoku,
the rabbit's-fur black running down, feldspar, iron, copper, and the ashes
from bones, calcium and phosphorous, ball clays and kaolin, all
for his huge hands to make into the empty containers others filled
with flowers, the vitrified glass, what he was proud of, a frail red rising
out of a deeper brown, the black, the impurities, the polluting elements,
and the beauty of his making. He was German, come over after the war,
and the same age as me, his parents dead, I think, or if not dead
then never spoken of. His hand reached through the air for bread,
broke off the crust at the end, and then he ate it, slowly, between
sips of beer. We talked the way men talked back then when they spoke
of the past, a privacy only spoken to wives and rarely then, the older days
best kept where they were in the locked leather satchel of the heart.

His was a long story that came slowly out of silence
and told without his eyes looking at me, but staring instead
out the window at the stubborn apples ripening, a pale brush of fire
flaring under the hard green. Summer in the Okanagan. The heat
and a single fly he caught in the middle of the telling, his one hand
holding what was left of the bread and his other, the left one, coming
behind the fly and then sweeping slowly, catching the fly as it rose
backwards as flies do when they first lift from what they rest on, bread,
the crumbs fallen on the slick surface of the table, a lick of wet butter.

He held his fist to my ear so I could hear the buzzing
then flung the fly to the floor, the single sharp click of its body
breaking there. And the story going on, the fly an interruption
he seemed unaware of except for the holding of it to my ear
to hear its frantic wings, its sharp death, and the bread almost gone.
I spoke of the war and how it had shaped who I was, the years
forming me, had told him of my childhood and my father
gone to fight in Europe and of my playing what we called
as children, War. How we would choose sides, the smallest kids
the enemy, the Germans, and how we would come down on them
with our wooden rifles made from broken apple boxes
and bayonet them where they lay exposed, choosing to ignore their cries
of *It's not fair*. We pushed the thin blades of our rifles
into their soft bellies, their shouts and cries meaning nothing to us
and then their tears, shameless, little kids broken in the shallow trenches
we had made in the clay hills, imagining what our fathers did each day
in the sure glory they never spoke of afterward, no matter our begging.

And his story.

That he watched his father and uncle come home to their farm
in the Black Forest, the horses pulling the short wagon in the night,
nostrils breathing mist in the cold, the wagon back piled with straw.
And the bodies of children under the straw.
That they had hunted them down in the forest, children
run from the gathering of jews and gypsies, tattered clothes and rags
wrapped round their feet. He remembered the small feet hanging
from the back of the wagon, the rags like torn flags fluttering.
His father and uncle had lifted the bodies one by one and fed them
into the grinders with dry corn and rotting turnips and blackened potatoes
the pigs clambering over each other and screaming.
His mother had found him watching and carried him back
into the house, swore him to silence, said what she said and said again,

and he had not spoken of it these past thirty years and why
he spoke of it now he did not know, but that I had asked him of the war,
and of children playing, and that he had played too, but what games
they were he didn't remember, it was so long ago, those years, that war.
But what he remembered most were the feet sticking out
from under the straw, the horses' heavy breathing, the rags fluttering,
and his father sitting beside his uncle, tired, staring into the dark barn,
and the wagon pulling heavy through the ruts,
and the rags wrapped around the feet sticking out from the straw,
and the rags fluttering. That. He remembered that.

In the desert hills the ponderosa pines have grown three hundred years
among blue bunch wheatgrass and cheatgrass and rough fescue, and
there are prickly pear cactus in spring whose flowers are made one each day
and among the grasses are rabbitbrush and sagebrush and antelope brush
where the mountain bluebird is a startled eye, the grasshopper sparrow,
and the sage thrasher, and the woodmouse and harvest mouse,
and the kangaroo rats who come out at night to feed on seeds and moths.
There are these living things, and they are rare now and not to be seen
except for the careful looking in what little is left of that desert place. And I
list them here in a kind of breathing, the vesper sparrow, the saw-whet owl,
and the western meadowlark, and the northern scorpion and the western rattlesnake,
now almost gone, the last of them slipped away into what I remember
of that time when I lived among them. I name only what I can,
my friend, the potter who lived above Swan Lake, who made pottery
from kaolin and ball clay and the glazes from the yellow clay of the hills,
and who was but a child in that far war almost no one remembers
now, the warriors dead, and the people dead, the men and women dead,
and the children dead, and the children of those warriors and those people
who remember are now fewer than they were, and that is how it is now.

Sage thrasher, woodmouse, western meadowlark, and saw-whet owl,
and the meadowlark, and the vesper sparrow, and rough fescue,

The Collected Poems of Patrick Lane

and I must tell you so you understand, that we sat there at that table
with cold glasses of beer and the remains of the bread we ate together
and he showed me how to cup my hand and come up slowly
behind a resting fly and then sweep my hand through the air
perhaps two inches from the tabletop, the fly who lifts backwards
when he flees, caught in my fist, and then flinging it to the floor, the click
of its body breaking there. And that I learned how to do that,
and it was important I knew what I was learning, though it was
only a kind of game between two men killing flies, and then
we went outside under the weight of the heavy sun and talked a moment,
and he did not speak of his crying at the table and I did not speak of it,
for we were men of that time and we had learned long ago not to speak
of tears and of the stories that bring them, and that in this only world
there are things that must be remembered, and that they be spoken of,
scarlet gilia, parsnip-flowered buckwheat, white-tailed jackrabbits,
and balsamroot, and the rare sagebrush mariposa, and all such things
that are almost gone, and that I can still catch a fly the way
he taught me, and that we stood there by his truck in the dust and the heat
and said nothing to each other, only stared out into the orchards
and the green apples ripening there, and then he was gone into the desert
and I can tell you only this of what I remember of that time.

Weeds

1.

And the woolly burdock blooms in the yard and beside the grey boards of the fence
and in the wasted fields beyond and the absinthe and the nodding thistle
also bloom there with pigweed and tumbling mustard and prickly lettuce
and they are weeds and the poor live among them
and believe them flowers just as they believe the quack grass and the wild oats,

the downy brome and foxtail barley, and the witchgrass are lawns,
and the children of the poor pick the tall buttercup and the low larkspur,
water hemlock and wild carrot, death camas and yellow locoweed,
and bring them home to their mothers as bouquets
and their mothers place the blooms in milk bottles
and the children look upon the blossoms there in the kitchen and laugh
as children do when they have made their mothers happy
and then they go back out into the wasteland and play their games,
for it is summer, and it is good to be a child there on the beaten clay
among the glacial stones and broken branches of poplars and aspens
and I can see them there and part of me is made glad by their fierce joy,
and part of me is not, for I know what it was to endure there and that happiness
was rare in that world and not to be imagined or wished for. The poor
do not make wishes for wishes are seen as luck and luck is by its nature
always bad and brings consequences and so wishes are not made,
and the small bodies of the children who do not wish and so have
neither bad luck nor good luck move in the waste places and seeing them
I am taken back to the broken bones and lice, scabs and scabies,
ringworm and roundworm and tapeworm, cuts and scrapes and bruises,
fractures, blindness, and lameness, and that the parasites and injuries
and deformities are what they know and they cannot imagine their not being there
for they have always been a part of their lives and that is how it is
for them, just as it is for their mothers and their brothers and sisters,
and the screams and the weeping in the night are also what they know
just as the beaten heads of their fathers and their huge hands and oily clothes
and the drinking and the fighting and the silences are part of them,
but there are days when the children break the thick stalks of burdock
and bring the blue thistle heads home in bouquets to their mothers
and those are the days when beauty is made possible and that is enough for them
for the children do not know they are poor and they do not know they suffer.

2.

And when I was a child in that world, the wasteland of barren fields,
the deserted shacks and burned-out houses, and the creeks
with the rusting bodies of Fords and Packards drowned among the cattails
and milfoil, the clasping-leaf pondweed and marsh horsetail, and mosquito larvae
and the broken bottles jutting their jagged necks from the mud,
and pieces of machinery, transmissions and oil pans, gas tanks and differentials,
bled their oil and gasoline into the puddles
where it made rainbows that would burn at the touch of a match
and my friend and I would sometimes light the edge of the creek on fire
and watch the flames reach up into the cattails
where the red-winged blackbirds had their nests
and watch the birds shriek up into the sun as their nests burned,
and in the wastelands too were silent places
where men sat around thin fires and cooked their food at night
and we were told never to go among them, though never why,
and the days were bound by the brown hills and the blue hills beyond them,
and the fires of the town dump, and the alleys of the town, which were
also our playground with their huge garbage bins and the sleeping bodies
of drunken Indians and drunken white men curled up under cardboard,
and we would roam among them, and I know we were seen as wild children,
for at seven in the morning our mothers would send us out into the world
and tell us not to return until suppertime when our fathers would come home,
and we never questioned why we were sent away and why we could not return,
for such questions were not asked by children of that time, and our days
among field bindweed and dodder and ivy-leaved morning glory
with their white trumpets were known only to ourselves, and how we would
take the white flowers and make chains with their beauty,
and sometimes we would drape the chains around the necks of the little girls
with their cotton dresses and bare feet, and sometimes we would tear them off,
and our fires and fights, our crimes and misdemeanours, were known only
to ourselves, and such knowledge as we had of other mothers and girls,

the idiots and cripples, the deaf and dumb, the hunchbacked and the goitred,
the chinks and japs and bohunks and wops, and the rapes and tortures
we witnessed, the beatings of boys and men, and any and all of such things
that occurred in our wandering belonged to us and our interpretation of those
things, our understanding of those things, were given to us in our days
only by circumstance and event, by what happened, and never by admonishment
or praise, and never by our mothers and our fathers, for to speak was to implicate
ourselves in where we had been and what we had seen and so invite punishment,
and our silence was their silence and they told us nothing of who they were,
and so we expected nothing from them, and the only thing we knew
was that we should never bring home anything but ourselves
and sometimes not even that and never and never a mistake, never a thing
that would cost our family shame, for shame was the greatest sin and not to be
endured, and the punishment for it was not to be imagined or endured,
and that shame lived in a child just as it lived in a family,
and so we did not, for the world of our lives was without words,
and things were not spoken of, things were not said, things were left out,
and that is how it was with things, and that we knew people were things too
just as cleavers and dogbane, locoweed and puncture vine, were things,
and even the smallest child knew that, and that was how things were.

3.

And there are stories that can be told of such times and about such children
but they are long and all that is known is that things happened in those days
and there is little that can be said that will make anything clear
and there are no reasons and no excuses and no explanations
because that would mean understanding what happens inside a child
and there is no understanding what happens there,
only that there was a child,
and he was killed by his father
and he was only six years old
and I was only six years old,

The Collected Poems of Patrick Lane

and anything I might say,
anything I might write here
to explain why he was killed will not help anyone,
for a child's death is a child's death
and a half century makes it no clearer than it was
when that child's father raised his huge arm in the blade of the sun.

4.

And children die and sometimes they die when you are there
and such a death brings a kind of shame that cannot be understood,
for anyone who has known shame cannot explain it and so it is just a word,
and the boy who was my friend is dead and it was a long time ago
and that is the end of it, and there is no explaining
the beatings in the shed and my watching them
any more than I could explain why the wild carrot flower gathers itself into a clench
that is called a *bird's fist* and the fist cannot be undone without breaking it,
and that only the plant can undo itself and it only does that when it is
ready to let go its many seeds, and my friend's death is like that weed
and there is no undoing it except to say I saw him die
and that my father did nothing and my mother did nothing,
and the man who killed my friend was the father of my friend,
and I accepted my friend's death just as I accepted a dog kicked to death in an alley
or a shot grouse in its bloody feathers or anything else that was not allowed to live,
and after my friend's death I went out alone into the secret places,
and some nights I walked among the men by the fires down by the railway tracks
and ate their food and listened to their songs,
and I don't know why I disobeyed my father,
but I know that I was afraid my father would kill me too,
and that the anger of fathers was not to be understood,
not by a child, for I remember my fear and the hugeness of my father,
his silences, the hunched shoulders and the bowed head,
and the fists his hands made, the scars and dried blood,

so I stayed far from home, far from the world where I lived,
and I went out alone into the waste places
and I learned to name the things I found there,
and that somehow I knew it was important I name things,
and why it was important I do not know now,
just that I wanted to know what things were,
and I would wander the night with weeds in my small fists
and that is why I remember burdock and bugbane,
and jimson weed and mouse-ear chickweed,
and pygmy flower and rough cinquefoil and stinging nettle and poison ivy,
and all the other names, dogberry, barberry, goat's beard, and cocklebur,
and that what happened in a family could happen in my family,
but whatever happened it belonged to the family and no one else,
and that a man's shame was his to own,
and that what I could tell here would only be a story,
and my telling it now would have been like my telling it then,
because I had seen my friend being killed by his father and I told no one of it,
and it was because I knew that telling it would have made something happen,
the story would have led to some consequence,
and that was how it was in that world
and a little boy under the sun is a boy under the sun
and no more and no less, but sometimes there is no boy and there is only the sun.

5.

And that is how it is with stories and sometimes the teller of the story will
try to make the story better, make it more real, and sometimes leave someone
out, or describe something different from what it was, and he will say it was
a day when the sun was huge in the summer and the sky was a pale blue
because of the hugeness of the sun, and there was a creek
with cattails and duckweed and painted turtles say, and a rusted car in the water,
and the teller of the story will make the car a Ford coupe
instead of a Nash or a Packard and no one will notice for no one is there

to correct him, for he is the only man left who knows of such things,
and everyone listens carefully, and nods their heads at the right places:
the sun in the sky, the brightness of it falling through a shed door in a blade of sun,
a stick of firewood, and a father striking his child, and the right moment to speak,
to say things, as when he places a child among death camas and yellow locoweed,
or says how a child has ringworm or roundworm or tapeworm, or has had his arm
broken by his father, or has seen a child killed by his father in a shed full of sunlight,
or has curled in a ball under his bed in the farthest corner of his bedroom
and held his hands over his ears to stop the shouting
and the screaming and the sound of fists
and breaking things
and slammed doors
and how the child holds his hands tighter
when everything becomes quiet in the silence that follows such things,
for that is what stories are
and that is how they happen,
and that is why there are weeds named cleavers and dogbane and puncture vine,
and that there are such things in the world, death camas and locoweed,
and that children inhabit that world, quack grass and water hemlock,
and sometimes a child goes out into the night to the forbidden places
because he is afraid of the sun and the blade of the sun,
and there are men sitting around a stolen fire
and a child will go to them and listen to their songs
and the stories they tell of places and of the names of places
and there he will be fed beans and burned potatoes
and he will sit by the thin fires there
and return home safely with the songs and stories of those men in his mouth,
and he will try to sing them and sometimes at the corner of an old yellow house
he will stop in the night and he will stand beside blue burdocks and repeat
the sound of their song and the few words he remembers, and the storyteller
will say that sometimes now he will hear a song on the radio and it will bring back
the nights he went among those men and returned safely with their song.

6.

And that childhood remains far from us even when we are children
and to remember anything is a kind of wonder,
and to speak of it at all is to begin with names and places
and the things that inhabit them, the children and the weeds,
and so they become story, but stories are not to be trusted,
for they are like the pictures children make with crayons of a beautiful day
and there is always a sun huge in the corner of the page the child colours with chrome yellow
with great rays shining from it and there are green fields and round faces
though sometimes the faces do not have ears and sometimes they are without eyes,
and sometimes there is no one in the picture and the child when he is asked
says no one is there, there is no one in that world, but the sun is there,
the sun is always there, bright in the right corner or the left corner,
and there are no clouds and the sky is always blue,
and there are flowers that grow only in pictures
and the flowers are not the same as the child knows in the waste places,
but always there are children, though sometimes there are none,
and the mother of the child who makes such a picture tacks it to a wall,
or leaves it out for the father to see when he comes home, in the hope
that the father praise the beauty of what his child has done, praise the child,
and no one asks why the child in the picture of the beautiful day
has no eyes or no ears or no mouth, or why the legs and arms are sticks,
or why sometimes there is no child at all and only the sharp blade of the sun.

Shingle

"He should not place himself in a position to lose.
He should find things he cannot lose."
          —Ernest Hemingway, "In Another Country"

When he was a boy he attended well to the men in the Cenotaph Park
who spoke of the war and of the friends they had known in their youth
in the rubble of Caen and Dieppe, in the camps of Burma and Japan.
Their stories were simple stories and though he knew now
much of what they told was hidden inside the words they spoke,
that their fears and shames were never voiced, still he listened,
loving most what seemed their joy.
In the cool shadows of the elm trees at noon,
on the granite steps of the Cenotaph at dusk,
the men shared their bottles of wine and beer
remembering for each other the best of days.
The boy saw them in their medals and dress, the old ones
weeping on their day, though never when they spoke
on his father's porch of the war that would surely come
that would be like all wars and the wars they had known.
The boy with bare feet and ragged cotton pants
would sit at the edge of their sprawl and listen
and sometimes know their stories were meant for him.
That meant and meaning were different by degree if not intent
did not occur to him. He could tell by their smiles they loved
the life before. What puzzled him was the moral world, though
he would not have known to call it that, and how
it never included them, that the hero of every story
was never themselves, but a man who never returned
and their hush in speaking was always to the side and not the centre.
They had made themselves storytellers and took
their joy in infinite detail, as in the story of Tiny,

his father's closest friend, who burned alive in his tank
in a Holland marsh. His father spoke of the heavy water and the mud
and of a single flower floating among broken reeds, a blue flower
like a strange star floating there, small and blue as if fallen
from the sky with its broken clouds stumbling in from the sea.
It was true because his father was not there at the dying,
his story told by what might have been, not was.
That the boy's father believed Tiny would have lived
had he been there and that what he meant was his own death
more sweetly made by sacrifice frightened the boy.
On the day his father wanted to die,
he was in southern England in a seaside town
buying brass candlesticks to send home to the boy's mother.
As his father told him the story of Tiny's death,
he took the brass down from the plate rack
polishing them absently in his hands.
He spoke of that day and the death he wished was his,
how the weather was dark upon the Dover coast
and that after he bought them they were wrapped
in cotton rags, there being no paper then.
He had placed them in his kit and walked down to the sea
and stood alone on the shingle far from the war.
Listening to his father or sitting with the men at the edge
of the Cenotaph circle, the boy learned that children
are what you leave behind, that women are never
what you have but always what you have left,
that the friendship of men was the only beauty,
that loss, not gain was the measure of a man,
and regret was in the living, not the dying.
That the teachings were in the stories
and that they were believed, that the small boy
would carry the joy of men to sorrow in this life,
and that loss was the full teaching to be learned

on the steps of the Cenotaph and in the quiet
kitchen of his home was his inheritance.
Now what remains are the candlesticks in his mind,
his father looking absently for meaning in the brass,
and *shingle*, a word he thought
meant his father when alone
stood on a wing of cedar, not on stone.

Choices

The apple tree in the garden is thin and black and without leaves
and the birds, the chickadees and bushtits,
siskins and juncos, come and go among its pruned
branches at dawn. It is another tree enters you in the night,
a pinyon pine secure in the blue granite outcrop
at the top of a scree somewhere south of San Francisco
and high above the Big Sur coast, a place your body
made among stones and needles where you rested
in a hollow and stared at Rexroth's stars and saw
Aldebaran glittering in the cold night sky of his poems.

West of the west the light is pure and you look
behind, knowing what you see is everything
you have left. Constancy is what you promise. It is
what you ask the stars as they filter what light they have
through the thin air. Last night the planets lined up
and you went out to Mars and Saturn, Jupiter and Venus,
and thought you would not see them again like that
in this life. More and more you are promised less.
First light, cold iron, thin blue, the stars diminishing.

Regret is one way to understand things, your mother
bringing you Scotch Mints as you lay ill and still
faking it a bit by the narrow window that looked out
upon the transparent apple tree with its golden fruit,
how your body still feels that thin autumn light, the red
Indian blanket wrapped around you, coughing just enough
to keep you home forever. *Golden, narrow, thin, red.*
Regret for what is remembered, *transparent apple.*

You think for a moment you understand
that the particular can heal into what you call
proud flesh, a raised scar, white and hard,
that has no feeling, something you can know
only by touching it with the parts of your body
that still have nerves. There was the long wound on your chest
you received when you ran into a barbed-wire fence
at the United Church Summer Camp for Boys
on the beach of Otter Bay in the summer of 1948.

You picked at the scab until it grew into a long scar.
You were nine and the pain was exquisite, the blood
you licked from your fingers in dazed boyhood tasting good.
Later when you were older you told women
you had received the scar in a knife fight
in Mexico City or Santiago or Whitehorse,
wherever you thought they would find romantic,
and how the women would reach with their fingertips,
their gentle, tentative touch a sure sign of your suffering.

When they asked you to tell them the story of the wound
you became quiet and stared past them at the window
above the cold streets, past them into the distance
of the city you were lying in, as if what you remembered was

too terrible to speak of and how they would sometimes
kiss that scar with their lips and murmur words like:
How terrible! A feeling, you think, is what you try to achieve
and mostly fail at. A story is what you require, a plot,
where what you leave out is more important than what you tell.

It is what passes between a man and a woman,
the general, *love, pride, flesh,* and the suffering
at the heart of it, the quiet that follows the carnal, the questions
about scars, *hard, white,* so that in order to know
she is touching your wound with her fingertips
you have to see it, there being no feeling left.

In the same way, when you are reaching the end
of a poem, there is always a moment when you stop
and go back to the beginning and read
what you have written. And as your eyes travel down
through the words you begin to make the choice
that is just one of the many choices possible and you
feel a certain regret, turn to your hands and write:

The apple tree in the garden is thin and black and without leaves
And the birds, the chickadees and bushtits,
siskin and juncos, come and go among its pruned
branches. It is another tree enters you in the night
from the cold, blue, iron of the last sky. Clouds obscure
everything but the knife edge of light that rests
hard on the horizon that in a few moments will be
riddled with startled blood, what you turn away from
before it arrives, leaving to the many small birds,
chickadee, junco, siskin, the cold night sky of poems.

My Father's Watch

My mother, drunk again, her nightgown pulled up to her hips, raised
her legs and scissored them in the still air of the room where we had
all lived once in the great confusion of family. I didn't know what she
did there alone in the years after my father's death, what mirrors she
stared into, or what she saw there, what rooms she paced or where she
placed her hands as she gazed into the test pattern late at night, the
rye whiskey bottle beside her, and the golden glass she drank from.
Bare calves and thighs and the dark willow smudge of wet leaves
between her legs. *Daddy loved my legs*, that coquette wince of voice,
the sound like something dropped among steel blades and minced
there. I didn't know then it was not my father she spoke of but her
own. Or perhaps it was both and she was only drunk again and lost in
time, her memory a face she might have known and did no longer.
There are stories so simple they elude me, their meaning lost in the
telling, so that even now I miss the words, the *or* and *if*, the *but* that
makes all questions possible.

Or was it the willow above the pond
where I saw her last, that flash of red babushka
above her hands deep in the earth?

If, if, if? In time I will tell you of the wind
in the willow if you hurry to the garden,
if she is still there on her knees by the pond.

But you didn't see her, did you? So furious
her scraping at the earth, the willow flailing
in the last great winds of spring. Oh, yes.

My return to her was to a garden, the orchards of the desert hills, I
would pick my steady way through the trees above the lakes in the

fall until the cold branches were empty of fruit. A dead marriage, children gone, a continent to wander, and always leading back to her. *What if*, I might have said. Nights after the bars closed I would walk drunk the miles back to her dark house, the only light from the window a flutter of blue, the comedies and tragedies over, the news finished, the test pattern a flicker on the screen in front of the couch where I knew she sat with her whiskey and her glass. How I would wander outside saying this was the garden of my father, that is his tool shed, there is the place where he parked his car, and here is the well, the root cellar, the sawdust bin, the steps leading down into the basement — here, there, this and that, and not going, yet, into the house.

I wanted to place the word *sorrow*
in a poem so that it was no more
or less than *and, if,* or *but.*

One crow for sorrow, two for mirth
I know I have it wrong, but willow leaves,
are they what fall through her slow fingers?

It is not a willow leaf, nor can it be, but that I
make of it a sorrow. The form of, how I know
the wind by the shape willow leaves make in fall.

I don't think she waited for me. I was a ghost as much as anyone in that cold autumn. I could tell by the way she looked at me I was a stranger kind of son. It wasn't a question I could reach into. *Oh, it's you,* she'd say, as if there was anyone else who might have come. I'd drink her into dawn. I'd drink her into sleep, my body folded on the faded couch, dreams of apples tumbling from my hands into bins that never filled. Each fall I'd come and stay the harvest month. The living room was full of the gone, too many to count, the shadows of my family, my father, his breathing quiet in the chair I never sat in. *That's the man's chair. Sit there, sit there,* she'd say. I could hear his lungs hiss, quartz crystals like stars inside his chest. When she pulled her nightgown up and raised her legs it was as if she fell backwards into a darkness all her own and the flutter of her calves and thighs what a body does before it dies.

So white, so white, her dance
in that room of shuttered light.

Dark earth, a staghorn's prance
among the fallen leaves at night.

How small her gentle feet, her glance,
wet willow leaves, her hands, their slight.

Should, must, will, all words. Who was it I served as I stared at her white flail and the damp I call now leaves for lack of a better, other word, between her legs? *Daddy loved me,* she'd say, her flirtation not with me but with some ghost that walked inside her eyes. A father's night in that steady sorrow of straggled lipstick, the giggle of a girl as she lowered her legs, her nightgown awry, and looked at me as if I knew. Flirtatious, thin coquette: she stood and walked to me, and dropped into my lap my father's watch, then swirled around the room until she slumped into my arms, a little thing, her body like a child's, thin bones and wretched flesh.

A stone fell five thousand years through ice
to find its way to this garden. First things,
where nothing is that is not nothing.

I crawl on my knees to find the trace
of her hands in the wet earth. I have a stone
to place among willow leaves and rain.

Her ghost in the garden again today.
Sleep soon, little mother. Go to spirit
that this world at last might rest.

I carried her then to the bed she had shared with my father and
covered her, her face slack and wet. I sat in the light coming over
the blue hills, the watch on my wrist. It had begun again, the hands
starting their slow, methodical measuring. In the bracelet's chain his
sweat had congealed in thin grease mixed with dust, the fragile tick of
seconds counting the night into the day, my thumb moving across the
scarred face and hinge of links that bound me.

Tumbling Mustard

The dry ditch by the dirt road and the tattered leaves and stems
of the tumbling mustard grown spare and brittle with August
that scatter their seeds as they roll with the wind and their seeds
which remember the brown hills of North Africa and the sea
which remembers Carthage and the stones that remember
what we no longer remember, slip into the cracks of clay
and wait for the rains that will come when they come
and not before. A man has chosen not to be with a woman
and now he is standing beside the dry ditch and the wind
blows hard upon his back and he is going away to a place
he does not know. At this moment he is not trying to understand
anything and the woman who offered herself to him is not
in his mind. A tumbling mustard is caught on the prongs
of a barbed-wire fence and he is looking at the stems
as the mustard spins there in the wind, the orange seeds
falling into the cracks of dry clay. There is no one to tell
why he has refused her, except there is no rain.

He knows that the tumbling mustard came to this ditch
from North Africa and he knows that Carthage was in
North Africa and that at the end Hannibal did not live there
but in the back country of ancient Macedonia and that
he had gone there to live out his last days far from Rome,
and that the Romans hunted him down and killed him,
and that is what the man is thinking as he stares
at the tumbling mustard caught on the barbed wire
and the seeds falling. As for the woman he has refused
there is no telling, but for her brown hair and her crying,
and his going out into the heat of the day and the wind
and that somehow the mustard and Carthage, Hannibal
and the Romans, are somehow connected to the woman
and that is why he is standing there by a dry ditch
watching orange seeds fall into the cracks of dry clay.
In the wind. And without rain.

Infidelity

Under the rain, under the spare trunks of Indian plum,
the faded rust of redwood needles and the club moss
grown thick from the winter feast of weather. On his knees
he picks the flat needles splayed there, gathering them
in the way he remembers the monk in the old garden
gathering, his quiet in Kyoto, and leaning down after sweeping
with a bamboo rake and picking up a single needle,
placing it on a swept pile, then turning, going up
a worn path that followed the thin creek, and gone.
It was so much what he had imagined in the old poems
of Issa, a kind of stillness, perfection being
what distracts us in the moment, something forgotten

in the ordinary harmony we strive for and almost reach.
That is why he is on his knees cleaning the garden.
He is thinking of his dream, how he was gentle with her,
touching only the curve of hair above the pale shell
of her ear, the dampness there. And then the wind
and the going out into the last dark, and beginning
the clearing away, his eyes a mist, how he remembered
that, on his knees, one needle and then another, thinking
it is what the old know, a slight turning, something
not seen, and reaching back for what was left behind
on the moss, something fallen, under the rain.

Cutthroat

A creek, brown water thick with spring runoff, and the trout
in the riffles come up out of the deep waters to feed. Cutthroat,
that red comma of blood, and the curl of thin water,
the elemental body, eating the eggs and larvae of insects
swept down from the banks high in the hills behind him.
When he was young he had read of a golden ring
found in the belly of a fish and standing there, so many years
later, remembering how he had thrown his wedding ring
into the same lake, he thought . . what? That happiness eludes us
when we apprehend it, that the fallen world is the peculiar dialect
of the heart, that a ring flung out upon the waters will return
wearing the blood of angels in a choir of water? He
had fished there, long ago, with his young wife and
their first child. He had turned only once and saw her
pick up the baby and walk away into the willows,
her body and the body of his child
going away from him into the shade.

It is how the high waters talk to us in spring, how we cast out
with every hope imaginable, catching nothing, and casting again,
the line falling upon the waters and everything below the surface
sinking deeper, a silence waiting beyond the riffles of the creek
where it meets the lake, the good food come down from the hills.

Coyote

He chose to eat in silence with the monks,
the oldest a man of perhaps eighty, lifting thin gruel
from a bowl, milk dribbling from his lips down his chin.
The monk's shoulders were hunched, his neck bent oddly
so his head hung over his food. Morning,
the joyful bells quiet now. He imagined the bronze
still vibrating, a sound so small only the bell could hear it,
and the stone walls and the heavy chain above it, the light
not yet striking the narrow windows of the high tower
and the cross. He had woken at dawn to the cry of a coyote,
a cadence that brought no answer but for his waking
into the night, the coyote restless, calling for a mate
who wasn't there. The monk had devoted his life to a god
who was chaste and poor and became obedient
even to the death of the cross. He wondered at the words,
not *his death on the cross*, but the cross itself a death.
The Lord be with you and with thy spirit . . . The light beyond
rose as the mountains rolled away in the slow turning
of the earth. A chickadee landed on his windowsill,
a wildlife high above the branches of a plum.
When he was young he had thought of a place
like this, the life away from life, the one Christ
might have given had he *died to sin with him,*

---

had Christ plunged into the paschal mystery of his body.
The chipped statue of Saint Benedict outside his room
had a plaster duck at his feet, a symbol he didn't understand.
Perhaps like pelicans they plucked feathers from their breasts,
their beads of blood a memory of Christ and his sure suffering.
Or perhaps it was because they walked on water? No matter.
The old monk has given himself to god. Close to his death
he has lived as he could without sin. Such were the beliefs
he himself had turned away from, wanting something other
than the heart. To live in a community of men could bring
suffering, he thought, for who knew what lay beneath the old
monk's breast? Bright laughter rose from the parking lot
outside his window, young women come to the monastery
to wander the grounds, the view from the cliff
overlooking the Fraser and the far mountains white
with the last of winter snow. He wondered what they thought
to see men who lived chastely away from the world
or did they think of it at all, young as they were in their lives?
He stared down at them through the plum branches
swollen with buds, girls really, not women, not yet.
They were beautiful in their bodies, sufficient to themselves
in this time before childbirth, in this time before men,
and he remembered the bellies of girls he had known
when he was young, the terrible beauty of their flesh.
How strange, he thought, the delicate bells of their voices
in this retreat he had made for the moment of himself.

The Spoon

He has picked up the spoon from among all the small things
on the table, the knife and fork, the salt shaker you don't shake
but turn and grind, the bowl with its applesauce, the glass of milk,
and how he hesitated between the glass and the spoon, but chose
the spoon, and his daughter's voice going on
in a low and steady murmur, her blonde hair cut short
and the bit of grey at her temples,
and how he remembers his old mother hating flowers
after his father's funeral, how she would never have any
in the house, and his daughter still talking to him
in her quiet steady voice about things he already knows,
but knowing it is important for her to say them,
important for her to make some kind of order
out of what must seem to her the chaos of what will be
his life now, and the dog barking outside, and the light
on the table, and the spoon in his hands, and he turns it
over among his fingers and marvels at how his hands
have been holding spoons all his life, and he holds it
by the end of the handle and looks carefully into the shallow
bowl polished so carefully by his wife and sees there
his face upside down, and how if he could understand
the spoon everything would become clear to him, if he
could understand something this simple, something
so small and ordinary that he has used every day of his life
and never paid attention to until now, something very small,
and very simple, and not a glass, not a flower, just a spoon,
and that without it everything in his life
would have been different if there had never been spoons, this spoon,
and he feels a sense of wonder at what he holds, and he reaches out
and takes a spoonful of applesauce from the bowl in front of him
and gently and very carefully lifts it not to his mouth,

but to his daughter's mouth, and he touches it against her lips
and she opens her mouth and it is very quiet now and the only thing
he knows he can do is in this moment, and that is what he does.

That Cold Blue Morning

Thin snow in the ruts and the men without work
rising from the ash and coals of the burner behind the mill,
the cleanup crews gone home and the long chains
no longer screaming. I wake in dreams and sweat, my mind still
shaped by a wailing woman on the sawmill road
as the trucks went by. Her song lives in me, her high thin crying,
and the girl-child in worn cotton pulling at the woman's dress,
the child's hand trembling, her mother gone mad again.
The woman's arms were raised into the river of wind
out of the North and her song rose on that wind
and was gone like the snow scoured from river ice.
The trucks went by and the men stared through starred glass,
ashamed as men were back then, the Coquihalla logs
heavy in their chains. *Good God, go home,* the trucker with me said,
his eyes straight ahead. *Jesus Christ, Jesus Christ,*
and I said nothing to what was as much a curse as sorrow.
The stories in my head are made from mountains,
they are made from cold four o'clock winter mornings,
from thin coffee in a plastic Thermos, from crying brakes
and broken ruts, and from the chains and groans
of the start-up early mill, that late fifties moan of just enough
wood, just enough shelter, just enough food to live another day.
That woman on the late dawn early road was some man's
daughter, some man's wife, and though I thought
I knew the thing that drove her onto the frozen ruts,

still it had no name. *Jesus Christ, Jesus Christ,*
but it does no good except for the crying out.
I come out of the Interior and there were no words back then
but for the names of the gods and those who cried them,
staring as they did through the broken glass and diesel smoke.
Back in those nights I struggled to make words
turn into poems, but I was young and it was no good.
It was hard to make things right. My wife huddled in our bed
and there were nights I know she too might have gone
into the road to sing her song. There were dead butterflies
and blue stones, a gut-shot doe in a spring meadow, a headless dog
in a ditch, children picking their way through garbage at the dump,
and the cold winds, and the spring breakup, and the nights
alone with words. I don't know now what drove me into poems,
what dream I had or where I was to go. I have tried to make sense
of it and so made sense of nothing. There are men who think
the stories are not them, men who've spent their lives in books
and offices. I curse their luck tonight.
Tonight I place that woman on this page
in the hope she'll give me rest.
And me?
I want the cup and the cold coffee. I want the last of night.
I want the truck's roar and the shapes of the shadow-men
rising out of the ash and the rush of wind that follows them
when the kerosene explodes under the falling bark and wood.
If I could, I'd end her song. That's what I want.
I want the song to end that shapes me still. These words
make no sense but I write them anyway that they be said:
Jesus Christ, Jesus Christ, but the snow still blows
and the ruts freeze hard and the burner's smoke still rises grey
into that cold blue morning I called the sky.

Wolf

Wolf prints on the estuary and the long, slow mutter
where water breaks on sand, the broken crystals,
stone reduced to the myriad confusions we call chaos
that comes clear only when we reduce it to the few,
an eye staring into a hand that once was mountain, sand,
thin shells, and stone. And the wolf who passed through
in the night, his paws leaving a steady track, stopped
here and played a moment with a bit of driftwood
in the tidal wrack. I read the simple signs,
where he turned and leaped and turned again
like any animal in love with the dawn, his belly
full of a deer he brought down in the ferns by the creek
beyond the stand of firs and cedars. Then to play.
A solitary animal, no other tracks beyond the early
claws of crows and ravens. On a tidal stone a heron
stares down into his beard. Hunched shoulders, long beak,
he waits for sticklebacks in the diminishing waters. Once,
I came here with a woman and we lay in the heat of day.
As sun fell away she ran naked across the sand,
the sweat of her love drying on her small shoulders.
I chased her until we fell laughing on this same line of shore,
her hands and mine and the curve of her thigh at rest.
Years ago now. Here is where the wolf played
and here is where his paws churned the sand
as he turned back to the sword ferns and the cedars.
I am sure it was here. That line of hills and that fir
leaning out over the waters. I am sure the tree is the same tree,
broken crown where an eagle rested, that one branch
where the kingfisher fell into the shallows years ago.

Things

"The loneliness which is the truth about things."
—Virginia Woolf

Under the chandelier of the wisteria, hanging Christmas lights,
plastic trout and Chinese lanterns. I stare up at the dull jewels
that are the seed pods in winter, each grey carapace holding
bright flesh, and wonder at the lights I am arranging. The solstice
is three nights away and last night I stood on the deck
where dark leaves shine in their decay upon the cedar planks
and wondered at the full moon among scudding clouds,
the night's bright seed. I am late with the season's lights,
my neighbour's house glittering among the black branches
of the cherry trees and the firs. In these dark nights I hang each year
the same lights and wonder what it is I am saying.
Dickinson said, *Water is taught by thirst . . . birds, by the snow.*
Each wisteria seed shines between the folded legs of the pod,
demure, waiting for spring. Their loneliness is not ours
though we try to escape the song that draws us to them,
the mortuary of art, history telling us what we try to elude
and can't. So I hang lights that the night be made brighter,
and the seed pods hold their lips together as they wait
for the long days of spring. The rain falls and my thirst
is greater than water and no one knows where the birds sleep.
I imagine them, among the green limbs of the redwood,
the branches of the firs, their small hearts beating like jewels.
That is my wish, for what the image says is always human,
and the stones we carry in our pockets are the burden
of things we have made our own. If there is snow I will know
the birds by what they leave behind. Even among words
there are bright seeds hidden; in the trees I imagine, imagined birds.

Dwarf Crested Male Ferns

You try to tell the truth without altering anything, a word
waiting sometimes days before appearing and even then, unsure
if it is right, if the word *whisper* is as strong as *shadow*
when it modifies a drunken junkie in a motel room:
his hand was a shadow . . . and you go to the west garden
still wondering and ashamed. You kneel among fallen needles
and plant beside a river stone the dwarf crested male ferns,
the ones you left under the cedar tree three months ago, thinking
there was time. The pale buds are the furled fists of a child's violin,
something you plant in the dream of what you think music might be
and rarely is, there being no child to play, the buds growing anyway,
pushing like clenched fingers into the mottled light, your own hands
delicate as they press the ferns into the earth at the dripline of the cedar,
giving them a chance to live at the edge of the tree's long shadows.
The shadows whisper in the false light that blights what grows beneath.
The junkie you are writing about lived a long time ago.
The motel he is in is the kind you see now only in movies
of the fifties, the kind left behind when the highway moved,
the kind they used to name The Shamrock or Dream Away or Day's End.
The names always promised hope or escape, some kind of luck.
But the man you are writing about has gone past hope and luck
and now is working on despair, a victim in search of himself.
You ask what you feel because you know
that without feeling there can be no truth.
His hand was a whisper . . . and you think that might be closer
to what you want his gesture to be, someone small and alone
in a cheap roadside motel room with curtains that won't open,
with only a bed and a lamp and a television set that is always
tuned to the porn channel, so that when he entered the room
what he saw was a woman on her knees, her head moving up and down
like one of those plastic birds you used to be able to buy, the kind

that would bob into a glass of water for hours without stopping.
And now you know you are getting close to him, and you
return to where your poem is waiting. You think of the man
and how he lay on that bed knowing his young wife was in the hospital
three blocks away and giving birth to his child and how he passed out
and never got there, how the only thing that mattered
was his own oblivion. That cheap romance, that loneliness.
The Shamrock or Dream Away or Day's End, names
that promised peace. Something like that, a place where,
if they made a movie of the room and the man, they wouldn't use violins
and they wouldn't use ferns. They'd use a desert and a bad saxophone.
It would be years ago. You would feel him all the way down,
see him in the kind of dark a curtain makes of the sun.
His hand was a whisper, you write, *a shadow in a small room*.

Bitter

Our vines have bitter grapes and we eat
and call them sweet. It is a pain in the mind,
intentional unkindness aimed only at the self.
Nitrate of silver, quinine, quassia, and strychnine,
vinegar, bad grapes grown too far north.
The caustic utterance is meant to burn. Unlike
bittersweet where you start with one
and end with the other. But you go on picking
and eating everything, horseweed and sneezeweed,
woody nightshade, monkshood, what kills you anyway
in the wrong fields of Arcady.

Uncle Jack

My uncle picked me up by the back of my neck
and shoved me into my father's coffin. I was
twenty-seven years old when I kissed my father dead.
Uncle Jack worked steel and stone, his fingers
big as kielbasas. My Uncle Jack, he loved my father.
I was still young enough not to know what love is.
But I won't forget my father's mouth, cold.
That's what bullets do to a family. As to my father,
he was all right. My uncle? He was mad,
but at what or whom I do not know.
I think he wanted me to love as much as him.
There was the powder, rouge, and lipstick,
and my face raked down my father's chest,
the hole in it singing, how everything breathed and me
trying to crawl away from those steelworker hands.

Backwards

You walk backwards in time because there's more
there than anywhere. You walk into the dark
diminishing, going without grace, steadily.
You think of your bright daughter,
her hair as much silver as your own,
and you fail away, your heart spoken, broken
like grit in a grinding mill. Old
is memory gone awry, silly and foolish as cold
men are when they burn. She was so pretty
with love. You too, who in the hours
make with your seed a child

as white as sorrow, think of her. She is
tangled up in eggs and emptiness.
She shone once with you, now she is without.
Bright little dancer, singing her one song.
What you leave remains, the last light falling
like a hurt hand shaken, careful and afraid.

Ash

She was ash-white and broken by the North,
three kids and a logger who never came home.
She was moon and wanting more, a slip of silk
she never had. When she came to me with her
artificial pearls I tore them off and they danced
like beads of sweat across the floor.
She was young and I was younger. Ash flies
in the dark. You search for fire
and mostly never find it.

Campbell's Mushroom Soup

Sometimes she's naked, wanting you.
You think about that. You look at her and all
you want to do is drift away. She cries real tears
and you know enough to stay just long enough
for her to stew cheap hamburger, gum rice,
and Campbell's mushroom soup.
Your life with her is mostly
thinking of a bar and pool table

playing for money and not for her.
That's why she cries
and that's why you keep leaving.
It's the tears and then
in the night when late you see her,
butcher knife quiet in her fist,
saying what she thinks a man won't hear:
This's the last damned man who's going to leave me.

Sign Language

Her left foot high in the Ontario night,
she swings her white panties like a flag.

Whiskey Jack

A metal flume for love in the desert hills.
You love her flailing following snow water
into the apple fields, naked as a whiskey jack.
First times cure loneliness, that waiting,
wanting. It's when she goes dancing by
herself through the dust, just alive
with her body. A man can love that,
white breasts, bronze flesh, the flume
calling out to the valley the sound of wet,
three small drops on her belly below the navel,
watching them vanish above that golden bowl.

The Working Life

We blew the grave with sixty-percent forcite,
The holes punched down with steel in the frozen ground.
He was old, belonged to no one and was dead.
The boss watched as they pushed him in
and back-filled with the Cat,
the curved blade tamping him down.
The boss said, *ashes to ashes, dust to dust,*
then stopped a second and turned away.
That's all I know, he said, *and that's enough.*

Digging Ditches

Eight feet down and digging not a grave.
The foreman's daughter lays her body in red dirt
and with her arm string-lean in torn cotton,
white as wax and melting, holds down a canvas water sack,
cold from riding the truck grill thirteen miles.
You look up and for just a moment don't reach.
Just look up and see her thin arm trembling.

Sorrow

There was a girl-child small as song
sung in a room where no one but her was.
Her mother was my once or twice lover.
Her mouth tasted of blood from her lungs
and I couldn't love her enough. One day she was

gone to the bar and I woke up in the wreck
I called my body then. The girl-child came in
and sat on the floor at my feet, her honey hair
like breath coming clean in the high country.
I was barely awake and sick, naked to my waist.
She crawled up my body, barely twelve,
and touched me thinking love,
though she knew not what that meant . . . pray Christ,
I grabbed my shirt and boots and ran,
going anywhere away. I wanted her
and her just barely twelve. Love is mistaken
sometimes. Sometimes you run just out
of wanting, and not touching, her back on the floor
afraid and me so wild at what I might've done,
her crying, *What did I do wrong?*
This's for her if she ever reads it. Honey,
there is no fault a man can't fall into. It's why
it's called a fault, a crack in the rock that waits for you,
crying for love and meaning only sorrow.

Chevys & Fords

Red Ford Fairlane, right fender gone, spiderwebs
scattered on the shield like startled hands, two fists,
one with a golden ring, the other bare, and a face
eaten by shadow, riding down Field toward the Crowsnest Pass
and east, and you clamp down, the foothills just ahead
and the flat country for a thousand miles stretching
to the Lakehead and a thousand more to Toronto
where you will cruise down Spadina to Queen and turn
west again, your '67 Ford with its Slant-6

and bald tires moving, knowing you will meet that Chevy
again somewhere near Pile O' Bones,
your fists holding hard to the road. You stop
only when you need gas and a grease of eggs,
coffee mug trembling, the waitress not looking at you
from under her bruised and beaten eyes in Medicine Hat,
then back in your car, warm vodka like oil between your legs,
Hastings & Main a place to go, if only to turn and drift
again, your eyes marking that same Chevy truck
ten miles west of Moose Jaw, no hand raised
in passing, nothing but your eyes talking to his eyes
making it the fourth time you've passed each other
in the last eight weeks of rage and knowing
he knows you through the smoke and broken glass.

Wildfire

Wildfire, that ghost walking the rotted stumps.
Things dead and things not. A fire so blue.
You put your hand in the cold and walk away
in flames. Friends come and go. Women too.
I looked around just now but no one's here.
Strange how the heart never sees itself.
Wildfire ghosts and an owl step-dancing like Molly,
your hands on fire crazed blue in the grey bush.
That was before the coming down hard.
Her leaving. And you nothing if not sorry,
wildfire alive in your wretched hands.

Tight Smoke

Her closed eyes talked to the walls in a bar
I don't want to remember, her man
with his one hand held to her throat
like tight smoke burning,
her broken bird wings
thrashing above the sawdust floor.
Some nights you just keep quiet. Some nights
you lean over the table and make the three-ball
in the corner. You know she'll go
where the darkness is and there's nothing
you can do. A little thing no bigger than
a child from where you stand, held up
and shaking. Two hours from now
she'll be laughing, all the scare gone deep
inside her eyes, while you ride your cue,
lean down to a rack you know will break.

His Own Sweet Own

Trouble is hard. Not finding it is harder.
The cat close-walks the edges of the room
finding the trail out, the circuit past the strewn bottles,
a jump over the sill and gone. You go limping left,
carrying a book you don't remember writing,
find the cat licking his left paw under the plum tree,
yellow eyes like hooks in birds to come.
He's on his own sweet own.
There isn't anyone you want right now.
Not the blonde with the pull-down mouth

and not the one who cries. It's cold and early on.
The day is barely begun. In the room
there is a knife with a broken bone handle
in the freezer that's never worked, wrapped
in a pair of dirty Stanfield's, put there by someone,
and on the lino floor by the mattress, a wig
you can't remember anyone wearing, long
black hair uncombed and matted. Every day
is like a number you divide that's never even,
something left over every time. Trouble
just keeps walking, crazy and clean, sideways.

Go Leaving Strange

You sit watching hounds go leaving strange
their nails clicking swift the wooden floor
as they slide like narrow smoke away.
They know. They have the smell on them.
You see it move in folds, the slack jowl
flutters pink and the tooth comes down
cutting stiff and the ear upraised. The door
is one way of knowing the world's gone wrong.
You let the hounds out and they go leaving strange,
even the one you call Slip tracking quick
on the heels of his wretched dam without a sound.
When a hound goes quiet into the night
you wonder. Head down and the long ears
lifting scent into the nose, she leads, he follows,
the young ones coming last, the little one
jumping vertical to see what he can't smell.
Hounds run silent till they catch the spoor.

It's why you close the door
and when your woman asks what's wrong, say
nothing, the sky inventing clouds
where no clouds are, the light in the thin pines
turning pale and the hounds lost in their steady run.

Profane

You grow up at last and regret it all. You sit cornered
so no one can get at you, your knife in its scabbard
hanging from your belt, whetstoned to the same edge
as your eyes. There are two rifles in the truck
and miles of road. You live in a place
where a rifle is safe unlocked and loaded. There are
two Kispiox boys coming with five hundred pounds
of salmon in an hour. They don't give a rat's ass
for anyone. Don't tell me they think the world is sacred.
I've seen them dance. They dance the same as me.

Death

I think of death sometimes, my own and others.
Purdy told me the worst was having no one
you could tell the story to who was there, no one
to dispute, to say that wasn't it at all, no one
to laugh in the pure knowing of it. A poet
once said *it* was the strangest word we know.
Agree or not, lonely is when the story runs out,
old is when the people do.

Stiletto

After each cigarette you save the butt stub
and store it in the old can.
When you run out of tobacco
you take out the butts, break them,
and begin rolling again,
saving each new butt. When that tobacco's gone
you go back to the can, take out the butts,
break them and roll again.
There are only twenty butts now
and you have out of them five cigarettes.
When they're gone you roll the last
five butts into two thin stilettos.
There are five days until you get paid.
There are two butts and five days.
It's a dilemma with grief at the edges
and there's nothing you can do.
That's why it's called tragedy.
Or you could call it poor.
There's one left and four days.
You sit in the room thinking.

The Truth

The truth is I saw what I saw,
I did what I did. So what do I feel?
I feel sometimes my heart in its cage
not screaming, just going on steady,
one beat and one beat going on.

The Collected Poems of Patrick Lane

For Red Lane

When I left you on the side of the road after I kicked you out you
were already practising your death, your cards laid down in Patience,
that solitary game still in your mind. Jack of hearts on the queen
of spades. Nine on the ten, two on the three . . . Christ, what do I
remember? You stuffed your hands into worn pockets, your jacket
bunched against the wind coming cold off the Nicola River, the wind
out of the North, your red hair, the fear I understood and still can't
name. Johnny knew it too. Brothers. I tried to find that road today,
write now on my knees beside the dry hills where the pine trees reach
for water. It was somewhere around here. Hell, the old road is gone
and now there's nothing to hold on to. Your death was singing there
in the gravel. It sang to you as a boy. You were always somewhere
gone, your punishment the friends who loved you, no matter the
loss. Brothers are strangers to the world, all blood and crazy laughter.
Today I drove the new highway, pulled off into the dry stones where
the river used to flow. I found a dead girl upcountry once, twenty
miles east of Spences Bridge, but that was long ago. Right around
here. The little cutthroat trout were lilting in her hair. Sometimes
water is the last place you look to find a home. She was so lonely
there and then the walk out, the telling what's become a story, the
where? the *why?* the *how?* Like her, having nowhere to go, you went
there anyway. *It's okay,* you said. *I'll see you later.* Both were lies, the
truth just another kind of terror. Two months later you were gone.
It's like the dead girl. Sometimes at night the bodies come back, if
only to tell me what they couldn't say. I thought my life was mostly
luck. Looking back, most of it seems bad. You thought I should
stay in the North. You wrote me from Vancouver. Never come out,
you said. I couldn't wait to leave. That was '63, the year before your
death. The road was dust. I could barely see you looking back, the
mills below, the burners spewing ashes into sky. Every few years I
almost find the place where we had been. I drive down old roads,

most of them changed. Trying to find the lost places I sometimes
have to climb higher into the trees. The dirt and gravel roads are all
in pieces now. Remember driving Cat on the Rogers Pass? It was
'58, I think. What do numbers mean? It was summer and there were
so many mountains. We were pounding down the new highway.
One time after work you took me up a creek to where a single pool
gathered falling water. There was a doe drinking deep, her soft face
delicate among the stones come down from mountains. I can see her
now. There was always somewhere if we looked for it hard enough.
That girl was beautiful, caught in the broken poplar limbs. O, your
death's alive in me! Poets say love goes on after lovers die. But what
of brothers? Was it you who stopped the darkness? Was it you who
tried to save me? And Johnny? What of him? Who were we back in
the days of the little boys? You're still somewhere, the pebbles and
dust you touched with your worn boots. Was it here? The wind comes
hard down the valley. It did that day. I think this place is where you
hitched away. I think this is where I left you.

For Al Pittman

With you Newfoundlanders, everything came down to the sea except
your father's boat. It ended in a field rotting in the sun after he died,
you sitting in the wheelhouse with your bottle, staring across the
withered summer grass, both of us drunk. You told me through tears
of the outports and the years. What I remember is the withering of it
all, that boat pulled out of the water, the hull dry, the cabin windows
broken. You tried to turn the wheel but it was frozen by the sun,
rusted out by weather. It was like you to be running rough water on
land, the right tears in the wrong place. All those years. We could
both find a metaphor in that now, or I could, now you're gone. The
last time I saw you, you were hunched over your drink in the bar

in Corner Brook and couldn't be moved by words, told me to leave
you alone. The bartender shrugged. There were too many echoes
for me. I thought of all the poets I saw die with their hands clenched
around a glass or puking booze and blood into a toilet bowl; the years
I tried to drown, the bottles as empty as the times. Christ, we went
back a long way. I think it was '67 we met, you in Montreal, and me
the first time in the East. Did we fight? Probably. You Newfies were
always troublesome, proud, and vulnerable, with your gift for the
insult of love, the tenderness of hate. I thought your wife a pretty
one and likely made a pass at her. Those days I wasn't much good
for anything but trouble, and poetry. It was the same with you. The
many times together, the night in '82 you locked yourself out of our
house in Regina and got lost in the dawn alley as you searched for a
cigarette butt to light. That you were naked but for your underwear
made little sense to the kindly neighbour woman who guided you
back. You passed out on a lawn chair. When I found you hours later
you were sunburned to a salmon. I think it was the only time your
skin was ever touched by the sky. Jesus, Al, I loved you, but I couldn't
bear the dying, the steady day and nightness of it. I was dying too, but
that doesn't mean much now. I'm still dying, just more slowly. We
were always drunk together, Al. Always, with Nowlan or Newlove or
Acorn, or whoever happened to be around, strangers like ourselves.
I remember guiding you off the stage in Vancouver in '98. The
audience was laughing at you, your wandering jokes and stories. I
knew you were lost up there and couldn't find your way back. I went
up and put my arm around you. You whispered in my ear, *Thank
Christ*, and then you asked, *Where are we?* I still don't have an answer
to that. Some questions leave me reeling. Maybe where we were was
in a boat in a dry field far from the sea. Maybe that was the best we
had together. If I close my lids I can see you in the red light the sun
makes of my eyes. You're up there at the wheel with a good sea and
a fair wind. Someone's laughing — your father, me — and we're
heading into harbour, the light falling across a Canada far to the west,

and there's a life to be led on the waters, in a dry field, with no one to
hurt us, and tears enough to go around.

For Al Purdy

It wasn't the brawling man who wrote of *dangerous women with
whiskey coloured eyes*, it was the other man I read in '62, the awkward
one you hid inside the Contact book, the one who spoke of lines
that never end. That's what I heard first and that's the man I knew.
It was the uneasiness you had with the myth you'd made of yourself.
You were a mama's boy and spoiled like only children are. Even your
ride on the freight train back in the thirties wasn't a real struggle,
was more adventure than endurance. Survival had nothing to do
with it, though later you'd learn, picking through Air Force garbage
with Eurithe to keep food on the table. Three days in Vancouver
and you couldn't wait to hop a freight back to Ontario, homesick, a
little scared. Suffering was never your strong point. It took Eurithe to
help you with that. But I remember '66, the night we left the Cecil
Hotel to visit Newlove on Yew Street and giddy with drink I threw
a full bottle of beer at the sky. You stopped dead and waited till the
bottle fell and smashed. *Only throw empty bottles at the moon*, you
said, shaking your head at the waste of a drink. It's a metaphor I've
lived with in this life, that moon. Or the time we stole books at the
McStew Launch in '73. You told me to stop taking the poetry. *Take
the picture books*, you said. *No one will give you money for a poem.*
Jack McClelland was railing at us and Newlove was dancing drunk
on a table while Farley glowered in a corner because he wasn't the
centre of attention. Clarkson was prissy and Layton was trying once
again to get laid. God knows where Acorn was. All names now, men
and women either dead or getting closer. And you? I could talk with
you about the attributes of *Rubus spectabilis* and Etruscan tombs.

We could go from there to a discussion about the relative venom of *Laticauda colubrina*. You liked the leaps and made a poetry from space. You went from the yellow-lipped sea krait to the eyes of Eurithe and found love at the end of your complaint. I think love was at the heart of all you did, the only loss you knew. Not knowing what you should learn, you learned everything. An autodidact (I loved that word when I was young, it gave my ignorance a name) you put in everything you could, your mind moving like your body, a poem too big to fit into the world. Sitting at the kitchen table three months before your death you told me you'd never had a friend. *Are you my friend?* you asked. *Yes, no,* I said. I'll never forget your eyes. There were never any cheap tricks in your art. It's the one thing you taught me. *Don't tell it slant,* you might've said. Your poems were Möbius strips. Following your mind was like my wandering in South America years ago. I knew there was no end, it was the going I had to learn, the nowhere we all get to. I split the word these days. Right now I'm here. You liked the story of me almost dying from a centipede sting in the jungle east of Ecuador, the little brown woman who nursed me back to life as she fed me soup made from boiled cuy. Like most men you liked stories. All your confessions were metaphors, those tired horses in the dust at Hundred Mile the measure. Or the time you made coffee in the frying pan in Toronto for Lorna and me, the bubbles of bacon grease just something to add body to the day. With you I could almost make it through. I fixed your deathbed, the second-hand one you and Eurithe bought at a garage sale. You stood in a reel while I hammered it together. Three days later you were gone. I could say I still have words but none of them add up to you. Whispers mostly in the racket. Poems go round and round, this one too, never quite getting there, but I still live, and your *ivory thought* is all that keeps me warm some nights, still writing, still alive. It's a cheap out, Al, but where else to go but back to you grabbing the picture books, telling me once again that poems don't sell. They never did.

For Alden Nowlan

There's a dark river in both our lives and poverty not always of the
spirit but the flesh. The cold waters drag the salmon to their deaths
in the great pools up the Miramichi. Those born in forests know
what shadows are. I always imagined you walking a dirt road, me
behind you, writing down the details of your life, the footsteps you
thought would lead your body out. No mention of the soul. There
is no common usage for that word. It's one we've lost or if not lost
then buried under the porch planks of the shacks we grew up in.
Still, I see you walking down that road wearing the clean shirt your
mother ironed for you, the collar turned and the sleeves shortened.
Something handed down like the stories of Culloden and Ypres.
"Bannon Brook" still catches at me, that bobcat coming wild through
the smokescreen of your words. I watched the pages roll out when
I printed *The Jesus Game* in Trumansburg, your poems laying
themselves down. I bound them. Now, my copy barely holds its cover.
I was never much good at permanence. My hands have opened your
poems so many times and now my hands are worn just like the paper.
Things slip away into the gentleness big men know. Touching anyone
could hurt them. I'm not sure whom the pronoun refers to now,
you or sweet Claudine. Her and Johnny. We always drank too much
whenever we met. There was always a party, Ray and David, Louis
and Al, the young men who worshipped you. Only David escaped,
though he carries the old scar deep in the ball of his thumb. It's the
hook his country left him. You never fished for anything but poems.
Your Nancy searched the roads for you but you had left by then,
gone down to the city. You waited for her in the poems, half-afraid
she'd read herself into your life. The last time I saw you it was two
months from death. It took ten minutes to find your way from the
sleeping room upstairs to the living room below. I could hear your
body smack the walls as you blundered drunk to see me. It sounded
like someone slapping the belly of a dying cod. Claudine was bright

---

and beautiful as she served me beer. *He'll be down in a minute,* she said and chatted the years I'd come and gone. You sat there with your orangutan face so swollen I barely knew you. It would be easy to say the moose was you, mysterious, naked, come down from the hills to die, but things are never that easy. I've tried to write this letter twice before. Maybe I'll get it right this time. You raged at me the night we met in '67. You made me an honorary Maritimer at sundown. At two in the morning you stripped the gift away, cursing me for being from the West. We almost came to blows, you swinging the empty gin bottle and me trying hard not to spill my whiskey, ducking out the door for a cigarette with a girl I didn't know, but for her mouth and her tumbled hair. Like Purdy, you were our love poet. No one can touch your tenderness. It was as if you were ashamed of what you wanted most, no one listening to your whispered, gentle words. Do we ever escape the past, Alden? Tell me if you know. I keep walking behind that kid on the dirt road, the one with the ironed shirt and the gumboots. I never catch up, but I know that's what the dream is all about. It's enough I keep walking knowing nothing changes and only the details hold. It's the way things are that matter, nothing altered, the boots leaving their scuff in the mud, the clouds coming hard out of Maine, and the fists of the boy swinging in the cold wind of that rocky country as he goes down the river, full of anger and something he thinks is love. Despair when you're young is always taken wrong. You knew that in "Pimlico," the flow of those dark waters leading you up, not out. It's why we go where we go, the Ithaca at the end of a Cavafy poem, everything we need on the journey that takes us home.

For Anne Szumigalski

In the bar at Fort Qu'Appelle we danced country and western, a couple of Cree or Sioux guitars and a white man on the drums. The beer glasses rattled on the tables while Hank Snow rose from his grave to sing our hearts. You were so huge, your dewlapped flesh white mountains in that lake-locked cut of land down from the old asylum where plains poetry began. You floated across the floor. The farmers and cowboys gaped as you twirled light as a red fox angel, your dip and weave as much invention as my own imagining. I loved you best in my arms, your smile the wicked grin of the bad little girl you were. I used to dream of being buried in your flesh. I always asked why you never wrote of the war. You nursed the bone racks from the concentration camps when you were a girl. It seems a century ago now. You took the first workshop I ever led in '76 in Saskatoon. I remember saying there was a problem with your poem about a girl giving birth to a fox. The middle was all wrong. You argued with me, your eyes telling me you'd wanted praise, not blame. I'd never heard of you. Then you sent me your book, *Woman Reading in Bath*. I read it that winter. You were a poet. But you never did get the fox poem right. The next spring on the Sunshine Coast I sat under my old cedar tree down by the tumbled stones. She was the one I prayed to when I left that marriage. Old Cedar Mother. The man who bought the land cut her down. I think grief rises from neglect, the wish to save a part of the life you leave. I never wanted to save you, but I still grieve for that tree. She was always there for me. The strangest part of you was your desire for acolytes. You loved their loving you, their admiration, and, more, their hopefulness. Like the ghosts that summer. You came late to Fort Qu'Appelle. How you missed talking to the dead. Your daughter, Kate, and I called up a ghost from the Ouija board. I thought I was going to die but the ghost didn't want me. I'd just come back from China, tired and spent, full of temples and tragedy. I needed ghosts that year. I don't know where I'm going here. There was a misery in you, a shard of ego stuck in your bright eyes. I always thought you went wrong when you started searching for a place that would admire you. I loved your first poems best, your garden too. And the loneliness. You carried England the way a bag lady carries rags. Story was the thing you trusted least. Your lyrics thought too much. But, O, Anne, how you danced! Up on your toes you'd cross the floor like the tiniest angel, the one who stood first on the holy pin and danced all heaven to her perch. I think your body took the life you should've had. A prima ballerina lived in you. And that sounds like your poems were something less. And that's not true. Like the cowboy songs Hank Snow wrote that weren't meant for cattle drives, your poems kept trying. It's all a matter of tone, the way you spoke your world, not what you said but how you said it rearranged. Mostly I remember the time of the ghosts at Fort Qu'Appelle, you and I walking down by the lake and you telling me of the war years, the men who died in your hands, your Polish man, the eccentric little girl who had no friends but the ones she imagined. They were who you wrote for. There's room for everyone on the head of a pin. *Just come,* you said. I did and that's how I danced you, red fox angel, you.

For Bronwen Wallace

Your poems are stories with common lines, cadence the guide that turns a people into a map of your heart, a history made from prison stones, everything in the details, letters that asked for grace and caught it with the lifelines you threw out. We sat out on the lawn back of the house in Saskatoon, you with your joint and a beer in the other hand. I used to wonder how you could make sense stoned. I never could. Two tokes and I'd be under the bed hiding in a corner like a dustball afraid of a broom. My world was cocaine and whiskey. I could ask how *I* made sense. I don't think I ever did.

You just kept on talking about the women you knew, the ones in prison, the ones just dead, the ones who were your friends. All that fragility, the blown glass ornaments that were their lives, you juggling them in the wind, trying hard not to let them fall. I liked your anger and your stubbornness, the way you'd tense your jaw as if you had to worry something in there, some hard candy heart that wouldn't melt. But all the struggle never gave me you. You kept your tears for poems. Back in the League days you were always tied up with Mary, Roo, and Carolyn. There wasn't room for a man. I kept my distance, watched your feminist moves, and danced what steps I knew in the suites where men punched each other out or got left in gutters, too drunk to understand your voice, your quiet rage. It was the common plight of men who misplaced love, thinking change could be made with a boyish plea for mercy. You'd seen enough of that, a beer bottle smashed against a wall, a woman beaten by the man who loved her. *There's only so much anyone can say*—or do. This learning to love is hard and common magic is mostly shared on sidewalks where the furniture gets piled, in safe houses where a woman finds what love there is among her kind before going back to the storm. What I loved most about you was forgiveness and your need to find a common truth in a common touch. And maybe that's it, a touch and nothing more. I wasn't around when the cancer ate your mouth. I hated my thinking it was ironic a poet could die in the place where words were made. How cheap a borrowed pain in the limits a body is. Rooms within rooms, a lawn and a man and woman talking about Levine and Wayman, Purdy and Acorn, the men you said had given you a place where you could cry the time. Neruda too. And Lowther. It was the fists of men, the women bruised and broken, the indignities that dogged you. But who was it I knew when I knew you? Facts get mixed up in poems and fictions are a poet's safest bet to change a world. You were all stories, beginnings, middles, ends, and the means was in the measure you ladled out. You said, *we carry our lives in our hands*, and we do, an open hand held out to hold another, simple things so fragile even a breath can break them, a word, a poem, the cadence in a woman's voice, like a rocking chair someone's left. It moves by itself a while, then stops.

For Earle Birney

It was words like *skree* that got me, *pika, grizzly*, creatures I'd never seen before in poems, the Rockies, lands I'd walked and mountains that were not a problem, mine nor yours, until you told me so, the *otter rocks* then changed, and what I knew was what I'd lost, childhood and the wilderness, both foreign lands where I had to learn there was a trance called men. Or maybe just a man. There was that party at Livesay's house in '66 when you made a pass at my wife. You weren't the first and wouldn't be the last. I hardly noticed, my life already moving past her into what I didn't know. You wrote me back in '62 and told me to keep writing. I was up north, a first-aid man in a dead-end milltown, nursing the dregs of cheap whiskey, tapping out poems about bears at burning barrels, a cougar at the door, a man with his hand cut off, ordinary things in the tired nights when my children slept and my wife had given up on me. Strange how I thought you were already dead, but that's how it was back then, the only poets I knew long gone, their ghosts looking down off Westminster Bridge, words from another country. You said: *no man sees where the trout lie now*. I missed the first two lines. It took years for me to find the lady. These lines, long and wandering, are how I knew you. Poetry is a different kind of slowness, the break in things taking forever to happen. I remember sitting in Lionel Kearn's room and listening to you talk about Trotsky when you were his secretary. History was always just around the corner with you. *I am my own clown*, you said, and now I think I understand, for every clown has a false face under the mask. That's why they frighten us so when

we're still young enough to believe that nothing can save us from
the dark myth we can't be severed from no matter our trying. I think
that's why we make a past from ourselves. When we're far away the
only truths we have are inhuman. It's funny, Earle, how much you
mattered then. I never thought I learned from you, yet tonight I read
"El Greco: *Espolio*" and think I got my carpenter poem from you.
Lines live in poets. You wait long enough and everything you've read
gets said again. The father of a poem is what you write. Still, with
the creek outside my trailer door purling, the wind in the fir trees,
and me a little tired staring down at the river David Thompson never
saw, the one Simon Fraser named for him, I hear the black bear
rummaging among the burned pork chop bones, the green bread
crusts, the rotting bits of food in the ashes, and think how near a few
words can take us to another time. I stopped reading you back in
the early seventies. I'd grown tired of local masters. I think it was the
old contempt for what is known. I needed an imagined master, not
the one I knew. That's where the quest began, I guess, that looking
everywhere else for what I'd already found. In this early book of
yours I read today, some sweet student's written under "The Road to
Nijmegen," *War memorials are synechdoche for people.* Yeah, I know
it's spelled wrong, and the poem isn't about war memorials anyway,
yet I know my father's friend was burned alive in his tank on the
salient near Caen. Maybe that's it, I don't know. Like most letters to
the dead, this one's gone too long. Like the lines, it's wandering. It
was words that started me. There's no easy end to them: *pika, grizzly,
otter, ice.*

For Gwendolyn MacEwen

I was teaching "Dark Pines under Water" today and now it's almost
too late to wonder what anything means. I used to think I understood,
but everything's imperfect, mostly us. Isn't that what you taught us?
A *close reading* is what this teaching's called, students lowering their
hands up to their wrists in your dark imagined lake, the numbness
that comes so quickly in February, the ice broken and the body
learning what cold can do to the mind. To them they were only
words, to me too, without the *lonely*. Remember the time we sat in
your apartment drinking Scotch and talking about the poets and their
poems? You kept brushing a lock of hair away from your eyes. I loved
your laughter. Me? I had nowhere to go again, slept on your floor.
It was Toronto, back in the day. I loved that you let me sleep alone.
I paid for my beds back then, that one you gave me free. Later, we
talked about Lawrence and his *Seven Pillars of Wisdom*, his years in
the desert, his sordid soul in ruins. Your 'Manzini.' I kept going back
to him. Like all good poems he offers no escape beyond the listening,
beyond the circle your words draw around me still. This computer
keeps telling me I'm doing things wrong. It draws coloured lines
under the fragments, tells me there's no *u* in colour, no structure
to my lines. It says there's no Manzini. Perhaps there isn't except in
poems, circuses and sideshows, the tattooed man, the bearded lady,
the dwarf, the albino, the freaks I loved when I was a boy. You loved
them too. How you laughed when I told you the story of the lady with
the goitre. I followed her when I was a child and she stopped and let
me up to touch the growth that hung from her throat, that pendulant
bag of flesh. I was seven years old and thought beauty was the
suffering you gave to little boys. I think you wanted Lawrence to be
simply a man. How strange a woman's thinking is. When I was in my
last room trying to swallow a mouthful of blood I thought of you, the
bottle of vodka almost gone, morning coming on, sleep the only thing
I could imagine, the kind of sleep only the dead drunk know, the

dreaming so terrible there is nothing to remember no matter how far down you reach. The closer I get to your poems the worse I feel. My students try, but there's no telling them they have to go deeper than their wrists in dark water. I remember so little now, Gwen. *Listen, there was this boy* . . .

For John Newlove

I lost the epitaph I wrote for you years ago. Strange how things have a way of coming true. It's as if everything has a way of getting to the end, the lies, how you balanced truth on the end of your pen. Did you wait long enough? Spare words from you would arrive and I would read through them to what silences there were. What to say? O, say nothing. You told me to listen to the snow, the misery in the sound of the wind as you looked for that tired, halting song. I think everything becomes a story in the end. You would have muttered about loneliness at that. I still have your baseball bat, the one you kept by the door in Regina in case the Indians came for you. It's a child's bat, chipped and scarred, as if you practised with it by hitting furniture pretending to a bravery you didn't think you had. But what good does that image do? I keep it by my front door in memory of you. If they ever come for me I'll let them have it. Memories like that don't do much good and stories are only things I tell my students to amuse them. Did you really know John Newlove? Did, not do. The better answer is probably, no. Imperfect flowers are the best we get. They die a little, watching us from the bookcase. Maybe that's what beauty is, fear at night, the cold, the diminishing hills, what must be done to endure. What must be done, John? Is it to write the old poem again, speak words in the tired arrangements, knowing the aridity, dead branches, imperfect flowers? You tied a yellow one to the carriage of your typewriter so its false petals would remind you of elusive lies.

Things keep getting taken away, people, poems, the words we both
got tangled up in. Hell, I keep getting tangled up in the tenses, past
and present, the future imperfect. You told me once you learned
a trick from Creeley and so dismissed your poems. But you always
diminished your art. It was a kind of self-loathing, the one without
definition, the one the philosophers go on about, thinking the perfect
is attainable, that negative dialectic leading us to believe in nothing
at the end. I published "White Lies" years ago, mimeographed it up
in Vernon at a lawyer's office. They lent me their Gestetner for free,
amazed a poet needed them. Do you remember the little white cards
you wrote on in a script so tight even Ondaatje couldn't read it, so
small you could cram a thousand words on a page? They were the
notes to books you'd read, the histories, the facts of this land and its
people, the explorers and the Indians, the men who had been gallant
in their time, heroes so perfectly lonely in their quests. Gentleman
John, they called you in your white shirts and shiny shoes. One night
you called me drunk from Ottawa, told me your suit cost a thousand
dollars. That's all you wanted me to know. And the day in the Plains
Hotel when you spit in my face. You were so afraid, wanting only to
be alone with your glass of gin and tonic with a twist. Ah, John, what's
the use of going on? The poem reels out in its long, uneven dance.
I miss you. But then, I miss Acorn and MacEwen too. You were all
drunks. I miss me too at times. Does that make sense? Today I feel
I'm just filling up a page and nothing is being said. Strange how I
lost your epitaph. It was about the Spartans at Thermopylae, their
combing their hair and you picking up the broken combs, selling
them at a loss in the markets of Asia. Something like that. I think
it was better years ago. I think all I have to hold onto are imperfect
flowers. I can hold onto them, I think. It's easy enough to do. As you
said once somewhere, weeds are flowers too.

For Milton Acorn

Today I'm under the Seawall at English Bay where we both fell
asleep drunk under the sun after watching swallows chase a feather,
the birds passing it one to the other in a game of catch. The crows
watched us from under their helmets, almost amused, dark centurions
waiting for the inevitable slaughter, the barbarians come down from
the trees, Chaka and his warriors with their spears, all the history you
raged about, the inequalities, the people's needs. I think of you in
my kitchen eating peanut butter, gouging it out of the jar with your
fingers, eating it in gouts. My kids loved you for that, a man like a
child, breaking rules they always knew were wrong. They called you
Uncle Miltie. Is that where everything began? You were dried out
three days from triple sec, sleeping on the couch in my living room,
me piecing out your Percodans and Valium one at a time to keep you
almost sane. There was no talk of the night I washed the shit off your
body, the filth a thick cake on your thighs, and you screaming Gwen's
name and my brother's. I loved your loves, but hated your crying
so. Poems stumble sometimes. Yet there are times they catch at us
much as swallows do feathers in the air, the feather almost but never
falling. I sit down by a piece of driftwood and remember us sitting
against the same seawall. It was back in '65, you weeping over my
brother, Red, his early death. It was strange how you never thought I
felt anything, but your world was mostly about you. I cry too, but at
other, simple things, a scarred stone in the sea, the tide baring its dark
shoulders, swallows in the air as much a god's calligraphy as birds,
my tired hands. *Bright warriors*, I called them once. My father liked
you, perhaps because you'd been in his war. Who knows? I think you
tripped going up the gangplank in Halifax, hurt your head, and by
the time you got to England were sent home a little worse for wear.
Shaughnessy Hospital looked after you, a veteran you said, but the
psychiatrist told me quietly it was because you were a poet. *It's why
we give him the pension. Poems, you know.* I remember the ones you

wrote on my porch, "The Natural History of Elephants." Hell, the stink of your cheap Cuban cigars, your muttered arguments and the rages against those who betrayed you, Trotskyites, Marxist-Leninists, Stalinists, all the sad, petty miseries of our leftover thirties life. They still don't read you, Milton, though I've tried to change that. Little things, a poem as small as an elephant, as large as your heart. Today I'm trying to find a piece of myself I lost. Instead I find you. And the birds, of course, the swallows gone into the mist lifting from the wrack, the crows in their infinite patience, strutting at the edge of sea and land, an old bird slightly tattered in its mourning cloak turning a crab shell in the hope of a meal. It makes me think of you at the White Lunch down on Hastings Street. Sometimes I find what I'm looking for, but it's never what I wish. Getting older is like that, things creep in, a memory, your tears, your tired flesh clean at last of shit, the rags I washed you with thrown from the window onto Fourth Street, their falling like smudged bodies into the gutter. Sometimes it's like that, the times I remember, you telling me I'd never be as good a poet as my brother, and loving you anyway as best I could, the sea all around us, and the crows like dark children, never quite believing you.

For Roy Lowther

1.

I could ask the old question, but I know there's no answer to why a man carries a hammer to his wife's room and bludgeons her to death. Maybe it's not an answer I'm looking for. A question, perhaps. One night back in '65 bissett and I went up to your house to talk poetry. Milton Acorn told us about you, a communist, a man who believed in the worker. When I met you I saw a man who'd never worked hard in his life, just talked about it. Neither of us had heard of Pat and

then in the middle of a boring night she read three poems. She was
so beautiful, so young, her girls just babies, her poems full-grown and
shining. It was a woman's voice I heard. She was a poet. But you, Roy,
with your pomp and bluster, put her down, dismissed her verse, told
her to be quiet. It was too late for silence, Roy, too late for listening.
One night last year I went to where you used to live and stood on the
sidewalk as two children played on the lawn and wondered if their
parents knew what happened in their home so many years ago. I hope
they don't. Who needs to sleep in a house of blood? I remember you
raging on the phone, telling me you'd kill her if she dared to read
to the ironworkers at the hall. *She's got all the rest,* you said. *She's
got no right to take my only audience away from me.* All that jealousy
and rage, all that self-pity, that misery of the male when he has no
power left. You used to lord it over her, that ordinary girl from North
Vancouver, the shy one you controlled, the one you said you taught to
write. You spoke of her as if she'd been a monkey in a cage. She was
almost free of you.

2.

I think it's time I learned how to forgive you, think I've carried things
long enough. Like the Carrier Indians of the North, I've packed Pat's
ashes from Prince Rupert to Isla Negra, from Furry Creek to the
Finger Lakes to Firenze and while there were times I put them down
in fury or futility I always found them on my back the next go-round.
Christ, why did you have to kill her? What reason did you have? Roy,
that's where I always got it wrong, there being no reason at all in what
you did. I've never killed anyone. I've used my fists to beat strangers
in anger and once a friend out of love, and once I used a knife, but
the guy didn't die and two months later we found ourselves in the
same bar laughing over beer and counting his stitches. I've carried
the wounded down mountain roads I travelled at night so I could see
another's headlights coming on the hairpin curves. And I've buried
children, friends, my mother, father, brother: hell, death seems to be

most of life when I look back, the graves so many. What's an elegy
for? I should be writing in distichs with hexameter my drum to carry
words into song and sorrow. I should be a better poet. Sorrow is never
long enough for me. Like a dog I keep going back to my own vomit,
circling a wound I can never find. There's that thing called *phantom
pain*. Maybe that's what I have. In the end there are two deaths and
I lie between the two of you like some child who doesn't understand
the dark is everywhere.

For Pat Lowther (2007)

I almost forgot you. It was as if your dying wasn't a death, as if my
refusal was the kind of mourning only water understands, its long
falling and the wait before it becomes what it was, quiet and flowing,
how I hide what grief there is. I never expected you to live. How
many times did I beg you to leave the man who killed you and how
many times did you refuse? You never said I didn't understand, you
just said no. Yours was a different kind of death. Two days before
Roy put the hammer to your skull he told me you'd no right to take
the workers away from him. *She's got everyone else*, he said. All that
anger because you were going to read with Trower and me at the
Ironworkers Hall. Old history, him saying he'd kill you unless he
read there too and me saying there was nothing I could do about the
reading. Strange how simple language is and how we never think it
real. To be murdered over poetry. I remember Roy running across
your kitchen and smashing his head against the wall, Acorn coming
up from his basement hole, watching in the hall as he chewed on his
cigar, then you holding Roy, his broken head, his wretched self-pity,
and you telling me you couldn't leave him, saying, *Look at this blood*.
Today I read your early poems, the ones I published years ago, your
chant, the one that begins with the lines, *Hands are beautiful things*

/ *grasping a hammer* . . . your world *more precious and terrible* than I made sense of then. What's love but addiction. Pain too. I've known them both and know there's no leaving anyone or anything until you kill something in yourself. It's odd how tired a cliché is until you stare at it awhile. You've got to live with words so long they come back new. It's like falling in a dream, the never landing part. They say if you land the heart breaks. It's too easy to read in poems what we want to find, the prophetic reduced to easy choices, "Kitchen Murder," the false biography the future makes of the past. What I hold on to are the years. Back in the early sixties you thought promise wasn't forbidden. Now you lie with the others *under the scalpeled earth*. Do I hear your cry in poems? In Newlove's "The Weather," tears are just another word for love. Like you, like memory. But we sat once on your front step in that last spring with the first bulbs blooming — snowdrops, crocus, daffodils — and talked about poems, how much we loved Neruda, Sexton, Plath, and how, if you got a grant, you'd leave him. You stayed and stayed and stayed. A hammer! Christ. I try to imagine it and fail away at the image, him crushing your skull then dumping you naked in Furry Creek. What could have been in his mind as he took your clothes off, the body in his hands one he had loved. It's all suburbs now, a road leading to Whistler, and there's no plaque or bench by the creek to honour you. I go round and round, your bad teeth, your poverty, your children, that man running down the hall with his head a battering ram striking the wall and you putting down the phone and going to him, perhaps holding him in your long arms, cradling his hurt head in your lap and whispering to him that it was okay, that you had him now, that you loved him, really loved him. Was that how it went? Or did you throw him a rag and walk away? No, you never walked away. There's a white stone in my shade garden. It's a crooked one, a single piece of shattered quartz. It glows in the night, the stars giving just enough light. Bright stone. It makes me think of you when I walk the mottled path under the cedar. It's a pebble path pretending to be water. Each time I look at it I think of your body, the

wild creek crashing down from the mountains and your white body in
a pool, a single steelhead fingerling swimming through your fingers,
another touching your lips and me in the dark under the trees,
wondering at the silence that is the story of men. They put an arbutus
on the cover of your last book, Pat, the bark peeling from the tree as if
scraped by the sun. It's a tree that only lives where water hides away.
It's why you can't transplant them from the wild. Their roots go on
forever even as they lose their skin. I'm sorry I almost forgot you. The
years for me get gathered crookedly. I remember only what I can. I
keep lists of what I need to remember: I must buy milk and bread
today, work in the garden while the sun shines, feed the cats, place
flowers by my woman's bath, talk to a friend, write a poem. If I call
you, will there be an answer?

For Irving Layton

I.

Maybe this letter is dead. I know you're not, but I expect to hear
you're gone each time the day arrives. It's the stumble light makes,
faces reaching out to us in the dark. We call it waking up, unsure
who we are in the false dawn. The older I get the more confused
I am. Dying seems much a simple thing. I'm amazed it takes most
of us so long to get it right. You live in time and the dead still to
accumulate. They're like trees I used to see in spring up the North
Thompson when the ice went out, the ones whose roots gave way
to water. Their falling was so long and slow, all whisper going down.
And then their rolling into the hook above Mad River where the rocks
were. The trees hung up on them, their bodies for a season green
among a hundred years of trees. Strange how fir and spruce turn
white from water. They're like the thoughts the canyon has, things
beaten to the colour of old bone. Fear makes us brave, Irving. I'm not

afraid anymore. The dark is just the need to make something out of nothing. There are questions I could ask, but like old Socrates, they always lead to a kind of foolishness: *ambition, pride, the ecstasy of sex,* lists that make no sense. Just words. Old Nietzsche had it almost right, the part where the poet walks a wire above the street. I always thought it best to walk those wires in the dark. Seeing things has always made me fall. It's your snake keeps coming back to me, *its last silent scream.* I'd seen the same in the hills above the lakes, seen the wisps of grass in its mouth, the twists and turns of pain. I killed the first rattlesnake I saw, thinking its suffering made easier by death. But that's the thing a young man does to hide his fear. I know I'll pay for that death after I'm dead, some god taking me to task. Is that what transformation is? Tell me if you know. I'm weary these days. There's a riddle in my skull and I was never good at riddles. Being born is enough to make a man wonder what a meaning is. Maybe that's why I keep writing poems. This letter like all the rest is full of questions. I'd send this to you but what good would that do? I remember having coffee with you in '68 up "The Main" in Montreal. You talked about poetry. I didn't say a word. Young men don't speak to heroes, especially the ones who talk of freedom in a poem. You and Yeats on your stilts. I keep trying not to lie, imagine butterflies and Buddha, twist and turn. You're not dead and so my grief is greater. The dead are breathless swimmers. Remember that night at York? Eli was talking poetry while you kept trying to get that girl to go to the hotel with you. You never got the girl. I did later, but I never told you. I loved your trying though and want to say she was as marvellous as you imagined. Such breasts she had, such thighs. I was just young enough to interest her lust, that's all. But Irving, you showed a way for me to write myself toward a paradise and though I never got there, still, it was all in the reaching. I too have wanted to sing *in the throat of a robin.* And though it is a furious path where black dogs howl I walk it anyway. You told me that. I think you'd tell me now if you could speak. The gods aren't dead, not yet, though their bodies lie in the rivers, stripped of flesh,

while all about them is the great noise of the waters as they take
whatever they can reach to a darker sea.

2.

I went out to Maimonides to see you after I wrote that poem. In the
hall I got confused and couldn't find your room. I turned to a group
of people sitting in easy chairs. They were watching television with
the sound turned off. I asked them where I was going and they all
turned at my voice with the looks of the demented and deranged.
Such smiles they had. A little ashamed and confused I shrugged and
stepped away. One old lady waved at me. There was no *waterfall of
grief* in her, just a simple joy at being asked anything. Like Jarrell's
cry of *Change me*, I saw what I might be and so waved back, a little
foolish, a little less ashamed. You were in the room in your chair,
staring through your window, intent on Montreal, just houses and
apartment blocks, streets and cars blinking through the rain. There
were photographs on the tables and on the walls, you with Leonard,
and you with your mother, a picture taken years ago when you were
still your mother's son. You didn't look at me, just sat there staring
at that pane between you and whatever world there was. I picked up
your book and it opened to your poem, the one I loved when I was
young. I remember promising myself that poem back in the sixties
and swore I'd never lie, but like all poets I failed at truth, thinking
rhetoric an easier disguise. How quiet whispers are. I told you I loved
you. You just raised your hand to your lips and stroked a knuckle
across the place where words get made. They told me your skull still
holds your body alive. You don't speak anymore, your poems all in
your head. There must be such beauty there. I read to you the words
that started me down this long road of poetry. You said the death of
your father sent you toward what you feared most. In the end we all
touch a knuckle to our lips. I made a whisper of your poems. That
was enough. In the hall outside I waved to the woman in the chair.
She stared at me. She had the look I've seen on every broken thing

I've touched, querulous, her hands asking me who I was, palms out, the name of what kept hurting her, the sound turned off, the images flickering just beyond her eyes.

Under the Sun in the Dry Desert Hills Where the Rain Never Falls in August

In deep sand a beetle shoulders her way toward paradise.
A sunflower, wild with yellow, covers her with one shadow.
Among the grains of quartz, one bruised garnet, a cone of pine.
The beetle clambers. There is nothing like her in the world.
Almost blind, I get down on my knees.
My bare feet have the same soles they had when I was born.
My mother is dead.
Among many things I am alive. Still.
A single drop of water falls.
The beetle stops for a moment, but she does not drink from the salt.
There is somewhere she has to go and she goes on.
Mightily.

Forms

Decline, the way
things slope, lessen,
there, the angle of
the scree, things
held in place, a note,
a diminution, as of
the breath, what

builds from what
fails, fallen, what
bends under, what
gives way, diminished,
as the dying do,
the lessening, as of
last days, limbs
moving more
slowly, a decay,
without violence,
the mountain
revealing the
light I could
not see, abated,
abandoned to
this fallen stone
at rest, inclined,
unearthed.

The Shrine

You think of the boy opening the casket in his father's bedroom,
the one where he kept his regalia from the Shrine and wonder
at what secret he desired, as if secrets were all buried
things, an archaeology of love he dug for, holding up the apron
with its scimitar and star, the scrolled Aramaic text that told him
nothing, the books with their ritual responses, what he does not
remember now. Like all things of his father's, they were a mystery.
He'd heard his father memorizing pages of text,
the mutter of his tongue going over and over the arcane lines
he needed to repeat to the circle of men down at the Temple.

The fictions of his father were many, all hidden, so a boy
crying out for the story was given only shards, bits of broken clay
in the till that was his father's living. Death was far away. The boy
had no thought of that, living as he did in his immortal flesh.
It as if his father's mind were a broken thing
spilled out were only shattered pieces, things
an archaeologist might have put together to display
in a locked, wooden case where a boy might hover and imagine
this fragment of wood, papyrus, vellum,
bits of goat skin that revealed nothing but an image,
a mysterious verb that told him to run and hide, a bird's head
that might have been a hawk, some raptor made into a god
to guide the dead to that other world.

Teaching Poetry

Certainty, fidelity
On the stroke of midnight pass
Like vibrations of a bell . . .
Giving the student three lines of "Lullaby," and wanting
her to hear the bells in the first line,
knowing she must come to it alone or not at all,
walking after in the Nitobe Memorial Garden alone,
having to place my feet carefully on the stones
leading down to the water, the last stone
where I stopped and looked out upon the world,
water leading to water and the trees above,
their leaves, koi showing their backs to the sun,
thinking what I know now is what I didn't know
back then, buried as I was in Job
and Ecclesiastes. Just eighteen, I lay beside

my first wife and read aloud to her from the Bible
those old words from centuries ago. High school nights,
my first child inside her, my son, who hasn't spoken
to me for twelve years now. This stone, that stone,
my student who's reading Auden's poem and is
or is not hearing the bells in that first line, old
hearts, that certainty, the bells.

Not Going to the Nitobe Garden, Choosing Poetry Instead

In the white coffee mug a yellow flower, nameless,
picked at dawn. Her sleeping in the muscled dark, bright hair
thick with sweat. Him sitting in the wicker chair, silent,
staring at the flower with the old regret. A wasp
rages at the window, the glass between its wings and paradise.
It crashes its helmet head against what can't be reached, cedar trees,
magnolias, penstemon, and the last blooms of the foxgloves.
In the redwood tree a grey brain thinks among the branches,
a wasp nest where eggs lie in cells, each one a thought, each one
what he can only imagine. He doesn't open the window,
wonders instead at her dream, the click of the wasp's blunt head on glass,
what she's translating now, what dream of hell she holds,
the *click, click . . . click, click* of the wasp, and her shifting,
the hair falling across her cheek. All this and waiting,
the wasp in fury on the flower, the only thing
resembling, nectar pooled below, the flower still
alive in spite of its death, and her waking, slow to morning,
him in the wicker chair, its brittleness creaking, and
not going to her, the wasp under its bright wings, watching.

Miniature

A man sleeps in a chair by the wall, his bare feet out
on knotted pine grown dark with time, the left one
with its bit of blood hooked carefully over the right.
The quiet light in the room is pale, reflected
off the blue hills to the east. In the corner
a woman patches the worn heel of a sock.
Through the thin strands of worn wool a china egg
glints like the single eye of a bird at twilight.
Her hands slide the darning needle in and out.
It seems to be flying there, a small whisper
like the bird inside. The day is almost gone
and she squints to see what her hands are doing.
They know their way.
The sock she is darning is one of a thousand, thousand socks
she's mended in her life.
In a moment she will wake him.
The sock is almost done. His work boots — the leather worn away
on the toes so that the steel plate shows — sit side by side,
placed carefully as if the man might leap into them
and move stunned to the door
to find what lies beyond in the coming night.
We're sure we've been here before, the story
an old one of a man in a chair, a man
who has worn the socks she mends. We know
he will wake and step out into the night.
She waits, her hands moving in a silence
broken only by the clicks of the needle
against the darning egg. We're sure.
There is her breathing, her small bird-like chest
rising and falling, the man in his chair, the needle moving
with its pointed beak so much like death's sharp snout,

the tip of it blackened because it was heated by a sulphur
match only an hour ago to sterilize it before she took out
the wooden shard from his left heel. It's what
she waits for now, his leaving. Death's sharp snout,
yes, that's what we're seeing, a little bird of death coursing
over the egg under her hands. In and out, the steel beak
flies as the light, almost without regret, waits quietly away.

The Sooke Potholes

A tree frog's creak and croak are all that beauty is
when we're alone. Sometimes a song is all we have.
And the water swirls in the potholes down in the canyon.
The people are gone home to bed and I'm sitting on a stone
at the forest's edge listening to a tree frog's only song.
Out here in the dark alone I think of my woman.
A saw-whet owl calls from the other side of the canyon.
The frog answers back, happy there's someone he can talk to.
Above me the moon holds onto her bright daughter.
She wants to fly away from here, her curved arms wings of light.
I came to hold what is left of the wild and found
a blouse, a running shoe, and the torn cover of a book called
Natural History. But there's nothing natural about history.
I listen to the waters.
They say they've travelled far to find this place.
I say little, having little to say.
The waters go on to the ocean, busy,
happy to find the place where it all began. I think water
knows more than I of love. Old Hugh Latimer back in 1549
told his king, *The drop of rain maketh a hole in the stone,*
not by violence, but by oft falling.

Sometimes a gentle soul is what we want.
What can be saved, I ask, but the moon and the stars,
the owl and the frog tell me nothing of salvation.
If my woman were here she'd say all will be well,
knowing I need love at times a little.
Her song saves me tonight, no matter love.
She tells me there are living things.
I listen to the waters far below, the scour of stone on stone.
Like the tree frog's song, I think the earth is singing.
The owl knows he will starve if he waits for the mouse
to crawl under his talon, and the tree frog knows
no lovely frog will come without a song.
Nor pray for tree nor frog nor man,
but praise that *we* are a living place,
the whisper of these waters ours to hold,
however brief our stay.

Lookout

Sometimes you look out over the great plains
and see a faint light falling between what we think are mountains.
It is then you know you are living far away from the world.
As the abandoned hulk of a turtle you found once in a field
far from water. How you squatted on your bare heels and stared at the bulk
of that green dome. The body a thought inside that emptiness.
Or the night you stood by the redwood tree on the street outside your home
and stared through the burden of heavy needles at your wife
as she stared out of the light. How for one moment you were afraid.
Sometimes we live far away from the world,
bright sunlight, a heavy dark. Without thought, and waiting.

Two Crows in Winter

Two crows on the fir tree after days of rain.
They click beaks, lean to each other, blue shoulders touching.
They preen the blades of their wings, the long stretch of hollow bones
the arch they hang their feathers from.
The sun glints from their sleek heads, little servants of war
whose life is the fallen, the forgotten.
One drops to the street and returns with the body of a dead rat,
so small, the thin tail hanging like a dropped thread.
The other cowls and rolls its head, bright eye to the sun.
It leans its cheek against the wet fur,
its beak cleaning the skull of its last thought.
They are in no hurry to eat.
The day is longer than the night, the rare sun a blessing,
the rat a later meal, a death to share in some other, farther tree.
Their wings hold the sun as they fall into the blue.
They drift beyond my sight as I, as if in prayer, bend
down, returning my hands to the earth.

August Light

White sand and the gold running deep in the sun
at the far bend where a spring run jammed the wrack,
branches and leaves, an old tire, and a bit of cloth caught up
like a sail flung hard against still air, the bed of the creek deep
where no wind moved. The path did not wander. It followed
the land of Mississippi, each footfall as much animal as man,
around the hill, not over, stump and root, rock and hump
as distance, not discovery. This way, the worn bridge
over the creek old, the boards ground grey and curved

by foot and paw, hoof and claw, how many years, and how
many bridges over this dry creek and through this forest,
the path one path so one could in the oldest days
follow them from the north to the south or east to west,
an intricate map that covered a continent—so long ago,
as I, moving south of the Nechako, followed the trails
through the mountains to the Cariboo plateau.
I sat there in the forest looking down upon
the first man I had seen in a month and didn't move,
bushed, on my haunches behind tamarack needles,
my rifle butt on a stone, and watching him
as he moved from barn to house to truck and down
the road away and how I slipped back into the trees
for three more days, my fire small in the night, thinking
my way back into being a man again. The last night
I brewed coffee in the pot while a blue grouse baked in clay.
Broken open, the meat of the bird I thanked the land for.
And now this old creek bed, deep and waterless, white sand,
and going on through the wood behind Faulkner's Rowan Oak,
and onto Oxford in this far Mississippi I never thought
I'd see. I'd read *Light in August* in the hotel the night before
and found the creek in his book exactly as it was, the trail
he took from town to home and back again how many times?
And the time I sat behind green limbs
and watched another of my kind, quiet for three days,
thinking by the fire that I might kill someone and not
knowing who. That man I was followed a path southwest
leading me I knew, even as I wished to be lost, back to myself,
the Cariboo, late August light. I stare at the sand
shot with gold in Faulkner's dry creek bed,
each journey old as the trails that lead us again to the world.

Billiards

Light approaches from the east and I go out into the dark, wanting, a late raccoon scrambling over the fence, surprised by me or just in a hurry, a beetle in his mouth. Something about fear. As if there was a way to explain sound in the garden larger than a chickadee worrying the carapace of a sunflower seed.

And then she died, well, and that was the end, the nurse pulling the curtains and then an orderly trundling her body out. I heard the rubber wheels, one of them bent or twisted so it rattled as it went, skittering like a grocery cart on the polished floor, the curtain in the way of my sight, the room, white. I sat there and thought it was deliberately painted that colour because death could be better seen against its light or that light becomes us in the extreme, like the blonde hair of an early lover, someone young, and she, abashed, shy, but with desire, did what?

Yes, and the light caught in her hair, almost white, as was hers though she was old and the hair, thin, flared against her skin, the scalp freckled, and I thought of islands—the other, light in her blonde hair, I didn't think, after, astonished at what my body had done, could do.

To my left a Kodiak bear, harlequin duck and bull moose argue about how much I'm willing to salve my guilt over a wilderness that isn't there, not anymore. Some wilderness committee sending me notepaper with their dreadful visages staring out. Mute testimony like the poems I write in my sleep, my wife turning me over when I cry out.

So the man whose mother had just died sat in the chair in the corner of the hospital room and waited for them to pull the curtain back and when the orderly did the bed was empty. It was like what a magician had done back when he was a boy, a showman who vanished a blonde girl on a stage in a mountain town in the old days. A place where a moose would sometimes walk down Main Street.

The men in the bars and on the carved granite post office steps would talk about such a visitation late at night over their last beers, saying, *Imagine that*, and sometimes, when there was a silence, Old Jimmy, the blind guy from Salmon Arm, would say, *Can you imagine?*

And you can't.

When the blonde girl vanished up there on the stage, my father said to my mother, *I'll be go to hell.* Smoke and mirrors, girls vanishing, a moose on Main Street, that blonde girl when I was not yet a man, standing there in her panties, arms crossed upon her breasts.

I go outside and take a small broom to the meditation garden and begin sweeping the redwood needles away. The raccoon that scrambled over the fence stopped long enough to take a shit on the zenigata stone and I wipe it away with a bit of moss and then sit on the cedar stump and sip warm coffee. I think about maybe going back in to finish a story, my cat Roxy watching me from the safety of the porch, she having been found down by the docks, a feral kitten, the others dead except for one male, her brother, and her mother dead too, Roxy at four weeks suckling on her brother's tiny penis, and now five years old, careful, still not trusting that I will let her back into the house, sure I will take her back to the docks down at the harbour where the rats are, and me going back into the house, Roxy crowding through the door and then hiding for a moment under the dining room table as she always does. Staring out.

My mother looked up from her deathbed and I did not know who she saw, perhaps a shadow only, something between her and the sun.

The cat made no move until I sat down in my chair. Only then did she come out from hiding, belly low to the floor, not crawling, but as a cat does, as if without legs, as the old comics used to do or Russian or Ukrainian dancers in their skirts in a half-squat scuttling across the stage, the cat, like that, moving.

As much desperation as discipline, I said, and my wife told me to write that down or else I would forget it and I got pen and paper and sat back down and asked her to tell me what it was I had said, my mind between the couch and the telephone stand, having gotten lost entirely as it seems to do the older I get and then writing it down, folding the scrap of paper and stuffing it in the back pocket of my jeans.

If you don't use it, I will, she said.

I look out the window and a redwood frond, pale red, falls from a branch into the pool of water in the hollowed stone.

Desperation, and that got me going.

When I was still a boy I married a girl and she gave birth to a son, and I sat by her bed in the hospital after the birth I had not been allowed to watch or even be near, the nurses telling me to go away and only come back when it was all over, the *it* being something I didn't want to think about, happy a decision had been made that excluded me because I had not wanted to be there anyway, and she, my wife, the girl I'd married in high school, was afraid — and the story she told me, because fear is at the heart of every story, the unknown always just ahead, was about an old man who had come into the ward, made his demands and had made love, no, *fucked* his young wife, the girl in the bed beside my wife, the girl saying, *No, no, no.* It was just after the woman had given birth. And me, a boy, looked at my wife, barely eighteen years old, her blonde hair streaked with sweat, and frail after twenty-nine hours of labour, crying, telling me of this, and I, also eighteen, afraid of her story and knowing that somehow her telling me meant I had to do something about it, looking across the bed to the other bed where the girl, younger than my wife, who had been raped by her husband, lay staring at the ceiling, and I had been afraid as she told me what had happened and, strangely, excited by her story, my wife weeping, and me suddenly hard in my pants, ashamed and afraid, asking for details as if by her giving them to me I could, in her eyes, know more and so somehow better able to do something about what had happened, but also wanting to hear more of what the man had done and how he'd done it, *What did she say?* And, *What did he do then?* And loving my new wife, this girl, our son who I hadn't seen yet, somewhere else in the hospital being washed and cleaned and checked out by the doctor or whoever it was had taken him away . . .

The ellipsis which is railed against, that moment in romance novels when the girl with the blonde hair, almost white, steps out of her panties and stands naked as he moves toward her, dot, dot, dot, etc., the black boots, the quirt he slaps against his leg, his thick hair tumbling across his forehead, dot, dot, dot.

Oh, tell someone, walking down Mission Hill, a father now, looking for a game at the pool hall, my friends all still in high school writing final exams that would take them away somewhere, to university or college, or just to some good job somewhere, and no one in the pool hall except Paul Rivard staring across the scratched glass countertop, dust in the air, a Tuesday, my boy's life refusing to end, some other life beginning, and like all the old stories, ending, *kind of,* as in kindness, or the right kind, the word so strange suddenly, I write it down again, *kind,* as if it might help explain anyone's tears, and telling no one, of course, of my jerking off in the pool hall toilet, ashamed, wiping myself, and then shooting balls around the table, practising bank shots, a billiard game for one, Paul telling me how to use the carom and how to keep the balls clustered in one place on the table, working them against each other until I had to leave the cue ball safe for the invisible man I was playing against.

The raccoon turns the beetle over and over in his paws, as if it was a bright jewel or as the frog in that poem translated from Ghengis Khan's time and which a friend used in a poem: *O frog, jewel of the water.* And staring at the raccoon staring at the moon's light in the shining disc of the beetle's shell, such wonder, that bright bauble, that fragile testimony.

Pale Light

Pale light through the windows. It fell upon the white floor, a living
thing come from the night, the moon a far wandering. I watched
it become thinner and thinner, a curved blade diminishing, the
shadow of its other body a weight only the sky could hold. Swollen, it
obliterated the stars as it passed to the mountains of the west, a dark
belly held in arms of light.

I remember my mother holding her belly the same way when she
carried her last child, my brother, five years after the war. I saw her
standing back from the wringer washing machine, the piles of clean
and dirty clothes on the slat bench, clasping her hands below her as if
holding a stone. I watched her from the porch door and saw what was
a mother, mine.

Like that, her tiredness; like those, her days.

The hours don't exist.

I lift her out of the past. Her bones are potsherds found in a till,
fragments of time plowed under.

In the hospital room the only measure was her breath. Her
hair was a fall of grey on the pillow, the colour of a heron's breast
at dawn above the tide. I had come to be with her in death. There
had been others die before her, too many, my brother with his skull
full of blood crying crazy in his bed, the drowned girl I found in
the runoff waters of the Nicola River, her body tangled in a net
of roots and branches, cutthroat trout lilting in her hair, the old
remittance man I helped bury up the North Thompson. I was barely
a man back then, the backhoe gouging the grave he would lie in,
unnamed, unmarked, forgotten but for my going back years later
and laying a stone where I thought his bones might be, thinking
apology a remedy for grief.

Who can be forgiven?

My murdered father?

My Uncle Jack pushed me bodily into my father's coffin as he

---

shouted at me, *Kiss him! Kiss your father goodbye!* It was the first I knew of love between men, Jack's tears, my struggle, the lipstick and powder on my father's face marking me, I think, forever.

And there were other deaths before, but what do they matter to me who watched his mother fail? I'd seen the old ones walking in the park outside the hospital. They passed by with such slowness I could see through them to the trees and the towers of the city. The ocean's light turned them diaphanous, thin mist their shroud, bowed heads and tentative steps the measure of the lives they'd lost, the last to fail themselves. Once I reached out as if to touch a woman's hand and she stopped a moment and looked at me, O, from such a distance. No, not a stranger's hand, my mother's, and she rocked her head a moment as if to wonder who I was. I touched her hand and helped her back to the bench and sat her down.

What's wrong with you?

Her question old as life. A few weeks before she vanished, thin smoke, a mist rising.

A woman's hand, my mother's.

Who am I that I should write now of her death who carried me gentle in the waters of her womb? Too long ago to tell and today I'm older than my father and in ten years I'll be older than her and I'll know less and less until at last I'll know nothing, nothing at all. What did she know who blessed me at the end?

Blessing, warning?

Grief is a deep well. We dive into those waters until we become the rings that radiate from us, pale circles vanishing. I circle my grief, as the poet said of his mother, *quietly.*

Years ago I watched a tidings of magpies surround a young gopher come early from his burrow. Unlike the old ones he didn't know to sleep through the cold, and restless rose to the earth and the betrayal of the winter sun. The magpies trapped him outside his burrow. There were seven birds or nine, some uneven number, and they sported with the gopher. Confused, he seemed not to know why they held him there. Each time he tried to get to the safety of his burrow one or another of the birds would peck and drive him back.

Such play was theirs. I couldn't stay to watch the death and I didn't drive the birds away. Surely I am like that tidings of magpies. I won't let go what I hold. I play with it, my life a coin in a magician's hands. It seems at times I play with death.

I'm weightless, grief itself.

The last night before she slept she put her makeup on. At first I thought she'd become so deluded she didn't know if she was going to sleep or waking up and then I knew she was making herself beautiful. She'd told me she couldn't wait. *I'll be with your father,* she said. *Your brother, too.* A lipstick slash across her lips, her hand trembling so she smeared it across her cheek. And her hair. She had so little, just a few spare strands, yet she combed them carefully down over her forehead, brightly, sprightly, as she had all her life. And rouge too on her cheeks, too much, but I knew her eyes had failed. What she saw in the tiny mirror I held up was a face as young and beautiful as she thought she'd always been.

As she was and would be.

Death eats us alive. I could see her skull. It was such a fragile thing, that bone cup I think held part of who she was. There was a time in the far past when people thought the soul lived in the groin and then they imagined it the heart. When did we decide upon the skull as a container for the soul? How far away from our bodies can we go until we lose sight of ourselves and think our souls reside outside us or don't reside at all?

Who did I see lying on the bed in that hospital room where the last light of the moon shone pale through the window? What does a mother know when a child resides in her? Is there a moment when the soul arrives? Does a mother place her hands on her still-flat belly and feel through her palms that first arrival? To have a soul within a soul?

What does a man know?

I feel at times a man balanced on canes at the edge of a park, someone last, lost, left behind. One day I watched an old one in the park. He stood by the far trees and like the trees he swayed with the wind come off the sea. It wasn't a heavy wind, just some light touch of air come weaving. He was still there when I left to go back inside the hospital and I wondered as I walked away if anyone knew he was there, if anyone was going to come and take him to wherever he was to go. Perhaps he saw around him angels in the shapes of magpies, a tidings of things to touch him to his rest.

I wish my father had lived long enough to die.

I wish my mother had my father longer.

But what are wishes but luck gone wanting? I seem to begin everything with a question. Perhaps there are only questions. But there must be more? Surely there's only a presence of things for lack of thinking further than I can. Back then I lost what lay before me, but what made me think she was mine to lose?

I am bewildered.

A year before her death I went into the mountains to lose myself. I walked back into the bush until the hills became rocks, the creeks thin rivulets born from the fingers of glaciers as they retreated through tumbled scree. There were no trails but for bear and mountain goat. I sat at the beginning of water. I saw the birth of rivers rise in the far mountains. I knelt on the ground and leaned my face into first water and I drank from a clear pool, took into my body what once was snow.

I'm made at times of ice.

I camped by a nameless creek and made my fire. I lay myself down on cedar boughs under the stars and thought I was the only man there was, I was that lonely. There were so many stars I thought there must be a god for what else could have caused them to flare so willingly. I think I'm that old man in the park.

The other women in the ward were far away in sleep. My mother was awake. We didn't speak. Her bright eyes stared at me, curious. She had the quizzical look, the kind that wonders. What do the dying see? On my knees was *The Old Curiosity Shop*. I brought it thinking it was her favourite of his books. She loved Dickens. She'd read him aloud to me and my brothers when we were children: *A Tale of Two Cities*, *Bleak House*, *Hard Times*, the rest. We lived those pages of the far past, that other, older century, the nineteenth after Christ. She revelled in words, loved the detail of a world that was still in reach when she was a child.

Who was she back in the days of the little girls?

I remember what she was like when I was a boy. The time she clasped her hands under her belly in the kitchen when she stepped back from the washing machine and the tubs and held her last, my brother, Mike, a stone in her arms. What did she think as she held his body in herself? Why can't I see her?

I swear I'll kill my sight.

She was tired of the days and nights, the long hours looking after a family on little money, a wood stove, a laundry tub for baths, linoleum on the floor curled at the edges where it met the walls and worn away under the pine table where we sat to eat the food she made.

She paused for breath.

I don't remember her laughing. The only thing she would smile for was a camera and that was a thin smile, deceptive in its sleight. It was as if she knew something the rest of us didn't. She had a magpie look, curious and playful, strangely, cruelly kind.

She closed her eyes when I read to her. The woman across from her never moved. She'd been in a coma a long time. The ward cat slept in the hollow of her legs and stared at my mother and me. I didn't look back. I wrote a poem the night her husband came into the dark and slept with her. The woman on the bed had no visitors but him that once. I think she was mostly alone by then, her family having given up on her. Her husband said nothing to me, so intent was he on love. It seemed I wasn't there at all. The ward cat at the foot of the bed knew. Like that cat was the old woman in her sleep. Like a magpie my mother. Like that man am I.

I'm sick to death of death. There was a time a man would hire women to wail for him. They'd come in their long dresses and black shawls and sit in a circle. They'd sit and knit, talk among themselves as women do, but when death came they'd rise up and howl as if with their bodies they could cry all grief away. Is that what death is, some god come calling?

Where do such women live that I might hire them? Are they called a grief of women in the way magpies are a tidings, crows a murder, orphans an abandonment? Is this what I do here, list things in their gatherings?

I'm sick of me.

I remember the night I left the bar at the Cecil Hotel. It was three years after my father's death, three years after the poets had deserted the place at the end of the sixties and the Cecil had become a country-and-western bar with strippers and pole dancers, addicts and drunks, pimps and johns and whores. I was drunk and stoned and tired of booze and whores. I walked down to False Creek where the ocean never moved. It's odd to think how I folded my clothes and placed them on a rock. How neat I was. I sank a dozen times and each time my body rose again to the surface, refusing to let go of its hold on things. I sank again and then again, each time thinking this was surely the last. At the end I lay on my back upon the dank water and stared up at the stars.

Death doesn't come to us easy. It's us, who must come to death. We're welcome then.

I think my mother was welcome.

I think she was good at death who wasn't good at life. Why do I say that? God knows, she gave birth to us three and raised us through the war and then two more, my sister, my little brother.

I saw her hold her belly in her arms as if her last was what she must endure. There were no more. Old Doctor Alexander cleaned her out. He promised her that when she asked for an abortion. *You have this one and I'll make sure you have no more.* I can hear him talking quietly in the kitchen. I was at the porch door listening. I think at times I was some kind of ghost child, a spirit sent to keep close watch on her. She never told my father what she did. Five was enough and she was tired of birth. He came hard, my brother, born at the end like that. Eleven pounds he was. She told me he split her open when he came. *He almost killed me,* she said.

I read to her there in the night. The past came stuttering, glimpses, bits and pieces of a film stitched together every which way. There's no order to me. There never was. I remember too much. I remember wishing my brain would die. I remember wishing as I read from Dickens, her eyes closed, her hair combed just right, the lipstick crooked on her lips, her breathing light. I reached out and placed my hand upon her breast and held it there. I felt the bone cage move. I swear her lips couldn't lift a feather. She was a whisper made of silk so strange as to be made by the ghosts of worms.

All of them came back to me. It was as if I watched the dreams she had. As if what was in her mind became mine and I could see back, through the war to some other, earlier time, the thirties and twenties, her in a jangly dress, my father with his foot up on the running board of a Model A Ford, a cigarette in his hand, a cigarette in hers, the two of them young and wild. And later, the Sullivan Mine and my father coming down the rocky trail to her, two children, me not born, not yet, her belly swollen.

She reared up from the bed and grabbed my wrist. Her tiny hand just skin stretched over bone, fine vellum pulled across thin sticks. Shining there, her eyes what the almost dead have, a bright and terrible burning, and she said to me as if to admonish, as if to warn me of my only life, as if to make of praise another kind of calling: *At every turn there's always something lovely!*

So I sit and hold onto what death knew and knowing gave to me that I might turn my life, to what? O, mother, who is it I mourn? Whose death did I wait for in that room? I'm alive in a kept silence and I turn and turn again upon your words and wait upon my

wanting. You died and I have nothing here but words. I make of them
a memory to you who sang to me and sing to me still, your voice as
bright as the sharp points of the moon before it's gone, that blade of
light that holds the heavens, crescent-shaped, like two arms holding
on to what it knows.

He Answers the Young Critic Who Demands That His Poems Change, Offering the Boy Blood and Tomatoes in Hope They Will Be Enough

When the boy lay bleeding from his temple
on the white kitchen table in the village shack
in the high mountains, the women kept washing
the clot away, their rags opening the wound.
The blood flowed, the boy's face bright
with the rose glint of his body starving.
It was as if he kept himself alive
only to stop their hearts from breaking.
As if their wailing could keep him alive.
As if the sickle cut of the moon
in the wine glasses the men raised up
could stop their women's tears.
In the mountains the river was huge
with ice, and the men in the night listened
to the lament as the women opened
again the wound of the boy who was steadily dying
in their care. All things proceed from such
attention and it is hard to be as hard as the young
when they admonish their elders. How difficult
it must be to ask the rust on the iron knife
to go back to the beauty of the blade in

its first fire? Surely rust is its own beauty.
It is the same as picking up a stone
from among the many myriad stones
by the river and holding it out to see
the lichens growing there. One white.
One red. They are eating each other.
It will take another five hundred years.
That is what the young critic wants,
I think, but what do I know
of such abstract wishes? Imagine
the loneliness in being just a man.
Or the boy on the table, how
I moved the women aside and stitched
the flesh to flesh, closing the wound, and then,
in the decorous dance a stranger must do,
drank wine with the old men on the porch, saying
nothing, their nodding as they filled my glass.
They were impressed labourers brought from Portugal
to work on the railway, the fallen moon,
the ice on the river, men and boys and blood.
None of us spoke of the women's singing.
They had heard it for many years and I, still
young, had nothing to say about such patience.
O yes, the boy brought me a bottle of good whiskey
a week later, something his father could ill afford.
The father could not bring it to me himself, shame,
pride, some kind of awkward love. I had refused
his money, you see, so he sent his son,
the one I stitched together in the shack. His mother,
she who had cleansed the wound over and over again,
bowed her head to me each time we passed on the road.
She didn't speak English, but in the late summer,
she brought me a basket of tomatoes she'd grown,

holding two of the fruits out to me, one in each hand, rich
and red, her hands worn from work, the steady
growing that is the lot of women who have laboured
beside their men for thousands of years
that their sons might live, blood and tomatoes,
a boy who followed me everywhere for the years
I was there in the North, as if with his presence
he could protect me from harm. As if it was that.

Bamboo Seeds

A bamboo screen and the bamboo above, the long wands
above the stone bench reaching in the long dream of seeds
that will not come for a hundred years or more.
Pebbles lead from here to the pond and the koi.
Deep in the water their brightness rests.
They eat their bodies slowly, spring far away and the snows to come.
Hard rains break above the earth.
The koi are deep in their blood.
I see through the bamboo leaves
the great death coming to this world,
the bamboo wands flung outward,
thin leaves, and the koi below.
So quiet. I am without tears.

Against Metaphor

He opened the book of a poet he loved in retreat, a man
who seemed to have spent his life almost afraid of everything,
love, life, sorrow, death, and how the man always approached
such themes as a small boy would, a kind of desperate
insecurity in the tone of the poems that always ended
with the man being somehow brave in spite of his fear,
as a small boy would who was forced to approach
something terrible and did, but at great cost to himself.
He thought the poet must be very attractive to women
because of his fragility and the sure beauty of his poems.
The man's poems were like an apple being peeled
very slowly with a knife. The knife had been honed
for hours on a stone like the one his father had once owned
and which he had lost in one of the many moves he had made.
He had been driving into the foothills
west of Fort Macleod, Pincher Creek behind him. The farm
his father had run away from when he was thirteen was near there
but he had never tried to find it. Paradise, his father had called it,
ruefully, half in bitter jest, but he was right, there being nowhere
on earth as beautiful as those southern foothills. His woman was asleep
beside him, her face slack in the deep world no one knows of,
except for dreams. He loved her sleeping.
To amuse himself he began to count
the houses and apartments he had lived in,
places where he thought he'd live
longer than a week or two.
Through the foothills and up into the Crowsnest Pass,
past the town of Frank that had been buried under a slide
back in the thirties, and then beyond into the Rockies,
so she slept, and he counted slowly and carefully, not wanting
to miss anywhere, his mind crossing and recrossing the continent

and when she woke he had reached the last place, the one
they had just left. Eighty-seven places, he told her.
She laughed in the tousled way women do
when they are not sure they are beautiful yet
and laughed again, serious, as she turned the mirror down
on the sun visor and touched her face. The last thing she did
was to run her slender fingers through her hair and then
shake it gently into place. Satisfied, she turned to him brightly
as women do when they are beautiful again, and said, *Really?*
Then, because she was no different from anyone else, she began
to count the places she had lived in her life, listing them out loud,
the place on Second Street in Swift Current, the rooms at university
she lived in when she was a student in Saskatoon, the other rooms
in a town called Glaslyn, somewhere in central Saskatchewan
when she was first married. There were only twenty-three places,
most of them when she lived with him,
and when she was finished she looked wistful and somehow
disappointed, as if there should have been more, not as many
as his, but more than just twenty-three. It was as if her life
had failed her in some strange way, then she brightened again,
for she was a woman and still is who never stays dark for long.
Later, at his mother's apartment in the Okanagan, his mother
has corrected his total, adding places he had lived when he was
a small child and had forgotten. That makes ninety-three, he said,
and his mother, not to be outdone, began counting the places
in her life and managed to beat twenty-three,
which irked his wife.
When his mother realized she couldn't
beat his total of ninety-three, she said he was lying,
that no one had ever lived in ninety-three places,
at least no one in her family.
When they left that afternoon to drive to the coast
and their new life there in his ninety-fourth house, his wife

told him she didn't like his mother and he told her he knew that
and it was all right, because he didn't much like her either,
though he loved her, had always loved her. *Of course*, his wife said,
she's your mother, isn't she? She said it in the way women do
when they think men are being hard on women, that
it was all right for her to not like his mother, but if he didn't
then there was something suspect about it, something male.
She said: *You have to love her. She's your mother.*
And instead of taking what looked to be bait on an argument hook
and telling his wife that he had said he loved his mother, of course,
who wouldn't, but that he'd only said he didn't like her, etc., etc.,
he just kept driving down to Merritt where he had
lived in four different places, all of them gone now, except
for the trailer park where he'd lived in a trailer, but the trailer
wasn't there anymore. He'd moved it up to the North Thompson in 1960.
When he left he sold it to a logger
who burned it down after his family left him.
It was a bad-luck trailer anyway,
he told his wife and she agreed, though she shook
her head at the trailer park. *If you lived there*, she said, *you were
trailer trash*, and they both laughed. Later on, up the Coquihalla
she fell asleep again and he'd continued on over the mountains
toward the new life they were making for themselves.
He'd forgotten all of that time until he opened the book
of the man whose poetry he loved. He was in retreat
and he was searching for something, anything to write about.
He had started a poem about humility because it was the subject
of the book the monks were being read at dinner, something written
about Hilaire Belloc, a writer he hadn't thought of in forty years,
but the poem he tried to write was pretentious
as any poem would be that started from the premise of humility.
When he opened the book a mugo pine card fell out of it,
a bookmark he'd used once a year ago, and he read

the identity tag he had used to mark the page of a poem
he loved. The tag read, *Pinus mugo Pumilio: A densely branched,*
broadly spreading evergreen shrub clothed in handsome,
dark green, needle-like foliage that tolerates a wide range
of soil conditions. Full to part sun for best results.
He thought of the poems in the book and how the man
who wrote them wrote as if he was almost afraid of everything,
his poems reading like an apple being peeled very slowly
by a sharp knife, the peel coming away slowly, revealing
the white flesh shot with veins of red, and he thought of how
his mother was dead now and how he'd loved her very much
all her life, even when she was bitter and old and angry at him,
he thought, yes, angry at him for being alive, as if somehow
he should have died like everyone else she had loved, her first son,
her brother, her husband, her father, all her sisters, everyone,
and for her, at the moment whenever it seemed he was there
with her, him too, dead and better off because of it . . . *but*
better for whom? he thought, the words running out and not caring,
not wanting to go much further, and muttering, ninety-five, ninety-five,
to himself, as if somehow a number could explain anything
like mother love, or a mugo pine, or a man whose poetry
he loved that he could barely read, and how it hurt so much to know
anyone who could keep going in spite of his fear, that almost afraid
being worse than anything he could imagine, anything,
and now that he was at the end of the poem he began to hate
the apple and the knife and the way they had slipped into the poem
through metaphor, and how he was against metaphor these days
and wanted his poems to be clear of artifice, and how no matter
how hard he tried, it kept getting into his poems, and he thought
of going back and taking that part out, but thought that would
somehow betray the poem, his father climbing back in, and
his grandfather burying his father's mother under the caragana
back of the farmhouse, the place near Pincher Creek

he had never tried to find, and couldn't now
anyway, everyone long dead who might have given him
directions, anyone who might have shown him the way.

Attention

How else, but the child in the ditch, so simple,
as she pushes a little wheel of lemon in the ruts,
the only wheel left from her carriage all of gold
that the stars shining see nothing of, so bright
their slow turning in the night. How delicate
she holds the yellow star between her fingers, the blossom
far away now, and the white seeds wet and gleaming
as they slip into the earth she leaves behind. How far
her journey in this small place she has made of her
riding, the horses plumed and lifting
their feathered hooves, the carriage all of gold,
and the barefoot girl in the shabby dress,
her gloved hand raised in farewell, as if
this was her leaving, a child going far away,
her two small fingers holding the yellow centre,
the wheel turning so delicate inside the image
she is, and how you are with her now
and so, by such attention, changed.

Seventeen Roads Out and Choosing

At the edge of the mountain road a toad crouches beside a yellow stone.
The pool of mud and water tells me nothing of my daughter.
I'm cold and wonder is not told by what I say.
I pray for what I know.
Somewhere in the rain my daughter stares through light.
I imagine her, slight and still, quietly.
Beyond the road, the fronds of sword ferns droop down below death camas,
a mound of white froth. What I see, I've lost.
The solitary toad squats like old leather beside his stone.
The road has no daughter. Here at the edge I pledge what I have to her.
Here, I say, *here,* knowing I pray for little, a pool of water,
yellow stone, a toad, my daughter in the first of dawn,
far from this place at the edge of her careful lawn.

Pygmy Owl

I think the moon
at the edge
where the limb
bends, quickens
night. My hunger
is for her. She is
unlike this owl
who, still, still
moves, the light
folding over
her wings: she
sings, a
dove note,

The Collected Poems of Patrick Lane

not mourning,
but only song
directed toward
who waits, with
me, the small
mole, mouse
and beetle, moon,
the limb bare
but for the cold
dark under her
bright wings,
the breath
I hold, I,
sudden, hear.

Across the Strait Thin Clouds Whisper above the Trees

Across the strait thin clouds whisper above the trees.
There is no rain. A dark age comes
and every silence we've imagined will be ours.
Sorrow and sorrow and sorrow will be ours.
Out of silence, woe upon woe.
The child in your arms will be taken from you
She will be dashed upon stones.
So too the child of your child.
And will you give solace to the one who cries out?
And will you?
O, I have seen us in the hours, in the long nights.
We will walk with nothing in our arms.

Last Water Song

It is not the water you tried to find when you were young.
That was the water that lost you.
You climbed trees to look and the water was there.
You walked on the earth and the water was nowhere.
That was the losing water.
This water is the finding water.
It is cloud searching water.
When you are old it comes down.
It stretches out on the earth.
It says follow this water.
First water is woman water.
The belly of woman has this song.
That water was the first learning song.
This water is the last learning song.
It is the cloud under the earth.
Now you climb down roots to find this water.
Now this tongue is a root.
Open this mouth in the earth.
Now sing this water song.
Now you are the last water.

What My Father Told Me

1.

The house was beside the sawmill and each morning
the floors were burdened with dust from the huge fires
that burned all night on the graveyard shift. The dust
blew through the cracks and crannies, the windows, doors,
through the broken places in the walls and roof. The dust

settled on the table and chairs, the crockery,
the children's beds, the worn blankets covering them, and them
trembling with each small breath they took, tremors of dust
rising from their mouths, thin, elusive trails in my wife's hair,
on her lips and cheeks. Standing by the bed in my bare feet
I stared at the dust in the cold of the winter night. Alive, it was
like smoke when it settled on snow, something grey
that crawled, writhing there on the white drifts
in the village, in that valley, in that winter, the mill
making its terrible music. A hurting song. You could call it
that, something a man might sing if he had lost
it all, his woman, his children, his truck, his job;
everything somehow broken, his life now strange and alone.

2.

Almost, I say, such songs as what we hear on empty roads
in the cold, the twisting ruts throwing us side to side, our hands
gripping the wheel for dear life. Not fear, just a machine
carrying us in the false, reflected light we call the moon
when it's alive on ice, and miles to go
before you get anywhere close to what you could
call home; singing along with the voice on the radio,
forgetting for hours it was you singing the song,
the radio not working in those mountains.

3.

The sound of the moon on snow is a whispering.
You hear it even when you know you can't,
humming the parts you don't know, the story that explains
everything, the refrain one sure thing, and shouting it in the dark.

4.

My father was drunk. It was twelve at night and he had come in
out of the snow, my wife in her pyjamas and me in my underwear,
amazed he was there, in that village, in that storm, his heavy coat,
and the thin icicles melting in his hair. My wife poured him a glass of rye,
and he held it in his two hands, cupped there as if it was some fire
he thought could warm him. I know now my mother told him
to visit us. He'd been in the village for three days, drinking
with his army buddies, the ones who came back, the ones who
made it after the war. He didn't want to be with us. He'd risen
from whatever shack or cabin, house or hotel room, and stumbled
out into the night, knowing he had to go because she'd told him to,
my mother. *Visit the kids*, she must have said, and him grudging, nodding
as he went out the door. Did I say he didn't want to be there? Yes,
and though I knew he had been in our village those days and nights,
I never thought him possible in that hovel we called a home. The fires
from the burner rose from behind his head, the window drifted
with dust so the glow of the flames seemed muted, another kind of fire,
the one you grow inside, the one that smoulders,
peat fire, a brown-coal fire, wet wood, damp dust, smoke.
He had no idea what to say or do, lifted to his lips
the whiskey I'd been saving for the Christmas months away
and drank it down, a single swallow, his mouth then lax, his lips
hanging from his teeth, the ice melted from his hair, the snow too,
gone from his boots, a puddle at his feet eating into the throw rug,
my wife standing then, smiling, a little shy, and going back to bed,
saying nothing, a nod, the kids still sleeping, and me hearing the door
latch behind her, imagining her curled at the edge of the bed, as far
away from me as she could get, as she often did those last years,
a body I could never find. And then, just my father and me breathing.

5.

I don't know now why I asked him about the war, except
I knew he'd been with his army buddies, the ones who came back in '45 and '46,
young men gone cold inside, or so hot the nights burned them.
The years that followed, the silences, my mother telling us
not to talk to him, and not to ask anything. He looked down
into his glass as if he thought he could find something there,
a small drop or two left, shivering in the bottom,
the glass he lifted to his mouth and held there long enough
for one last drop to fall upon his tongue. *That war*, he mumbled.
And I waited for what he'd never said before,
my father's head blundering then on his thick neck, a steer come up
out of a chute to the killing floor, that kind of heaviness, brutal
in its anger, its innocence. And I could tell you of what he told me then,
his friend burning alive as he tried to climb from the turret of his tank,
another friend quickly buried somewhere in Holland, my father
thinking he'd go back and find him and never did,
and later the woman in the ruined house. *A German woman*,
he said, one they found in hiding in the basement rubble.
And him looking slyly up at me, a look that was complicit,
that told me we were somehow
in the story together, that I was his son, a man now
though I was barely twenty-two, married, three children,
and I knew they had raped her, the German, that woman,
and my father seeing me staring at him,
angry, saying, *No*, and I knew
when his eyes slipped away, that he had lied.

6.

On the dusty floor were our three trails: the ones my wife made
coming in and going out, her trail to the kitchen and the bottle,
and the trail she took to my father when she gave him the drink,
the trail she followed when she left, the marks of her bare feet,

so small, one print perfect where her foot stepped a moment away
as if to run. I could see in the dust the curve of the arch,
the five toes spread, the track looking like something wanting to escape,
some animal that had tried to leap away from what pursued her,
her father-in-law, her husband, the room. Dust withered
around her, then a whimper she must have heard
from a bed, a child, I think now a son, troubled by the night
and the voice of his grandfather, a sound he didn't know,
not well, not yet, and, in the end, not at all. The trail my father left,
the wet prints leading in from the door, the swirls of burnt
sawdust he brought in with the snow, and the ones he took
leading out, his trail obscure, an arrival and departure,
his glass on the wooden crate by the chair, a muddy circle there
when I picked it up, and the smear inside
where his tongue had licked it clean. And the trail
I didn't make, the one I waited for, the marks my feet had left
coming into the room of my father, and the other trail,
the one I would make in what was then almost a moment and wasn't,
the door left open a crack, snow and dust withering
across the floor, so that I thought if I got down on my knees
and put my head to the worn wood, the dust would whisper me a song,
one I could learn about the night outside where the moon was
on the ice road shining, the music playing as loud as it could my heart.

The Green Dress

In the green dress, separate, the floor retreating
from her, so that it seemed she was farther away
than the others thought, around her white walls, severe,
and the doors white, and a single high window, a photo
on the wall of a horse's head, poorly taken, the light

wrong, the background cluttered, things
getting in the way, intruding, haphazard, and not
the fault of things themselves, the fragments,
old harness, a bale of hay, a man's shoulder,
his shirt with part of a floral pattern showing,
perhaps roses, and wrong. So the woman in the green dress
with her hands precisely on her knees, her face held up
so that her throat is exposed, the lines of the muscles drawn,
and her eyes, not closed, but open, and staring at the door
through which the undertaker will soon appear bearing in his hands
the ashes of her son in a plain white box, and her waiting
for that, the green dress not a special one, not one
she might wear every day, but a dress she nevertheless chose
and by such choice refused extremity, both simple and not,
reaching into the dark, and taking that dress from among
the many dresses and saying, terrible, yes, this one will do.

A Woman Empties Her Sock Drawer

Her hands stir among thin socks, sheer silks and coloured cottons,
the low socks and the high, tiny rabbits and ducks that danced
around the circle of ankle bones, pansies and peonies
fading, the calf-high sheers, the thigh high silks and nylons, the small,
delicate tears in the mesh, old scars where buttons had gripped them,
the faint discolourations where wine had been spilled, coffee and tea,
her hands remembering how they straightened out the long seams,
the faraway warmth now cooled, and then *this* into the bin, the bag,
and *that* refused and *these* discarded, the drawers emptying,
the scent of cedar and sandalwood faint on her fingertips,
the twist-ties bound, and finally the quiet as she pushed the drawer back
into the darkness of the chiffonier, the little baskets empty,

a single silk stocking on the throw rug by the door, curled upon itself
like a tangled sentence read over and over again, and memorized, forgotten,
her hands that touched them once, withdrawn, the high thigh
and slender calf, the ankle, foot, the glance that saw the stocking
cross smooth over its sister, a faint musk still in its woven mesh.

Threaded Blood Lichen

He is sitting in the old silence, having given up memory again
in anticipation of inevitable decay, holes in the brain, hollow throngs.
He thinks about the steady dispensations, the old and the new,
the way small children used to shine after weeping, their faces
round with hope, and him knowing it won't be like that again.
Tattered rag, frog pelt, lettuce lung, and the exquisite
peppered moon, him down on his knees, his eyes in the dawn
and naming the lichens no one knows anymore, the new children
afraid to touch anything. He remembers the white of his father's cheek,
the thin stiffness as of old china cups pushed to the back,
the thin brown lines inside caused by the crazing time makes
of things. How precious the broken. Who kisses the dead anymore?
Who cradles their slender fingers in their own, a hand
reaching out to touch cold flesh, the body just released
from the ice house, someone somewhere cleaning gas jets,
ashes and bits of bone crunching underfoot. He remembers his mother,
the opal ring lying on the ashes in the box he made to hold her.
The undertaker asked him if he wanted the ring to remain
inside. He said, *yes,* knowing as the undertaker went away to glue
the lid shut he would take the ring. Perhaps some child wears it
now, some girl, some woman, someone who loves
the antique setting. His hand brushes the lichen, frail hairs
clinging to his rough palms. How afraid he was back then.

       The Collected Poems of Patrick Lane

How impossible it was to remember: the polished grey slate
that he slipped upon when he turned away, the heavy drapes
he blundered into as he fell backward into the image in the mirror.

What Language Can't Reach

And the only way I know how to do that is to stand far off
as if on a low hill under a moon
watching a passenger train stopped
at a siding in the distance of a prairie night in winter.
In the snow and watching. That far away. That sure.

A NEW AWAKENING

Patrick Lane

*It was 1960, the year I began writing poetry. I began because
it gave me something I didn't have in my life. I had always
wanted to be an artist, a painter, but there was no money for
oil paints or acrylics. Writing was cheap. I had a tiny portable
typewriter, a worn black ribbon, and a sheaf of canary-yellow
paper. I had an* HB *pencil and a pink eraser. Where the
typewriter came from I don't remember. Late at night after my
wife and children were asleep I would sit at the tiny kitchen
table in front of our trailer and try to turn words into poems.*

*Never in my life had I tried to do anything so difficult. I
knew what a good poem was. I'd read the poets, but I couldn't
do what they could do. I couldn't write about daffodils and
skylarks or about Massachusetts, Black Mountain, or San
Francisco. They weren't what I knew, their words were not from
where I had been made. Without advice or help from anyone
I wrote about what happened around me. A dead baby in a
trailer, a woman who died when she tried to abort herself with
a coat hanger, the sound of the rivers that coursed down the
mountains I walked. A bear rummaging in my burning barrel*

in Avola was the subject of the first successful poem I wrote.
That was in 1961. I knew it was good, but why it was good I
couldn't have told you. It sounded right, that's all. It caught the
night in the mouth of the north. I sent it and some others off to
the Canadian Forum *magazine in Toronto and they published*
three of them.

My first publication and I was bitten and bitten hard.
From the moment I saw my poems in print for the first time I
never looked back. After that I never stopped writing, no matter
what happened. I disappeared inside words. I don't think my
wife and family ever found me again. I knew what I had to
do with my life. The early death of my brother Dick was three
years away. My father's murder was seven years away and
so was my divorce. Things were going to happen to me that
would change my life forever, but the writing stayed. I had no
teachers, no mentors, no education beyond high school, but I
had what all artists need and that was an obsessive and total
commitment to the voice I heard inside me. I think back to that
time, the mills and first aid, the poverty and struggle, the joy
and bitterness, and I know the only thing that kept me going,
the only thing that kept me alive, was poetry.
—from *There Is a Season: A Memoir in a Garden* (2004)

I wrote the poem "How the Heart Stinks with Its Devotions" one early
spring morning in Prince George in 1975. It comes close to what I
would call a poetics. Six months before I wrote it I had made my third
attempt at suicide. I had been working by then on my craft for fifteen
years and thought I knew as much as there was to know of life, of love,
of death, of all such immensities and their consequences. The poem
asked of me that a life's work be done, that the presence of one stone or
one leaf could be paradise and that the making of a poem, the making
of a beautiful thing could defeat time.

This past spring I was up in the Interior for a reading. The poet,

Sharon Thesen, spoke to me of how my poetry had been criticized over the years for what was seen as a preoccupation with violence. She said my poetry wasn't so much concerned with violence as it was with *the disfigurement of innocence*. Her comment startled me, the idea that one of my poems could embody the deformation of beauty. Yet the lines I just quoted from the "Devotions" poem illustrate what she meant.

> Empty your eyes of all save form.
> It is the green perfection of the space
> a leaf includes in its growing,
> the delicate birth baffled by the wind.

Sharon Thesen's comment explains one aspect of my poetics. The following lines from "A Murder of Crows" are another example of this.

> I have struggled
> tonight with the poem as never before
> wanting to tell you what I know —
> what can be said? Words are dark rainbows
> without roots, a murder of crows,
> a memory of music reduced to guile.
> Innocence, old nightmare, drags behind
> me like a shadow and today I killed again.

This poem was written a day or two after I shot and killed a doe from my front room window. She had been eating the windfall apples under the tree in my front yard. My wife had been laying out food for us, fried ling cod yet again, my small children at the table, me staring out the window as I wondered at my life. I spoke aloud to no one in particular, perhaps only to myself, saying that if the doe was still out there after dinner I'd shoot it. I spoke casually, absently, yet in doing so, I know I had trapped myself. My wife and children said nothing. As we ate our meal I wished the doe away. I wanted her gone because I knew if she was still there I'd go and get my rifle and kill her. We could have used the meat. We were getting along on next to nothing, the remnants of some grant I'd received, a bit of casual labour for the local Water Board, and my fishing, the salmon and clams, the oysters and rockfish, enough to keep us alive. The venison would be red meat for a month. I had shot deer before, shot moose, shot bear, but those killings had been in my twenties.

I didn't want to kill the doe. It was as simple as that, and yet I got up, helped clear the table, glanced out the window and saw the doe still there, nibbling at the apples. I went to the closet, got out my rifle, loaded it with .22 long cartridges. I walked back to the window, opened it, and lifted my rifle. The doe looked up at me as if curious about why I was there. She didn't scare. I waited a long moment, aimed carefully at that spot just behind the upper front leg, and shot her. The doe was the last animal I killed.

If I could tell you the silence
when the body refused to fall
until it seemed the ground reached up
and pulled it down, then I could tell you
everything: what the grass said
to the crows as they passed over,
the eyes of moss, the histories of stone.

But how, beyond the simple anecdote above, to explain the making of my poem? Did I write it out of guilt, to expiate a sin, to confess a murder? Was it remorse I sought? All of these and none. I simply made a poem out of what William Butler Yeats called "the foul rag and bone shop of the heart." The poem is, I believe, an emblem of my desire to salvage some beauty from a fallen world. In "The Witnesses" I say:

To know as the word is known, to know little
or less than little, nothing, to contemplate

the setting sun and sit for hours, the world
turning you into the sun as day begins again

To remember words, to remember nothing
But words and make out of nothing the past

This poem, written some years after "A Murder of Crows," is about my
father and his early life as the Macleod Kid, a rodeo cowboy from the
late 1920s, but it is also about my despair that the making of a poem is
no stay against the darkness surrounding us. Yet I also believe that each
poem I have made in this life "realizes a new awakening." William
Carlos Williams says this in his poem "The Descent." He also says, "No
defeat is made up entirely of defeat."

I read his poem carefully and long in the sixties and seventies.
I didn't fully understand it then nor did I feel it in its deepest emo-
tional and spiritual implications, but I knew it for what it was: a thing
of beauty. In his long poem "Paterson," Williams' lines "Beat hell out
of it / Beautiful Thing" made me believe that out of the wreckage of
a life a life could be made no matter its distortions, its disfigurements.
Williams' lines are the mature resolution of James Dickey's "wild to be
wreckage forever," in his poem "Cherrylog Road."

Williams says in the poem that "Memory is a kind / of accomplish-
ment, / a sort of renewal."

The descent
            made up of despairs
                        and without accomplishment
realizes a new awakening:
                        which is a reversal
of despair.
            For what we cannot accomplish, what
is denied to love,
            what we have lost in the anticipation —

a descent follows,
endless and indestructible.

Back in 1962 I worked in a sawmill in Merritt, BC. I remember sitting late at night in our house by the mill, my wife and children long gone to bed, as I struggled to make a poem out of a few simple words. I had been reading Arthur Waley's translations of Chinese poetry, poems derided by Ezra Pound as being full of bungling English and defective rhythms. I learned as much from my intense reading as from my writing. Even then I recognized the poems were not written with the simplicities of the North American idiom, yet I also suspected that Waley's versions were closer to the originals than Pound's inventive translations. Aside from that, what I remember is my immense struggle to get to the essence of what metaphor offered, to express the full power of an image both simply and directly. And while my early attempts were flawed, still the struggle was all. I didn't know then that it was through my failures that I was learning how to write. My early poem "Newspaper Walls" came close to what I aspired to. It is the unschooled work of a young man, but I remember writing it and the satisfaction I got from its rhymes and, especially, the pacing, the cadence, a vernacular, a simple speech replicated on the page, the lines a musical score for the voice. I delighted, too, in how a line could make a fragment from a larger syntax contain a meaning independent of the sentence it was a part of. My small discoveries in those desolate villages and towns helped me endure the poverty I lived in.

If there is a single poem in my twenties where everything I had struggled to learn came together it is in the writing of "For Ten Years." I wrote it a few months after my first wife and I separated, a year after my father was shot by a disgruntled madman, and four years after my brother died of a cerebral haemorrhage. It was 1968, six years after "Newspaper Walls." I'd gone with Seymour Mayne to visit Dorothy Livesay in Sechelt up the Sunshine Coast northwest of Vancouver. I hadn't wanted to go, but Seymour, a friend at the time, insisted he pay his respects. Dorothy was, as usual, difficult and contrary. I didn't have much respect for her writing then. I disliked her downward mobility, her socialist idealizing of workers, her arrogance and her sense of noblesse oblige when she was around poets like Pat Lowther, a working-class woman. I remember standing in Dorothy's living room and staring out the window at the sea. As I did a small bird flew into the reflection of the garden in the glass and died. Seymour, a city boy, asked me why the bird had done that. I replied: "Birds don't understand windows." And then I added, "They never did."

Of those two short sentences, Seymour said, "Now that's poetry." When I got back to my little apartment at the bottom of Yew Street in Kitsilano in Vancouver, I wrote the poem "For Ten Years." It laid itself down as one thing, and when I was done I didn't change a word. Even as I wrote it I knew I was doing something I hadn't done before. The ten years of my study and practise at my craft all came together and I'd finally written a good poem, one I could be proud of. It was an amazing moment for me. The rhythms and patterns, the metric beat of the lines, the rhymes, the presiding metaphor, all that and more made me sit there stunned after the poem was finished. Did I care about what I'd said? Yes, but that was of minor importance. What I really cared about was how I'd said it, how I'd captured an emotion, a moment of immense loss in a few lines, a few words.

But these are issues of largeness. If there has been a single, presiding constant in my poetry it is that the poem be present in the world of my senses. Williams' dictum "No ideas but in things" resonates in my work. I have always been suspicious of abstractions, preferring to trust images to carry the weight of discovery. Metaphor is my meat. In a late poem such as "Under the Sun in the Dry Desert Hills Where the Rain Never falls in August," I rely on descriptions from the natural world, images and the spare anecdote of a beetle who "shoulders her way toward paradise." The images of the beetle and my mother in the poem become one thing balanced on the tightrope of metaphor.

The poem arises from a small, intimate experience I had on the flatland near the high bridge across the Rio Grande in New Mexico. Lorna and I had walked along the cliffs and, like gods, watched from above the swallows flying below us in the canyon. I wandered momentarily off and, as always, having been a nearsighted child without glasses, stared at the ground, where I discovered a great beetle staggering across the sand and gravel. I watched the beetle for half an hour as it made its way to some near, some far-off place and was struck with intense wonder at its will and endurance, its implacable purpose.

Four or five years later the image of the beetle returned to me. Perhaps my poem was the beetle's destination. That said, what resonates for me is the strict simplicity of end-stopped lines, a desire to use the caesura sparingly and only when it enhances meaning as in "Among many things I am alive. Still." I also insist that the right-hand margin in its seeming chaos represents an emotional order based on musicality. That the plain statement, artfully rendered, contains multitudes of nuance, rhyme and other forms of repetition. In this particular poem my greatest delight was to end the poem with a single adverb as a line. There are moments when writing brings immense pleasure. That "Mightily" is one such moment.

The desert of New Mexico resembles in its moments as well as its monuments the desert country of the Okanagan where I grew up. Those spare, dry lands are my geography and its *beetles, pines, sand, quartz, sunflower, yellow, water, salt, bare, blind, still, drink, clamber,* are the my first words.

Faulkner taught me the value of the local, as did Eudora Welty, as did Hemingway in the stories that rose from his youth. Howard O'Hagan taught me to love my mountains in the many conversations we had, drunk and sober; Earle Birney's "Bushed" and "Pacific Door" were entrances to my geography. There were poems that changed me forever: Irving Layton's "Keine Lazarovitch" and "Whatever Else Poetry Is Freedom," Wallace Stevens' "Blue Guitar," D.H. Lawrence's turtle poems, Pound's "Dance Figure" and "The Garden," Frost of course when I was a young, Sassoon, Owen, all of Yeats, and Williams and Lawrence, Trakl and Bachmann and Celan, Charles Olson's "The Kingfishers," Phyllis Webb's "Poetics Against the Angel of Death" and Margaret Avison's "The Swimmer's Moment." There were Milton Acorn and Al Purdy, two men crucial to my thought and practise. My peers? Belford and Trower, MacEwen, Ondaatje, Robert Hass, Jack Gilbert, Charles and James Wright, Lorna Crozier and so many more.

I raged at others in my youth as they copied the imaginations of others, those who argued for the narrowness of schools and cults and cabals, the ones who dismissed humanism and its moral and ethical concerns, who relied on systems of critical belief that arose everywhere but in their hearts and souls. The child I was, the boy, the people I grew up with and suffered with, the people of the West I laboured beside, the people I healed and helped and hurt as a bumbling first-aid man when I was barely old enough not to be a boy; the women I loved who suffered the vicissitudes of their gender and geography, their lives at the hands of men, their fathers, brothers, lovers, sons and strangers, those who loved them and those who abused them; the children who died each day from loneliness and hurt, the men who staggered broken into the sun. The animals, the plants, the birds, the insects and spiders, frogs, rattlesnakes, the moss and lichens, the rocks, the stones, the suffering of the world and its peoples and the life I spent wandering among them, the "journey old as the trails that lead us again to the world."

—March 2011

FURIOUS SNOW SWIRLING: AN AFTERWORD

Nicholas Bradley

> What man that sees the euer-whirling wheele
>   Of *Change*, the which all mortall things doth sway,
>   But that therby doth find, & plainly feele,
>   How MVTABILITY in them doth play
>   Her cruell sports, to many mens decay?
> —Edmund Spenser, *The Faerie Queene*

In *Swamp Angel*, Ethel Wilson's great novel of the Thompson River country, the village of Hope is cast as the point at which British Columbia's coastal region ends and the rest of the continent begins: "Make no mistake, when you have reached Hope and the roads that divide there you have quite left Vancouver and the Pacific Ocean. They are disproportionately remote." Eastward lies the Interior, the vast expanse of the province inland from Vancouver, on the far side of the Coast Range. This Interior has been the setting for much of Patrick Lane's life and poetry. He was born in Nelson, on the west arm of Kootenay Lake amid the Selkirk Mountains, and raised there and in Vernon, in the Okanagan Valley. While these are sites of remarkable beauty, in Lane's poems the distant communities of the Interior are unpromising places for the growth of a poet's mind. The fickleness and cruelty of fate that Spenser decried is matched in Lane's world by the viciousness of men. His poems often portray injuries suffered and injustices committed: a father is shot and killed, a son is beaten by his father, animals are abused and killed, the lives of workers are disrupted or ended by calamities that Lane describes in unnerving detail. In "The Happy Little Towns," a grim, ironic reminiscence, the speaker repairs another man's body, "the stitches climbing up his leg / like small black insects," but he cannot rescue himself from his own sense of "oblivion."

Lane left the Interior for the coast—first for Vancouver and eventually for Victoria—and he would in time claim that "little is left of me in those far hills" ("Cougar Men"). But memories of his early life haunt his poems and provide his inescapable subjects, to which he returns as to unhealed wounds. It is tempting to discern a link between the injured man's "boot full of blood," in "The Happy Little Towns," and the wound of the mythical Philoctetes, whose "bandaged smelling foot," in the phrase of Lane's contemporary, Michael Ondaatje, is a lasting torment. (Ondaatje's poetry is also replete with wounds and scars, but his depictions of violence are more stylized than Lane's.) Several times Lane recounts horrific accidents at a sawmill: in "Just Living" he writes of the long drive to take the maimed man to hospital: "In the pink ice cream bucket between us / the severed hand sloshed in the melting ice." His task as poet has been to come to terms with these memories, with the "wreckage of that world," as he puts it in "The Happy Little Towns," and to make sense of his own life. It has also been to write that world into being, to give its conditions a literary presence. As he has noted in an autobiographical essay ("The Unyielding Phrase"), the Interior seemed to him to be considered peripheral:

> I remember reading through the popular histories of the time trying to find myself in them, trying to locate my place among the many words. That I didn't exist and that no one else around

me did either seemed very important. The town I lived in wasn't mentioned, the valley wasn't, even the mountains didn't exist, the Monashee Range an absence, the Cariboo country non-existent. . . . There was no evidence to suggest we were real.

His poems supply the missing "evidence." Like many Canadian writers of his generation, Lane understood that "place does not exist unless we imagine it." Yet the circumstances of his life — poverty, addiction, his brother's death, the collapse of two marriages — precluded simple celebration of rural ways and shaped ambivalent responses to place. His poetry fuses regional concerns with self-examination. The Interior is both his geographical subject and an apposite description of his perpetual theme: the bleak, remote regions of heart and mind.

At times Lane seems the Beckett of Canadian poetry, setting a desolate stage on which everything, including poetry, is meaningless. When, in "The Measure," "a magpie stuns his tongue against the wind / and the wind steals the rattle of his cry," the conventional association of birds and poets creates an image of futile persistence that verges on nihilism. At their most severe, his descriptions of landscape likewise border on despair, as in "Brothers":

> Sometimes when I'm afraid I walk into the hills
> where the trees are. Stunted desert pines
> the world leaves alive because they're useless.

Lane's works are so marked by carnage and malaise that some early critics were appalled. The self-revelation, however, despite its manifestly personal nature, reflects Lane's emergence in the wake of the so-called confessional poets, who, in the late 1950s and 1960s, broke decorum by writing about madness, depression and sordid family matters; Robert Lowell's *Life Studies*, the quintessential book of the time, was published in 1959, when Lane was twenty and soon to embark on his career as a writer. In Lane's "Held Water," the speaker admits that

I have discovered I cannot bear to be
with people anymore. Even the querulous love of old friends
defeats me and I turn away, my face staring
at the hard sleet
scraping at what little is left of the trees
in early spring.

The despair in the first line is nearly absolute, moderated only by the remainder of the sentence, "with people anymore," which follows the line break. Lane's "I cannot bear to be" is of a piece with Lowell's "My mind's not right," Theodore Roethke's "I dread the thing I am" and Sylvia Plath's "What I want back is what I was / Before the bed, before the knife." Lane's bare admissions of crisis also share in the characteristic plain-spokenness employed by Canadian poets such as Al Purdy and John Newlove in the 1960s and 1970s.

Lane's commitment to verisimilitude is accompanied by a devotion to craft, to the careful arrangement of details. His poems work colloquial speech into exacting formulations. The dismal conclusions of poems such as "Just Living" are made compelling by a sense of authenticity and the implication that stories of tough times in the Interior illuminate general truths. The autobiographical poems are not confessional in the sense of mere disclosure; they constitute a probing psychological study, using the stuff of the author's past to measure what a person can endure and what life can entail. Voyeuristic, the reader looks on, chastened and moved.

Though fate's cruel sports provide Lane's principal subjects, he also writes forcefully of the pleasant aspects of mortal life. His poems attesting to the restorative powers of gardening evince an experience of the world very different from that of his earlier work, not least because the garden affords a glimpse of connubial happiness — of earthly pleasures, and also Edenic and heavenly connotations. "Each time my lover / rises to walk in the early garden," he writes in "Stars," "I watch her from the window." In other poems, the mysteries uncovered by night are those of the natural world; in "The Desert," the speaker observes

> a beetle
> clambering from beneath a stone, a cactus
> moving its green paw to hold the flower
> it will grow from its flesh

Lane has been prolific—he has written or edited more than two dozen books in the fifty years of his literary life—and his body of work is varied. The poems hew close to life, but he has adopted various guises: not just the stoic witness to trauma, but also the wandering exile in South America, the cynical lover, the *poète maudit,* the traveller in Europe, the contemplative poet of *Winter* and the companion to Lorna Crozier. Consistent among the multiple personae is his distinctively stark style; he uses his unornamented, deceptively simple language to great effect. In "Moths," a poem of fifteen lines, all but a dozen words are monosyllabic. (The other twelve are disyllabic.) The poem seems diaphanous, like moths' wings; the apostrophe to the "soft birds of the night," a prayerful evocation of the dead, achieves a delicate musicality through subtle rhymes.

For convenience, critics and commentators lapse into generalizations about writers and their works. Lane's importance as a regionalist and chronicler of the working life is undeniable. Yet such useful ways of describing Lane obscure the range of his works and the wonderful strangenesses of individual poems. Auden remarked that "Like most important writers, Mr T.S. Eliot is not a single figure but a household." Lane is no different. Several figures keep residence in his household, but perhaps he is ultimately a domestic poet, despite the wildness and machismo of some of his poems. Taken as a whole, his writing charts a search for home, for stability and belonging, and a journey out of the Interior, both geographical and psychological. The assembled poems show the "wheele / Of *Change*" of which Spenser wrote, revolving inexorably, and a sense of order being made from tempestuous life. As Lane notes in "A New Awakening," his essay on poetics written for this *Collected Poems,* he acquired faith in a poem's power to "defeat time," in beauty's power to stave off disorder.

In "Winter 41," Lane proposes that "Being on a journey without knowing / you are on a journey is to understand grace." The journey that the poems in this volume trace has been long and hard, but this poetry achieves both understanding and grace in ample measure.

NOTES

These notes do not attempt to provide information easily found through an internet search. Throughout this edition, where titles of poems are followed by dates in parentheses, the title is one that Lane has used more than once.

Newspaper Walls

The way an early settler has used newspapers to keep out the drafts means the speaker of the poem is reading about the events following Germany's declarations of war on Russia and France on August 1 and 3, 1914.

Fireweed Seeds

Fireweed is so named because it is amid the first growth to return after a fire.

The Absinthe Drinker (1969)

This poem responds to Edgar Degas's 1876 painting of a woman, titled *L'Absinthe*. (Lane's 1966 collection, *Letters from the Savage Mind*, also contains a poem with this title.) A highly alcoholic liquor that was enormously popular in France during the nineteenth century, absinthe was banned in North America and Europe for most of the twentieth century as a dangerously addictive psychoactive drug.

On the Street

Sweet Thursday is a 1954 novel by John Steinbeck. It continues the accounts, begun in *Cannery Row*, of marginal individuals enduring the Great Depression.

Thirty Below

Thrown: that is, having been birthed. (This sense of the word is more usually reserved for farm animals.)

After (1973)

In an era of unregulated logging, a **gypo show** (or Gypsy outfit) was the term used for a small, independent operation, often lacking proper safety procedures.

For Riel in That Gawdam Prison

Gabriel **Dumont**—the Métis leader and brilliant strategist who participated in the North-West Rebellion with Louis Riel—took refuge in the United States after the Battle of Batoche; while there he performed in Buffalo Bill's Wild West Show from 1886 to 1888.

Sleep Is the Silence Darkness Takes

This poem is a dramatic monologue in the voice of Lane's father.

Still Hunting

Still Hunting is the stalking of game through quiet movement that allows the hunter to get close to the prey.

Machu Picchu

Quechua is the language of the native people of the central Andes. This poem is based on the understanding, current to the poem's composition, that Machu Picchu—a site in a remote area of Peru—had been abandoned before its discovery in the early twentieth century by the American scholar Hiram Bingham. He thought the complex was the legendary Lost City of the Incas, forgotten since the sixteenth-century Spanish conquest and the site of the traditional temple of the Inca Virgins of the Suns. **Manco Cápac** was the last ruler of the Inca empire; he took his name from the legendary "first Inca," a founder said to be the son of the sun god Inti. **Huaina Cápac**, Manco's father, had expanded the Inca empire; after his death his kingdom was divided between his sons **Huáscar** and **Atahualpa**, who struggled against one another for control, and then against the Spanish invaders. The Spanish installed Manco as a puppet emperor, but he rebelled and began his own war against the Spaniards. His forces, after years of struggle with the Spanish, were eventually defeated by the conquistador Francisco Pizarro. Manco's ancestor, the Inca patriarch **Pachacutec**, ruler of the Kingdom of Cuzco, was a poet and hymnist: the closing lines of Lane's "Machu Picchu" are, according to tradition, a poem Pachacutec composed on his deathbed.

Election Day

This poem is set during the 1970 election in Colombia, which was so disputed (there were four recounts) that it became a turning point in the nation's recent history. The party of the loser and former dictator, General Rojas, subsequently formed the *Movimiento 19 de Abril* (M-19), the first of a number of guerrilla organizations to make war against the government in power.

Stigmata

A response to Irving Layton's many poems about the deaths of animals (some of them inflicted by the speaker in the poem); these deaths function, in Layton's existentialist vision, as reminders of the brevity of life and the need to affirm the present moment. (See, for example, "Butterfly on Rock.")

The Trace of Being

In 1862 **camels** were brought to the Cariboo to serve as pack animals during the gold rush. (The experiment was unsuccessful.) The Wild **McLean Boys** were three brothers born in Kamloops: they killed two men while being pursued for horse theft; they were hanged in 1881.

A Murder of Crows

A **murder** is the collective name for a group of crows. Lane discusses the subject of this poem (the dressing of a deer) in "A New Awakening," his statement of poetics at the end of this collection.

From *No Longer Two People*

This sequence of poems forms Lane's half of the 1979 book he co-authored with Lorna Crozier (then publishing under her married name at the time, Uher): in the original, his poems alternate with hers.

Temenos

Temenos (from the Greek) is a piece of land or property — often a grove of woods or a temple — set off as a sacred place or sanctuary or as the official domain of kings and chiefs. Carl Jung adopted the term for a magic circle. The **Sibylline Oracles** were the enigmatic prophecies given by oracular priestesses in ancient Greece. Ezra Pound's "**Canto XIII**" (the last lines are quoted here) is one of his investigations of Confucian wisdom, emphasizing self-discipline and being true to one's nature.

Just Living

A **headrig** is the carriage and saw in a sawmill that shapes rough timber in squared-off logs, called **cants**.

Blue Valley Night

A **widow-maker** here refers to a dead limb on a tree, one that might fall at any moment.

Annie She

Snoose is chewing tobacco.

Indian Tent Rings

Leubingen, Stonehenge and **Mycenae,** three European sites of ancient ritual, are associated with burial.

The Killing Table

Chuang Tzu (or Zhuangzi) was a fourth-century Taoist philosopher. This epigraph is drawn from his story of the cook who, when asked why he was so skillful in the carving of an ox, replied: "What your servant really cares for is Tao, which goes beyond mere art. When I first began to cut up oxen, I saw nothing but oxen. After three years of practising, I no longer saw the ox as a whole. I now work with my spirit, not with my eyes. My senses stop functioning and my spirit takes over. ... when I come to a difficulty, I size up the joint, look carefully, and work slowly."

Monarch IV

The **crissum** is the feathered area around the hen's vent or cloaca (the cavity into which genital and anal canals open externally).

The Weight

Lane here responds to his sense of the neglect of the Canadian West by interweaving family history with myth, events in western Canadian (and other) history and allusions to Western Canadian music, poets (such as Sid **Marty**) and poems (such as Robert **Kroetsch**'s *Seed Catalogue* and "Stone Hammer Poem" and George **Bowering**'s poem about his grandfather **Jabez**)—as well as to other poetry. (The lines quoted at the end of Sections ii and iii of Part I are from *Shih Ching*, a collection of ancient Chinese poems.) The **rhetoric of Frye's image** refers to Northrop Frye's idea (in *The Anatomy of Criticism*) that literary archetypes, which are images that are recurring and typical, have a rhetorical function.

The Forbidden City

This and the eleven poems that follow are from the group of poems Lane published as his contribution to *Chinada: Memoirs of the Gang of Seven* (1982) and republished in his poetry collection *Old Mother*. They come out of a trip he made to China with six other Canadian writers. **The Forbidden City** is the Chinese imperial palace complex that lies within the city of Beijing.

Silk Factory

Ch'en T'ao was a poet of the ninth century, remembered for the poem "Turkestan":

> Thinking only of their vow that they would crush the
> Tartars —
> On the desert, clad in sable and silk, five thousand of
> them fell . . .
> But arisen from their crumbling bones on the banks of
> the river at the border,

Dreams of them enter, like men alive, into rooms where
their loves lie sleeping.

The Dream of the Red Chamber

The title alludes to the eighteenth-century novel *The Dream of the Red Chamber*, one of China's literary masterpieces. Its fifth chapter tells of the narrator's dream of a red chamber where the fates of many of the characters are revealed. The **symbol of the crane** is associated with positive traits—good fortune, happiness, success, etc. **The Ch'ing** Dynasty ended in 1911. The **wu t'ung** (or wutong) tree—known in North America as the Chinese parasol tree—has a delicate beauty and is associated with good fortune and blessings.

For Adele and Ding Ling

Adele Wiseman, one of the Canadian writers who travelled to China with Lane, was a left-wing activist and feminist. The dolls she took were examples of her mother's folk art (she wrote about them in her 1978 book *Old Woman at Play*). **Ding Ling** was a Chinese novelist and short-story writer whose work particularly concerned the rights of women.

From *A Linen Crow, a Caftan Magpie*

The poems that follow are selected from a book-length sequence written in a form influenced by the ghazal and the haiku.

"Who will explain the bones?"

The Japanese artist Matsumura **Goshun** (1752–1811) was a painter of the Edo period and founder of the Shijō school of painting. His "Spring Willows and Heron" is a painting of great delicacy.

"All that is left."

Saturn's breakfast alludes to the Greek myth about the

Titan Saturn devouring his successive children to prevent their overthrowing him.

"The natural man."

Yosa **Buson** (1716–83) was considered the greatest Japanese poet from the Edo period. He once responded to a pupil's request by saying that the student would "never see something as refined and clever" as the handscroll Buson had prepared.

Nunc Dimittis

Nunc Dimittis, Latin for "now let depart," are the first words of a canticle drawn from Simeon's speech in the Gospel of Luke after he took the infant Jesus into his arms: "Lord, now lettest thou thy servant depart in peace, according to thy word: For mine eyes have seen thy salvation" (Luke 2:29–30).

La Gioconda

Leonardo da Vinci (1452–1519) is said to have been so attached to his *Mona Lisa*, also known as *La Gioconda*, that, prior to its sale to King Francis I of France, he took it with him when he travelled. **Buonarroti**: Michelangelo, da Vinci's great contemporary, especially renowned for his sculpture, was known for his love of solitude

Dostoevsky

The speaker of this poem is **in retreat** in a monastery: see the note below on "Day." **Prince Myshkin** is the innocent epileptic hero of *The Idiot*; **Raskolnikov** is the guilt-tormented protagonist of *Crime and Punishment*; **Natasha**, found in Dostoevsky's *The Insulted and Injured*, is another figure of innocence.

Winter 20 (Winter is not Colville)

Winter scenes are the subject of several paintings by the Nova Scotia painter Alex **Colville**.

Winter 45 (The man without a name)

The man without a name: Albert Johnson, though that probably was not his real name; he became notorious in his flight from the RCMP as "the Mad Trapper" and his remarkable ability to survive severe winter conditions during his pursuit were central to his legend.

The Far Field

Originally published in *Exile* as "The Day I Burned the Far Field."

The Attitude of Mourning

Cardinal: Here, in the sense of *hinge*, i.e. the central joints of the wing.

The Firebreather

Marcel Horne, a Toronto performer whose memoir was *Annals of the Firebreather* (1972) and who appeared in carnivals as "Diablo the Human Volcano," was known for taking fuel into his mouth and exhaling it onto a torch, producing a large and dramatic fireball.

Stylites

Stylites were medieval ascetics who retreated to the tops of pillars as a way of renouncing the world.

Orpheus

According to myth, after the loss of his beloved wife Eurydice, **Orpheus**, the maker of enchanting music, was found in the woods by the Maenads, the followers of Dionysus (**Bacchus**), who, in their frenzy, tore him to bits. His still-singing head is said to have floated down the river Hebrus to the beach at Lesbos.

These Ones

Trakl's tiny aster is an allusion to the last line ("Blue asters bow and shiver in the wind") of the poem "Decay" by the Austrian Expressionist poet Georg Trakl (1887–1914). The aster in that conclusion seems a consolation for the "whiff of decay" that makes the poet tremble earlier in the poem. The remark that follows in Lane's poem, that this image "makes nothing possible. / Yet something is there," responds to Auden's famous statement: "poetry makes nothing happen: it survives / In the valley of its making" ("In Memory of W.B. Yeats").

The Last Day of My Mother

The lines the poet's mother quotes are from the opening of Thomas Babington Macaulay's "Horatius"—a gory Victorian pseudo-epic in eight-line rhymed quatrains about three Roman soldiers holding a bridge against the entire Etruscan army.

What Breaks Us

A response to the "Montreal massacre," the 1989 slaying of fourteen women by Marc Lépine at the École Polytechnique. Lépine separated the women from the men and identified himself as "fighting feminism."

The Day

Monastery: St. Peter's Abbey, a Benedictine monastery that is the site of retreats sponsored by the Saskatchewan Writers' Guild.

Choices

The **transparent apple tree** produces clear yellow (hence, the poem's "golden") fruit in the early spring.

Cutthroat

A **cutthroat** trout, so named because of the red markings at its gills.

Coyote

In medieval Christian iconology, the mother **pelican** was said to feed her young with blood drawn from her own breast. Thus the pelican was an image linked to Christ, his sacrifice and the sacrament of communion. Saint Benedict is often depicted associated with a bird (a raven or crow) that, according to legend, saved him when corrupt monks attempted to poison him.

Wildfire

Wildfire here refers to what is also known as will-o'-the-wisp, the phosphorescent fire seen in marshy areas, a product of combustible gases released by rotting organic materials.

For Red Lane

This begins a series of elegies for poets (and in the case of Roy Lowther for the man who killed his poet-spouse). Each contains allusions to the work of the poet being addressed (for example, "otter rocks" can be found in Birney's "Pacific Door"). Irving Layton was residing in the Maimonides Geriatric Centre, incapacitated by Alzheimer's disease, at the time his elegy was written.

Teaching Poetry

The **Nitobe Memorial Garden** is on the University of British Columbia campus.

INDEX OF POEM TITLES

The Collected Poems of Patrick Lane